Counterstreams in Migration

Hewan Girma

Counterstreams in Migration

Ethiopians' Choices to Stay, Leave, or Return

TEMPLE UNIVERSITY PRESS
Philadelphia • Rome • Tokyo

TEMPLE UNIVERSITY PRESS
Philadelphia, Pennsylvania 19122
tupress.temple.edu

Copyright © 2026 by Temple University Press—Of The Commonwealth System of Higher Education
All rights reserved
Published 2026

Library of Congress Cataloging-in-Publication Data

Names: Girma, Hewan author
Title: Counterstreams in migration : Ethiopians' choices to stay, leave, or return / Hewan Girma.
Description: Philadelphia : Temple University Press, 2026. | Includes bibliographical references and index. | Summary: "This book presents the motivations for migrating, not migrating, returning, and migrating again of Ethiopian subjects considering movement to the Global North who were interviewed by the author. The author presents migration emotions as a constantly evolving mix of pushes and pulls, driving the potential for different choices over a lifetime"— Provided by publisher.
Identifiers: LCCN 2025045542 (print) | LCCN 2025045543 (ebook) | ISBN 9781439925652 cloth | ISBN 9781439925669 paperback | ISBN 9781439925676 pdf
Subjects: LCSH: Ethiopians—Foreign countries | Return migration—Ethiopia | Emotions—Sociological aspects | Ethiopia—Emigration and immigration—Psychological aspects | Ethiopia—Emigration and immigration—Social aspects
Classification: LCC JV8997 .G57 2026 (print) | LCC JV8997 (ebook)
LC record available at https://lccn.loc.gov/2025045542
LC ebook record available at https://lccn.loc.gov/2025045543

The manufacturer's authorized representative in the EU for product safety is Temple University Rome, Via di San Sebastianello, 16, 00187 Rome RM, Italy (https://rome.temple.edu/).
tempress@temple.edu

♾ The paper used in this publication meets the requirements of the American National Standard for Information Sciences—Permanence of Paper for Printed Library Materials, ANSI Z39.48-1992

Printed in the United States of America

9 8 7 6 5 4 3 2 1

To all those that refuse to be bound by categories

Contents

List of Figures and Tables	ix
Acknowledgments	xi
Introduction: Migrate, Return, Repeat	1
1. Migration from the Vantage Point of Non-migrants	33
Interlude 1. Ode to Bolé Airport	55
2. Beyond the Myth of Return: Exploring Returnees' Motivations	60
Interlude 2. Passports Tell a Story	89
3. The Joys and Frustrations of Return	93
Interlude 3. Ode to Addis Ababa	115
4. Saviorism and Returnee Belonging	120
Interlude 4. Little Ethiopia in America	142
5. Repeat Migration: Ever Greener Grass or Next Logical Phase?	147
Conclusion	171
Appendix: Methodological Overview	185
Notes	201
Index	221

List of Figures and Tables

FIGURES

I.1	A 360-Degree View of Migration	8
I.2	The MSM Model: Migra-emotions in the Socio-ecology of Migration	15

TABLES

I.1	Migra-emotions: Types of Emotions That Can Affect Migration Decisions	12
I.2	African Diasporic Return Movements	18
1.1	Non-migrants and Their Prevalent Migra-emotions	54
2.1	Types of Return Migration	63
2.2	Push-Pull Reasons for Return Migration	87
4.1	African Terminologies for Returnees	121
5.1	Repeat Migrants' Motivations for Return and Repeat Migrations	168
C.1	Migra-emotions Summary	176
A.1	Non-migrant Demographic Data	196
A.2	Returnee Demographic Data	197
A.3	Repeat Migrant Demographic Data	200

Acknowledgments

This book has had a long, long gestational period, and during this time, I have accumulated lots of personal and professional debt. This work is only possible because I have been surrounded by amazing scholars, wonderful friends, and an ever-supportive family that encouraged me at every step along the journey.

My first shout-out goes to my formidable dissertation committee who nurtured my intellectual curiosity and guided me through my doctoral degree at Stony Brook. Kathleen (Katy) Fallon, Oyeronke ('Ronke) Oyewumi, Shimelis B. Gulema, and Tiffany Joseph: You have all seen the earliest iteration of this work and believed in its potential even when I had doubts. You have each massively contributed to my growth as a scholar and positively deserve the credit. Crystal Fleming, you have been a mentor unlike any other, and I always look forward to the next amazing thing that you do. I am forever indebted to Grant Saff, whose mentorship started in my undergraduate years at Hofstra University. He was one of the first to encourage me to pursue doctoral studies and even provided the unparalleled opportunity to develop my teaching skills in the Geography and Global Studies Department, where I worked for eight years. I would also like to thank all my colleagues in the African American and African Diaspora Studies (AADS) program at University of North Carolina at Greensboro, including Noelle Morrissette, Cerise Glenn-Manigault, Shelly Brown-Jeffy, Jazmine Eyssallenne, Sarah Cervenak, Torren Gatson, Elizabeth Perrill, Dominick Hand, and others. My deepest appreciation goes to Michael Cauthen and

Frank N. Woods, whose wisdom and conversation I value deeply. I also reserve a special mention of my friends and colleagues in the Ethiopian, East African, and Indian Ocean (EEAIO) Research Network, Omar Ali, Neelofer Qadir, and David Aarons. We will always have Zanzibar.

Throughout the years, my research has been supported by a number of internal grants at Hofstra University, Stony Brook University, and the University of North Carolina at Greensboro. I particularly want to mention the Dr. W. Burghardt Turner Dissertation Fellowship provided by Stony Brook's Center for Inclusive Education, which has been instrumental in getting me through the finish line of my doctoral studies. Moreover, while on the tenure track, I received a Career Enhancement Fellowship from the Institute of Citizens and Scholars, which provided a structured time away from teaching and administrative duties, enabling me to carry out significant edits to the manuscript. It was under this fellowship that I got to meet and work closely with the amazing and generous Onoso Imoagene and Chinyere Osuji. Thank you both for reading draft after draft of my chapters, gently pushing me to take risks, and encouraging me to develop my scholarly voice.

This work was also supported by the Carnegie African Diaspora Fellowship Program (CADFP), which enabled me to think broadly about contemporary African migration within and outside the continent. Their support enabled me to simultaneously work on a closely related project, coediting *The Global Ethiopian Diaspora: Migrations, Connections and Belonging* with Shimelis B. Gulema and Mulugeta F. Dinbabo. The two book projects breathed life into each other, and my appreciation goes out to my coeditors with whom I have crisscrossed the world, both physically and in our minds. Alpha Abebe, Mulumebet Worku, Netsanet Gebremichael, Tina Beyene, and Sara Derbew, my fellow Ethiopian-descent women scholars and educators, I appreciate all our random conversations over the years and our commiseration about life in academia. Helen Tadese, you are every educator's dream graduate student, and I cannot wait to see all that you accomplish post-Ph.D.

I am forever grateful to the multitudes of people who have opened their homes and lives to my probing questions. Readers will encounter their stories in these pages and be intimately acquainted with their emotions, desires, triumphs, and frustrations, which appear only under a pseudonym. Although I can never identify them by name for privacy and confidentiality reasons, this research would not have been possible without each and every single one of them. I also wish to express my sincere gratitude to my phenomenal editor Ryan A. Mulligan, who was patient and had faith in this project even when I felt discouraged at times, and the entire team at Temple University Press, who painstakingly saw this project to completion.

Finally, and above all, I am eternally grateful to God Almighty, through Whom I found amazing love and grace and without Whom all of this would be meaningless. My church families at Bethel in New York City and Immanuel in North Carolina have been amazing sources of love and support. I have been blessed to share the fullness of faith and life together with each one of you. I will refrain from naming individuals in either of these places as I do not have enough space, but you know who you are.

My family, like so many others, dispersed across oceans and living in Ethiopia, Europe, and North America, has been a steady anchor providing belongingness regardless of geography. My loving parents, I would not be where I am today without your never-ending love and support. Finally, my wonderful partner in life, love, and laughter, Abiy: you have seen the ups and downs of this project more than anyone else. You are my incomparable gift from God, and your love keeps sustaining me over the years. For me, home is wherever you are.

—Hewan Girma

Counterstreams in Migration

Introduction

Migrate, Return, Repeat

Three Lives, Three Choices, a Multitude of Emotions

Aida, Non-migrant, Addis Ababa

> Life in Ethiopia is boring! I don't want to live here anymore. I want the excitement of living in the U.S., Canada, or Australia. I can see myself having a life there. Chillin' and vibin'.... My sister moved to Atlanta in 1996, the year the Olympics took place there and not too long after I was born. I have been dreaming about it since. If I was living in Atlanta, I would work for CNN or Coca-Cola or Tyler Perry Studios. You know his [Tyler Perry's] baby mama, the gorgeous Gelila, is Ethiopian, right? Phew! Speaking of the life! My grandfather doesn't see the attraction of abroad, mixing with different people, eating foreign foods... the adventure. Abaye [Aida's grandfather] is stuck in his ways. "*Sidet kefu*" [exile is evil],[1] he says.... He is so emotionally tied to *Emama Ethiopia* [the motherland]. Oh, how he celebrated when my sister came back [remigrated to Ethiopia], dragging her entire family. He called her a true Ethiopian. If you ask me, the respect she gets is because she left [the homeland] in the first place.—Aida (F, 26)[2]

Aida, a young woman in her mid-twenties at the time of the interview, comes from a wealthy family in Addis Ababa. The youngest of three, she has one sister who settled in Atlanta and another one educated in Europe. Aida speaks mostly in English and inserts Americanisms when talking: "like," "you know," "yeah," "you get me," "for real," "you know what I'm saying," "true dat!" She stands out because I encountered mostly young men who imitate these Americanisms in the urban landscape of Addis. Aida's knowledge of Hollywood and Black American music is impressive, demonstrating both her cosmopolitanism and the wide reach of American cultural exports. She dreams of Atlanta sometimes, a big city, cosmopolitan and multicultural, but not the typical New York or Los Angeles. Aida has created an interior life with ambitions and a sense of self based on an American elsewhere, and she is emotionally invested in one day migrating. Aida's excitement about an imagined elsewhere is palpable. Even though she has never migrated, Aida's life is still affected by her sisters' migration and the anticipation of her own. She is very close to her grandparents with whom she lives, and she contrasts her own views with those of her grandfather, who she says is "stuck in the olden, golden days" of Emperor Haile Selassie. The reported generational difference between Aida's and her grandparents' views on migration reveals different emotional attachments. The pride and patriotism of Aida's grandfather contrast with the boredom Aida feels in her home country. The emotional landscape that motivates one's relationship to migration, the affective pushes and pulls that weigh on the decision to stay in a place of origin or strike out for a new destination, affects not only those who migrate but also non-migrants like Aida and her grandfather. This emotional landscape also continues to affect migrants like Aida's sister after migration, into and through return. The sentiments Aida reports here are only a subset from a wide range of emotions that affect peoples' relationships with migration throughout their lives, whether they never migrate, migrate and stay in their destination, or return and even migrate again.

Aida and her grandparents represent one of the relationships to migration that form the basis of this study: non-migrants. As individuals who have never lived outside their home country, Ethiopian non-migrants are still affected by the migration of their kin and the overall culture of migration that has seeped into Ethiopian society. While migration scholars are justifiably interested in the reasons people migrate and their postmigration experiences in destination countries, it is just as important to understand why people stay in their countries of origin, return to their country of origin, or migrate again. Defining immobility as an active state may seem oxymoronic, but non-migrants are agentic individuals who have made conscious decisions about where to live. The reasons for migration or nonmigration constitute evolving emotional landscapes, experienced over a lifetime by migrants and non-migrants alike. In fact, non-migrants, a group seldom studied in migration studies, represent the majority of people globally—97 percent of the world's population, to be exact[3]—and offer insights into immobility and mobility alike. The term "non-migrant" can be somewhat problematic, implying deficiency, since the group is defined by what they are not rather than by what they are. Some scholars and practitioners have used "stayees," particularly in forced migration circumstances. While I acknowledge the criticisms of the term, I still opt to use "non-migrants" to create contrast with the other groups I discuss. For this study's purposes, I define non-migrants as individuals who have never lived outside their home countries, and I discuss non-migrants, their views, and their sentiments in more depth in Chapter 1.

Alemneh, Returnee, Addis Ababa

As non-migrants can construct a persuasive imaginary of migration that they envisage until they depart, migrants confront the distance between that imaginary of the destination and the actual lived experience and in turn construct an imaginary of the place of origin, of home:

> This is home, and it feels good to be back. My lifestyle is definitely very different than what I had in LA. I was getting burnt out [in the United States]. Always worried about being sued for no reason, being the target as the only Black physician in my practice, always feeling like you have something to prove, the never-ending cycle . . . I had enough! Work cannot be the point of life. Work and accumulating more stuff seems to be the standard of the day in the U.S. And for what? You barely have the time to enjoy it. It is not just the physical exhaustion. I was mentally exhausted as well. Here [in Addis] I can live a more relaxed life. . . . My wife is also super happy to be back. I wasn't a good husband or a good father there [in the United States]. Here, it's a different story. There are also family members available to help with the kids. What can I tell you, we are surrounded by love. We have more time to ourselves, time with family and friends. It is not work, work, work all the time. I feel like I can finally breathe. . . .] I am also more needed and appreciated here than I can ever be there. Whatever I do is for my people. I can make a difference. This is home. This is where we belong.—Alemneh (M, 47)

Alemneh is a highly specialized medical professional in his late forties. He had relocated back to his birthplace of Addis Ababa about five years before I met him. He answered with the preceding words when I asked him to evaluate his return. In this short response, he repeats the word "home" twice. He expresses his contentment with his relocation. He also mentions his dissatisfaction with life abroad, particularly the rat race. While contrasting his life in Los Angeles and Addis Ababa, he highlights how much more leisure time he has in Addis, time for himself and for his family. He contrasts how he felt living in the United States (anxious, exhausted, disenchanted, and hyperaware of his racial identity) with how he feels after his return to the homeland (appreciated, relaxed, satisfied, and supported); these emotions kindled his return and his experiences postreturn. Alemneh also talks about feeling a stronger sense of belonging in Ethiopia than he did in the United States as a Black immigrant, despite his enviable economic success. He initially got the idea of returning to his homeland from a friend who had done so a couple of years earlier. Alemneh is now "doing his part" to encourage others to take the return plunge as he is happy about relocating to his homeland, calling it "one of the best decisions [he's] ever made."

Individuals like Alemneh represent the second group on which this book focuses: returnees, individuals who, after living outside their home country for a period of time, return to resettle. As return migration does not have a universally agreed-upon definition,[4] for the purposes of this study, I define returnees as individuals who have voluntarily[5] relocated to their home country for a minimum of one year[6] after a period of five or more years[7] in the Global North.[8] The experiences of returnees highlight the challenges of living as a migrant and the draw of home. Moreover, the phenomenon of return migration amply illustrates that migration is not a one-way street. Rather, return is a counterstream to initial migration, one that has not received its due attention, particularly in African contexts. Returnees such as Alemneh take up the majority of the focus of this book, and I discuss them and their emotional landscape at length in Chapters 2, 3, and 4.

Gash Mengesha, Repeat Migrant, Washington, DC

Just as a person who decides to migrate might confront a distance between their imaginary of their destination and the lived experience, the returnee might confront yet another distance—that between the imaginary of home and the lived reality of the origin country within the person's always-changing circumstances:

> Alas, this was not the plan when we returned. My wife and I both expected that we would live the remainder of our lives in Ethiopia amongst our own, but life does not always work out the way you plan. The kids and grandkids have been begging us to come live near them since we first moved. It was hard having that much distance between us, but we would have just continued to do what we were doing,

traveling back and forth to see them, spend a few weeks, a few months, and go back. Now our health forces us to live full-time here [in the United States]. If we could have gotten the type of medical treatment we needed in Addis, we would have stayed without batting an eye. Sadly, it did not work out that way.... [Washington] DC is not a bad place to live. There are lots of Ethiopians. We have plenty of friends. The community here is strong. We're OK, but this was not the plan. Our heart is still in Ethiopia. Our vision for retirement was back home, but now we have to settle for visiting once in a while.—Mengesha (M, 68)

Gash Mengesha relocated to Washington, DC, after living in Ethiopia as a returnee for a number of years.[9] Until he became an inadvertent repeat migrant, he fit a common trope of a retirement returnee. *Gash* Mengesha has roots in the United States, where he lived for over a decade. He relocated to Addis postretirement for a number of reasons. He felt a stronger sense of belonging in his country of origin, with all his extended family and kin group. He felt a strong sense of embeddedness and community in his homeland, something he missed while living in the United States. Also, his retirement income would stretch further in Ethiopia than in the United States. While he foresaw living the remainder of his life in his homeland, he was compelled to remigrate back to the United States after a health crisis. As he could not get the necessary life-extending treatment and continued care in Addis Ababa, both he and his wife reluctantly relocated to Washington, DC. While health was their primary reason, they also relocated to be close to their progeny—their adult children and grandchildren. In his description of his repeat migration, *Gash* Mengesha indicates that his emotions, his sense of push and pull between countries, surrendered to the circumstances that compelled him to migrate once again to the host country. While his children are surely a draw, even after return migration, he feels a sense of concession or acquiescence, not having anticipated the need to engage in repeat migration.

Gash Mengesha represents the third and last group included in this study: repeat migrants. For the purposes of this study, I define repeat migrants as individuals who fit the criteria of a returnee who have then chosen to migrate again to live outside their homeland for a minimum of one year. Repeat migration has been called many different things: circular, recurrent, secondary, back-and-forth, multiple, rotating, circuit, shuttling, revolving-door, yo-yo, va-et-vient, and pendular migration.[10] Although there are slight differences between these labels (some with negative connotations), the umbrella descriptor of repeat migration is large enough to encompass any migrant who moves between an origin country and one or more destination countries repeatedly for stays of varying durations. While repeat migration can be either planned or unplanned, it involves committed movements of migrants between home and host nations. This implies substantial periods of residence, ranging from a few months to a few years, in several locations. Although repeat migration gives observers an undue sense of indecisiveness or aimlessness, this migration can be driven by many motivations, including work, health, family circumstances, safety, and security, in addition to the changing emotional values placed on location and movement. Just as return migration proves that migration is not a one-way street, the experiences of repeat migrants underscore the impermanence of return. The emotional calculus that prompts a moment of action may change multiple times during a person's life. *Gash* Mengesha and his wife are inadvertent repeat migrants, a phenomenon I discuss in more depth in Chapter 5.

Counterstreams: A 360-Degree View of Migration

A stream is a watercourse or small river that generally flows in one direction, following a prescribed path or forging a new one. In migration, streams indicate the flow of migrants from source to destination countries. For every major migration stream, a counterstream develops, flowing in a different direction. Not to be underestimated, the counterstream contributes to the mighty rush of a water system—or a diaspora—the trickle becoming a deluge. Even though the volume and speed of the counterstreams may not be as sizable as the initial migration, they still warrant attention as they elucidate complex circuits of migrant comings and goings. Further, they speak to the affective forces sending the flow in different directions, reminding us that the people who flow in one direction are not fundamentally different from those who flow in another or remain in place, responding to their relative points of perspective, whether from a structural position related to health, laws, or finances or an emotional position of hopes and fears.

The most often studied migration stream flows from a sending nation to a receiving nation. Moreover, migration studies are overwhelmingly focused on receiving countries, and more specifically on immigrant incorporation in destination countries (particularly those located in the Global North).[11] On the other hand, the least studied group in or aspect of migration studies consists of non-migrants and origin-country dynamics. Moreover, although this is changing, most older migration studies give the erroneous impression that migration journeys are unidirectional, that once migrants have left their homelands, they are forever disconnected—or are now considered a categorically different sort of person, a migrant. This limited and limiting focus does a disservice to our understanding of migration as we need to fully grasp the conditions that lead people to stay or migrate over a life course.

Counterstreams builds on the work of transnational migration scholars who have spotlighted how migrants living outside their homelands maintain significant ties, bidirectionally exchanging ideas, goods, and services across national borders, thus extending economic safety nets and imparting social remittances.[12] Transnationalism extends beyond individual migrants and their kin to political organizations and civil society. Before the transnational turn in migration studies, scholars erroneously assumed a complete disconnection with the homeland. However, gains in telecommunications services and cheaper international travel have led to a more interconnected globe, enabling international migrants to maintain strong and regular ties to those they have left behind.[13]

If we conceptualize one's relationship to migration as a cycle, starting with nonmigration, followed by migration, the third and fourth potential steps are return and repeat migration. Of course, an individual may not take every step, but the cycle serves to illustrate the next step at each stage of one's relationship with migration. The focus on migrants as a category has led to a neglect of the other three states or stages of relationality toward migration: immobility, return, and repeat migration. In this work, therefore, instead of presenting migration as linear and unidirectional, I reveal more complex circuits of migration flows and the ways these different flows mutually affect and influence one another. The forces drawing someone away from or toward their origin may be felt in all three stages in different degrees. None of these stages can be taken for granted as "natural," but together they shed light on the benefits, pitfalls, and overall experiences of geographic mobility.

Employing the streams and counterstreams analogy, this study thus offers a partial look at a complicated issue, weaving together the stories of non-migrants, returnees, and repeat migrants. The concept of *counterstreams* emphasizes the often less studied but no less constant forces acting on people considering migration: immobility, return, and repeat migration. This book brings these flows and counterflows into conversation, highlighting multiple mobilities and the overall fluidity and circularity of migratory movements. Moreover, the notion of *counterstreams* seeks to complicate migratory movements by highlighting the complicated emotional landscape of individuals who are navigating multiple push and pull factors as they decide where to reside. *Counterstreams* thus offers a groundbreaking 360-degree view of migration, building on the inherent idea that mobility is a dynamic process and not a one-time event. By offering to provide a 360-degree view of migration, I mean to highlight that the study covers experiences of stay, exit, return, and

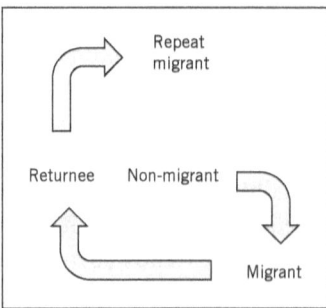

Figure I.1 A 360-Degree View of Migration

reexit and not necessarily that it covers all possible types of migration. Figure I.1 depicts a 360-degree view of migration as a process that may continue and evolve over a life. It represents an open flow rather than a full circular loop, as individuals do not end up where they started from.

We cannot understand these stages or flows in isolation. These movements and the people making them are in conversation with one another, if not directly, then indirectly. The comparative approach for considering non-migrants, returnees, and repeat migrants illuminates the multisided nature of migration and the heterogeneity of migrants. Together, these groups challenge the conventional wisdom that either migration or staying put is inherently and consistently desirable, affording social mobility and ensuring belonging. Indeed, the same people may reassess their needs and desires and flow back and forth. Moreover, all people, including non-migrants, live with the entanglements of migration. While the three vignettes at the beginning of this chapter are not meant to represent each stage—non-migrant, returnee, and repeat migrant—discussed in this book, they provide an initial overview and a starting point to the main themes of each.

In the next section, I will present my theoretical viewpoint on migra-emotions in the socio-ecology of migration (MSM) to assess immobility, return, and repeat migration. After providing the rationale for centering Africa and more specifically Ethiopian (non)migrants, I contextualize Ethiopian migration by offering a brief overview of its history over the past century. As the migra-emotions, migration streams, and counterstreams discussed in this book do not happen in a vacuum, I outline Ethiopia's recent sociopolitical and economic context, which serves as the backdrop of the country's and its people's complicated love affair with migration. I then offer a brief discussion of the research design and methodology before concluding with an overview of upcoming chapters.

Migra-emotions: Centering the Role of Emotions in Migrant Decision-making

Emotions are subjective feelings that form a fundamental part of the human experience, an aspect of human existence that we understand intuitively. Emotions are part of a dialectic process where they help us perceive, understand, and process the outside world, and vice versa. While there are still significant debates about the nature of emotions (biological, neurological, sociocultural), emotions are related to cognition.[14] They help us to process how we see and react to the world. Emotions help the inner being interpret and make sense of our outer environment. The intersubjective or dialogical nature of emotions makes them individual interpretive filters of the social world.

Emotions do not exist in a vacuum or ether. They are learned and managed, they are culturally variable and interactional, and they are therefore in and of the individual and also socially mediated. Emotions are part and parcel of the social worlds we occupy, socially constructed, culturally determined within a set of expectations, and context dependent. Emotions cannot be disaggregated from the sociocultural, economic, or political realities we inhabit. Rather, these dimensions are intimately linked as emotion can be considered a mechanism for socially mediated meaning making. Some emotions are considered to be socially acceptable, and some are not.[15]

Finally, we can conceptualize emotions as a precursor, prelude, or preamble to action, as they have a powerful influence on people's behaviors. Emotions are usually directed toward a specific person, object, or idea, which then engenders a physiological or behavioral change in the individual. An individual may not act on every emotion, but emotions generally dictate our actions. While emotions are seemingly intangible, they have tangible effects on the social world and real consequences. As Sara Ahmed aptly put it, "Emotions do things."[16] They produce actions and reactions, help us make decisions, and help others understand us within a larger social context.

Moreover, people sometimes experience a multiplicity of contradictory emotions (anger, joy, guilt, disappointment, frustration). Emotions are not static but can shift because of a number of external factors (family dynamics, sociopolitical situations, economic changes, etc.). Emotions can be transient and exist along a gradient (rather than in distinct categories). The dynamism of emotions can render them ephemeral. As such, emotions can be messy and complex, and they may not quite lend themselves to prescriptive social science analysis.

The study of human emotion has been relegated, for the most part, to psychology and, to some extent, social psychology.[17] Erving Goffman's work in the mid-twentieth century is one of the earlier explorations of emotion from a sociological perspective.[18] In his work on the presentation of the self and dramaturgy, emotion is a noteworthy part of managing the self and guiding people's impressions. The sociologist Arlie Hochschild, in her seminal work *The Managed Heart* (first published in 1983), introduced the concept of emotional labor, where workers in different fields are expected to display emotions specific to their field (e.g., undertakers are expected to exhibit sadness and sorrow).[19] Outside of work environments (and labor studies), individuals still manage their emotions in different ways depending on cultural expectations. Since Goffman and Hochschild, sociological research on emotions (from both a theoretical and empirical perspective) has burgeoned. While the study of emotions has expanded beyond the field of psychology to become more interdisciplinary, emotions are often neglected or altogether left out in migration studies. Part of the reason may be that researchers did not always consider the study of emotions as scientifically rigorous. In older theories of migration, emotions were dismissed as "irrational," fluffy, trivial, and altogether irrelevant, as opposed to the "rational" *Homo economicus*, the single male migrant who bases his migration decision on cold, unfeeling, material calculations. This gendered division perhaps explains the bias in migration studies, where emotions have not been accorded their due attention. While migration studies have been dominated by economic and political analyses of migration, we cannot underestimate the significance of emotions in migrant decision-making. Migration studies need to accord more attention to the role of emotion in migrant decision-making, as emotions have social value and social consequences.

In most migration studies, the emotional component is often left out in favor of socioeconomic or political factors. However, our understanding of how migrants engage in different migration streams is incomplete without an understanding of the emotional dynamics involved in those strategies and decision-making. People are not simply economic or political beings; they also have an emotional nature, and their feelings heavily influence their migration decisions. Consequently, understanding migrant decision-making and experiences requires an investigation into more than just the economic and sociopolitical conditions migrants face. It also requires understanding how they manage their feelings (joys, frustrations, anxieties, etc.), which are inextricably tied to their migration decisions and experiences.

A few scholars have examined the crossroads between migration and emotion.[20] The literature on migrant belonging in particular alludes to emotions as a key explanatory factor. For instance, Nira Yuval-Davis, Kalpana Kannabiran, and Ulrike Vieten explain that "an emotional dimension is central to notions of belonging."[21] Homeland governments also seek to tap into the emotional dimension as they attempt to mobilize their respective diasporas (for instance, presenting a rhetoric of responsibility and duty).[22] Governments' emotional pleas to their respective diasporas show that emotions can be instrumentalized for different ends. Similarly, migrant economic activities (such as remittances) or transnational political pursuits can be explained using the framework of emotional attachment.

Few book-length works examine the interplay between emotion and migration. Elizabeth Aranda's work examines the role of emotions in the integration of Puerto Rican migrants living in the United States versus returnees in the home island.[23] Ala Sirriyeh explores the central role of emotion in immigration policies in Australia, Europe, and the United States.[24] Leah Williams Veazey looks at the interplay between emotion and belonging in online spaces for migrant mothers.[25] While these are commendable works, they are few and far between.

In this book, I center what is usually relegated to the margins, looking beyond the causes of migration and processes of integration. I seek to complicate conventional understandings of the reasons for and the meanings of migration. In line with the recent encouraging emotional turn in migration studies, I posit emotions as a key lens to understand migration. I advance a theory of migra-emotions, akin to the theorization of crimmigration and migra-politics.[26] I define migra-emotions as emotions specific to migration that are central to understanding migration decisions and experiences. I adopt a broad constructionist approach to explore how migrants feel in particular situations and how they act on those emotions within the socioecology of migration.

Rather than seeing emotions as an unwelcome intrusion into otherwise rigorous academic research, I set forth emotions as a central component, recognizing their importance for human understanding. Migration scholars thus need to acknowledge and appreciate the existence of migra-emotions, become cognizant of how they function, and theorize their effects in and on different migration streams. By adopting emotions as a primary framework of analysis, I seek to move migrant decision-making beyond a sum of opportunities into a more sophisticated emotional landscape. This framework complicates conventional understandings of the reasons for and meanings of migration. I provide an insight into the nuanced motives, realities, and travails of migrants. Emotions are one lens through which to understand migrant agency. In a way, a focus on emotions can help us name or break down agency. Within emotions are subsumed aspirations, perceptions, and more generally migrants' subjective sense making.

Migration decisions and experiences are animated with all types of emotions, including positive (such as joy and happiness), negative (such as fear and sadness), and ambivalent ones. Table I.1 provides a nonexhaustive list of migra-emotions that can affect migrant decision-making. In the context

TABLE I.1. MIGRA-EMOTIONS: TYPES OF EMOTIONS THAT CAN AFFECT MIGRATION DECISIONS	
Positive	Joy, happiness, contentment, affection, hope, sense of belonging, duty to home, relief, honor, pride, excitement, optimism, sense of adventure, empathy
Negative	Alienation, fear, guilt, boredom, disaffection, dissatisfaction, estrangement, disillusionment, disorientation, agony, shame, embarrassment, anger, aversion, disgust, sadness, frustration, discomfort, fatigue, resentment
Ambivalent	Ambivalence, nostalgia, hesitancy, surprise

of migration, certain emotions can engender specific forms of migration or lead individuals to choose to stay within the home country. For instance, a non-migrant who feels contentment, pride, and optimism about the home country is unlikely to migrate. On the flip side, one who is dissatisfied, frustrated, and angry with the homeland is likely to consider migration. Similarly, a migrant who feels alienated and disaffected in the host country, while simultaneously feeling a sense of duty and belonging to the home nation, is likely to engage in return migration. Finally, a returnee who feels frustrated in the homeland may become a repeat migrant. These simple examples illustrate how migra-emotions can affect migration decision-making. These emotions are not unique to migrants but directly affect migration experiences and decision-making. However, emotions can sometimes exist simultaneously, resulting in conflicting emotional push and pull in (non)migrants. We can also discuss emotional push and pull factors, such as hope on one side and fear on the other.

Migrants undoubtedly feel the emotional weight of their migration decisions and experiences. Subjective cognitive imagining (how individuals think about their current location and how they imagine their future selves in different locations) significantly influences migrant decision-making. The role of emotions in migration is therefore a critical component of the discussion. More specifically, I posit emotion as a key source of motivation. At the same time, it is challenging to capture the transient nature of migra-emotions, as they can change over time.

In this work, one of my aims is to make explicit the emotional subtext of migration aspirations. I seek to provide insight into how emotions affect people's migration decision-making, their assessment of their migration journeys and experiences, and their sense of belonging to both homelands and host countries. Looking at migration through the lens of emotion enables us to offer a more nuanced analysis of the phenomenon. Leaving out emotions from the equation makes for an incomplete analysis as they are an intrinsic human feature that affects every aspect of our lives. This approach is cognizant of the effects of cultural globalization, which can fuel a desire for migration that is unexplained in purely economic terms. This work amply demonstrates the pertinence of emotions (positive, negative, and ambivalent) to every step of the migration process, starting with the initial decision to migrate or stay in the homeland.

Foregrounding emotional dimensions offers a fruitful theoretical approach that can help explain why individuals choose to stay or migrate, return to their homelands, or engage in repeat migration. By theorizing emotion, I want to contribute to the emotionalization of migration studies. Nonetheless, migra-emotions cannot be properly understood and analyzed without a structural understanding of the socio-ecology of migrations, the ecosystem of social, political, and economic factors that alternatively enable or prohibit migration. Emotional dimensions are thus only part of the story. Attention to the subjective, emotional, cognitive imagining element does not deny the socio-ecological realities and other contingencies that facilitate or impede migration. Capturing a full picture of migrant decision-making requires an engagement with the socio-ecology of migration, the larger structural factors that are exogenous to the individual.

The Socio-ecology of Migration: The Constraints of Possibilities

Social structures are the sum of all the interrelated parts of society, including different social institutions such as the family, media, religion, and government. It is a way to see the macro-level social system, the framework on which society is established, with its own norms and patterns. While social structures exert influence on people's individual behaviors, the rigid notion of structure is limiting as it implies immutability. For migrants, important structural factors can include national and international laws governing migration, employment opportunities, social welfare infrastructure, the immigrant integration landscape, ranging from multiculturalism to xenophobia, and so forth that encourage or discourage migration. Scholars have grappled with more malleable concepts to address what have traditionally been referred to as structural factors—broader political, economic, social, and environmental conditions that influence individuals' lives. Within the aspiration and capabilities framework, Hein De Haas and Jørgen Carling employ the concept of capabilities, which they view as less restrictive and rigid than structure.[27] While aspiration is the desire (or lack thereof) to migrate, capabilities are the socioeconomic, political, and environmental circumstances that allow or enable potential migrants to actualize their migration aspiration. According to De Haas and Carling, both aspirations and capabilities exist along a spectrum or continuum. It is possible to trace the progression of values along this continuum for those with high or low aspirations for or capabilities of migration. Migration aspirations emerge within particular contexts and macrostructures, and individuals' desire to leave or stay appears within this larger context. At the same time, these individuals may or may not be in a position to fulfill their desire to migrate or stay. In regard to structure, different types of resources, such as financial, social, or human capital, either enable or restrict the ability to migrate.

Other scholars have operationalized the framework of assemblage, which is similar to the concept of capabilities. As an analytical tool, assemblage can explain complex, dynamic, and perhaps fluid social and political realities, more focused on processes than on discrete events. With respect to migration, assemblage is defined "as the process within which various players, including prospective migrants, brokers and traffickers, state officials, and formal and informal institutions, link in a harmonious as well as competitive fashion to shape outward migration."[28] Scholars have thus found assemblage to be a productive analytical tool in migration studies as it also allows room for the agency of the migrants and a comprehensive understanding of migration.

While both the capabilities and assemblage frameworks reimagine the restrictive notion of structure, I find that neither quite captures the ever-evolving local, national, regional, and international realities that migrants must navigate. I propose a socio-ecological framework, which is a less rigid and more malleable approach than structure, capability, or assemblage. An ecology is an ever-evolving living organism constantly being affected and affecting those living within it. In a way, migration can be equated with a living organism with rules and a life of its own. There are a lot of moving parts to account for in the migrants' countries of origin, transit, and destination. I employ the term "socio-ecology," which encompasses economic, political, and sociocultural concerns while signaling that these are malleable forces. The socio-ecological analytical framework expands or supplements the capability and assemblage frameworks rather than supplanting them. A socio-ecological approach does not only focus on the immovable macro-level structures enabling or preventing migration but also encompasses micro- and meso-level concerns such as migra-emotions, family structures, and community groups.

Migra-emotions in the Socio-ecology of Migration

Migra-emotions in the socio-ecology of migration (MSM) provide unique insights into migrant behaviors. In this work, I am interested in the mediation between the emotional (intrinsic) and the socio-ecological (extrinsic) dimensions in migrant decision-making. It is meaningless to look at migra-emotions separate from the socio-ecology of migration and vice versa, as they are interconnected principles of migration. I challenge conventional ways of thinking in migration studies by positing the (non)migrants as agentic actors navigating complex and fluid emotional and socio-ecological landscapes. The dialogic approach between considering migrants' emotion and examining the meso- and macro-level drivers of migration sheds light on the unique nuances in a 360-degree view of migration. This model helps reconcile the micro- (individual migrant decisions) and macro- (socio-ecological factors, which include political, economic, and social structures) level analysis. Figure I.2 highlights the interplay between migra-emotions and the socio-ecology of migration. This framework allows a simultaneous consideration of both agency (migra-emotions) and structure (socio-ecology of migration) in decisions to migrate or stay put, enabling a theorization of complex and multifaceted social phenomena.

The complexity of migration makes it impossible to find rules or principles that explain (or predict) every situation, but the MSM approach enables us to respond to a shifting landscape. The MSM framework is a flexible and dynamic tool that allows enough room to address the complexities of lived experience. As a conceptual approach, the MSM framework is not constrained by the rigidity of other theoretical frameworks. The dynamism of the framework accurately reflects a lived reality where people's ways of thinking and the contexts underlying their choices are in constant flux.

By drawing attention to the emotions involved in people's migration decisions and experiences at different stages of the migration journey, this book captures the interactions between the large-scale socio-ecology of migration (structural factors) and individual migrant decision-making, with emotions as the mediating factor. This MSM lens provides an insight into how people "do" migration: How do they think and feel about their migration decisions and experiences? How do they assess their current situation (sociopolitical, economic)? How do they develop a strategy to migrate or stay put, to return to their homeland or to the host country? Illuminating how emotions mitigate migration decision-making extends our understanding about the inner lives of migrants and the ways migrants navigate the socio-ecology of migration.

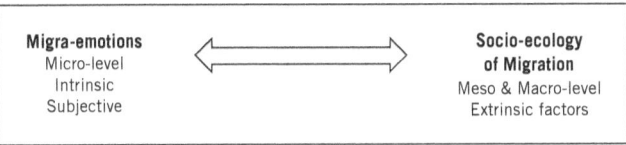

Figure I.2 The MSM Model: Migra-emotions in the Socio-ecology of Migration

The embodied accounts of migration in this work focus on how individual (non)migrants negotiate their emotions and understand and discuss their migration decisions. As the opening vignettes about Aida, Alemneh, and *Gash* Mengesha reveal, non-migrants, returnees, and repeat migrants possess, display, and discuss various emotions related to migration. Their emotional disposition then leads them to decide to stay or migrate within the constraints of the socio-ecology of migration. As a young woman, Aida is bored with her life in Ethiopia and filled with anticipation about her imagined life in the United States. Alemneh was tired of the rat race in the United States and is content with his family's decision to return to the homeland. With quiet resignation, *Gash* Mengesha has pragmatically acquiesced to the circumstances that compelled him to remigrate back to the United States. These three individuals—a non-migrant, a returnee, and a repeat migrant—have very different emotional responses to their circumstances navigating the socio-ecology of migration. Their feelings (boredom, hope, excitement, disenchantment, contentment, acquiescence) and extrinsic factors (divergent opportunities in the Global North and South, sociocultural expectations, health infrastructures) together shape their lived realities and migration histories. The stories in the upcoming chapters provide a multitude of situations and emotional responses that demonstrate the importance of the MSM framework. Moreover, as all experiences are mediated through different axes of identity, I infuse a race-, class-, and gender-based analysis throughout the chapters. It is additionally important to understand the intersections between these identities (for example, how gender and race work in tandem).

Labeling and the Inherent Paradox of *Counterstreams*

In this work, I employ various terms—"non-migrant," "migrant," "returnee," "repeat migrant"—to represent different stages or actions in a 360-degree view of migratory movements. I do not employ these labels to create binaries and discrete categories, nor do I envisage them to calcify categories or render them immutable. However, for a logical flow of my argument, I need to organize narrative focus around important stages and transition points along a continuum of emotions and mobilities. This book presents an inherent paradox where I am obliged to use extant labels, even as I seek to complicate their essentializing nature by highlighting the continuity, fluidity, and complexity of the individuals' emotional landscape and their ensuing mobilities. I acknowledge the inherent paradox in the need to impose discrete labels on a phenomenon that I am arguing resists labels for the sake of showing the complexity of the forces pulling people in and out of movement. I seek to show the fluidity between different stages and the circularity of migratory movements overall. However, to do so, I need to rely on extant, somewhat limiting labels. To coherently discuss the fluidity and emotions an individual experiences among different positions, decisions, and geographic locations regarding mobility, I must rely on labels to describe them, even recognizing that the labels are limiting by definition. This is the reason I allocate important space here in the Introduction and in each of the empirical chapters to discuss the definitions and limitations of each moment in the continuity: non-migrant, returnee, and repeat migrant. It is impossible to discuss these movements without accounting for the changing perspectives from which different subjects in transition between positions view them.

Centering Africa

Context matters, and the context for this study is the continent of Africa, and more specifically the country of Ethiopia. For a migration scholar, the African continent is a dynamic geography, encompassing both historical mobilities and contemporary movements. Historically, the continent has been marked by various major waves of internal and external migration that have shaped its people, cultures, and societies. The Bantu migrations, internal migrations of Africans from around present-day Nigeria to the West, East, and South of the continent that took place two thousand to four thousand years ago, have resulted in similarities in languages and cultures within the regions. The connections between Northeast Africa and southern Europe, the Mediterranean world, and the Arabian Peninsula have been well documented since at least the period of antiquities.[29] The eastern coast of the continent has historically been interconnected with the Indian Ocean world, leading to out-, return, and repeat migration, resulting most significantly in the expansive Swahili coast and a sizable Afro-descent population in South Asia.[30] Closer to our contemporary period, the transatlantic slave trade has led to the forcible removal of millions of Africans as enslaved labor to the Americas.[31] Contemporary African migration is a continuation of these historical movements and does not necessarily represent a new phenomenon.[32]

The African continent, however, has not been marked exclusively by emigration. In fact, return represents a significant migratory movement on the continent, and the two hundred million African descendants spread throughout the globe provide the source for diasporic and contemporary return. For example, Liberia and Sierra Leone are both modern nations created in the 1800s as sites for respectively American and British free (most of whom were formerly enslaved) Black people to resettle. Similarly, during this time, there was a significant wave of Afro-Brazilian returnees to West Africa.[33] The teachings of Marcus Garvey in the 1920s and the U.S. Civil

Rights movement and African independence of the 1960s also inspired return movements.³⁴ The Afro-centric religion Rastafari, born in the Caribbean, engendered its own diasporic return to the continent, with Ethiopia as the preferred destination.³⁵ In all of these movements, historical connections, ideas of homeland, and racial identification were significant motivators for the return to the African continent. The country of Ghana continues to attract diasporic returnees with events and programs such as the Joseph Project and the Year of the Return.³⁶ These different African diasporic return movements are summarized in Table I.2.

The continent has also received non-African migrants from other parts of the world, notably Europeans moving as part of European colonization to places such as Algeria and South Africa starting from the seventeenth century. Together with European colonizers came other populations, such as South Asians following the British and the Lebanese following the French.³⁷ All of these movements illustrate that the African continent has historically been connected with other parts of the world, as either a source or destination for migrants. This historical context provides a crucial backdrop for a

TABLE I.2. AFRICAN DIASPORIC RETURN MOVEMENTS		
Time period	Country / region	Context
Late 1700s into early 1800s	Sierra Leone	Place of return for free Black people from British territories (Jamaica, London, Nova Scotia) starting from what is now modern-day Freetown; return took place in waves until the territory came under British colonial occupation
Early 1800s	Liberia	Place of return for free Black people from the United States under the auspices of the American Colonization Society
Mid-1800s into 1900s	Benin, Ghana, Togo, and other West African countries	Afro-Brazilian return initially prompted by the 1835 Mâle slave revolt;¹ their communities became known as "Tabom people" in West Africa
Early 1900s	Ghana	Return influenced by Garveyism and Pan-African ideals
Mid-1960s	Ethiopia	Rastafarian return influenced by religious ideas
Mid-1960s to the present	Ghana	Return initially influenced by the country's first president, Kwame Nkrumah, followed by other programs such as the Joseph Project

¹ See João José Reis, Slave Rebellion in Brazil: The *Muslim Uprising of 1835 in Bahia* (Taylor and Francis, 1995).

full appreciation of the 360-degree view of contemporary African migration offered in *Counterstreams*.

Studies of contemporary African mobilities tend to disproportionately focus on forced migration (i.e., refugee movements) and the migration-development nexus, to the detriment of other types and effects of migration. The two main reasons for this narrow focus are interrelated. First, the existing research funding at the global level drives a lack of depth and breadth in information on African migration. Most of the research is funded by think tanks and not independent academic research institutes, which tend to view African migration as a problem to be solved rather than a topic worthy of investigation in its own right.[38] Second, the racialization of global migration contributes to the bias regarding the topics deemed pertinent in the study of African migration. African migration is often studied from a purely economic or political perspective. Moreover, the dominant story of African migration focuses on despair. This gives a skewed view of African migration in the ritual of Afro-pessimism. According to Marie-Laurence Flahaux and De Haas, there are three prevalent underlying assumptions about African migration: that it is "high and increasing"; "mainly directed towards Europe"; and "driven by poverty and violence."[39] They go on to dispel these assumptions one by one, and convincingly argue that "such ideas are based on assumption, selective observation or journalistic impressions rather than on sound empirical evidence."[40] We therefore need empirical academic interventions that provide a more comprehensive and accurate reflection of the reality on the ground.

There are new, exciting works examining Black and African immigrant experiences in the Global North, such as Tod Hamilton's *Immigration and the Remaking of Black America* (2019), Orly Clerge's *The New Noir: Race, Identity, and Diaspora in Black Suburbia* (2019), Onoso Imoagene's *Beyond Expectations: Second-Generation Nigerians in the United States and Britain* (2017), and Beaman Jean's *Citizen Outsider: Children of North African Immigrants in France* (2017). Cawo Abdi's *Elusive Jannah: The Somali Diaspora and a Borderless Muslim Identity* (2015) stands apart as it provides a comparative case of Somali migrants in the United Arab Emirates, South Africa, and the United States.

Most of these works can be classified as part of a growing body of scholarship examining the New African Diaspora, looking at the recent waves of migration (since the Second World War) that emanate from the African continent and settle in different parts of the world, including Asia, Europe, and Oceania.[41] The New African Diaspora goes beyond the historical African diaspora resulting mostly from the forced migration associated with the transatlantic slave trades. Contemporary migration mainly comprises voluntary migration driven by globalization, education opportunities, employment, and political instability.[42] This contemporary global migration of people of African descent leads to the creation of new and diverse African diasporic communities around the world, generating unique dynamics in the geographies of settlement.[43] Particularly fascinating is the relationship between the old historical African diaspora and newer communities that result from the different waves of contemporary African migration.[44] This relationship ranges from friendliness, cooperation, and solidarity to animosity and competition over limited resources.

Books that examine migration exclusively from the perspective of African migrant-sending nations are few and far between. For instance, Charles Piot's *The Fixer: Visa Lottery Chronicles* (2019) provides an ethnographic accounting of a Togolese visa broker. Similarly, Onoso Imoagene's *Structured Luck: Downstream Effects of the U.S. Diversity Visa Program* (2024) documents the multifarious effects of visa lottery programs in recipients' home countries. The edited volume by Lisa Åkesson and Maria Eriksson Baaz, *Africa's Returnees: The New Developers?* (2015), and Adele Galipo's *Return Migration and Nation Building in Africa: Reframing the Somali Diaspora* (2018) speak directly to African return migration.

While my work is located within the aforementioned conversations, *Counterstreams* is distinguished from the existing works in the following ways: First, *Counterstreams* examines three groups pertinent to a 360-degree view of migration. To the best of my knowledge, there are no studies that explore non-migrants, returnees, and repeat migrants in tandem. Moreover, the scope of the book extends beyond looking at these three groups individually to elucidate how they affect one another. As migration research is intrinsically comparative, it looks at the symbiotic relationship between these three different groups and their interactions.

Second, this book centers the African continent. This book corrects the imbalance of the existing lopsided analysis of out-migration and focus on destination countries, which has limited our understanding of African migration. This study can also expand our understanding of the interconnections and modes of incorporation of Black migrants in the host nations, as processes of racialization in host nations can motivate return migration.

Third, my study focuses on more privileged types of migrants. This research goes beyond an instrumentalist view of migrants as economic developers or sociopolitical agents of change as presented in previous research. It examines the counterstreams to dominant African migrant movements, paying particular attention to voluntary, lifetime, middle- and upper-class returnees.

This work presents an insight into a small but powerful group in African migration. I am heeding Laura Nader's call to "study up," to study the culture of power and affluence rather than a culture of powerlessness.[45] This is an attempt to recover and include previously unheard and excluded voices. In this sense, my work critiques dominant tropes of Afro-pessimistic African mobility studies and works against hidden Western imperialist assumptions.[46] Although this book does not shy away from the travails of migration or sugarcoat the lived realities and tribulations of African migration, it counters the prevailing Afro-pessimistic trope that characterizes African migration research. I locate my work within the emerging tradition of postcolonial sociology, which works against the epistemic legacy of sociology as a field developed in the context of colonialism and in the interest of imperialism.[47] In our contemporary "post-colonial neo-colonized world," using Gayatri Chakravorty Spivak's terms,[48] the global inequalities between the Global North and South, with roots in European colonialism, persist in the twenty-first century. It is important to formulate new knowledge that is centered on the Global South and taps into our global sociological imagination.[49]

Counterstreams provides the first large-scale in-depth analysis of three less visible aspects of migration—immobility, return, and repeat migration—from the perspective of an African migrant-sending nation, Ethiopia. By focusing on these under-studied flows of migration, I offer a more complete picture of African migrant stories. *Counterstreams* uncovers the complexity and the multiple facets of African migration, which will have a broad appeal beyond the case specificity. This book sheds light on emotions, socioeconomic conditions, and political factors to tell a more nuanced story of African migration where the agency of the migrants is front and center. *Counterstreams* therefore makes a timely contribution to the field of African and migration studies, increasing our breadth and depth of understanding of migration from the perspective of a migrant-sending nation. Within the context of the African continent, Ethiopia, the second most populous nation in the African continent, with over 120 million inhabitants (as of 2020), serves as a microcosm of African migrations and provides a unique case study to explore MSM.

Historicizing and Contextualizing Ethiopian Migration

Ethiopia's tumultuous love affair with migration is complicated, as illustrated by its history over the past hundred years or so. The country's migration history is symbiotically tied to the different administrations that ruled it over the years. Ethiopia had three distinct political systems in the past century. Under the imperial system, Emperor Haile Selassie ruled for forty-four years (1930–1974). During this time, Ethiopian elites sent their children to the United States and Europe in search of higher education.[50] The emperor, who was also the self-appointed minister of education, facilitated the overseas education of scores of elite children in the 1950s and 1960s.[51] The majority of them returned after receiving their first, second, or third degrees in Western educational institutions. Significant return migration of educated elites thus marked the migration history of Ethiopia in the 1950s and 1960s. Considering the strength of Ethiopia's political system at the time and its symbolic significance for Black populations globally, it is not particularly surprising that most Ethiopians opted not to stay in the United States or Europe, where Black immigrants were subjugated as second-class citizens. Rather, upon completing their degrees, virtually all the educated Ethiopian elites were anxious to return to their country and participate in its modernization. Stories abound of graduating students so eager to return to their homeland that they did not even bother waiting to attend their graduation ceremonies but instead opted to have their degrees mailed to them.

The post–Second World War period marks the beginning of a new world order, where a system of nation-states replaced the system of (European) empires, ushering in, in effect, a postcolonial world. African nations were beginning to gain their independence from European colonization. Ethiopia, a country that was never colonized, was extolled as the beacon of a Black independent nation. The decolonization of Africa also coincided with the Civil Rights movement in the United States, where Black people were reclaiming and proudly asserting their identities.

The perception of migration and settlement patterns of Ethiopian migrants changed drastically with the regime change in 1974, when Colonel Mengistu Hailemariam toppled Haile Selassie's monarchy (together with the centuries-old Solomonic dynasty). The Derg Marxist-Leninist regime that replaced the monarchy ruled Ethiopia between 1974 and 1991, enmeshing the country in Cold War politics and ushering in a period of upheavals that led to massive out-migration incited by political violence. This seventeen-year period was marked by unprecedented exile as Ethiopians crossed the borders to Sudan and Kenya, seeking refuge from indiscriminate persecution.[52] The elite students who were abroad at the time of the revolution, including some members of the royal family, were stranded and became refugees overnight. Ethiopian migrants dispersed to different corners of the world, forming the genesis of the global Ethiopian diaspora. This period also saw some (educational) migration to the former USSR and Soviet allied nations such as Cuba. The migration toward the Soviet Union and its allies were marked by significant return movements, mostly by design.[53]

The Derg communist regime ended in 1991, to be replaced by the Ethiopian People's Revolutionary Democratic Front (EPRDF), which has ruled the country until 2018. Although the arrival of the EPRDF slowed down the massive exile, the out-migration trend did not end completely. The forced political migration of the 1970s and 1980s was followed by an outflow of (mostly) economic migrants in the 1990s and 2000s. Networks that had been established in the previous era facilitated the migration of newer populations in the new millennium, leading to the growth and maturation of the Ethiopian diaspora. Additionally, migrant destination country policies such as the U.S. Diversity Visa Program, visa sponsorships, and family reunifications facilitated further out-migration.

There was an inherent contradiction in the political rule that governed Ethiopia after 1991. As former freedom fighters who liberated Ethiopia from the previous brutal regime, the political elite felt entitled to withhold power from opposing parties. At the same time, as a development state, the government poured its resources into modernizing the physical (transportation, housing, industrialization, etc.) and social (education and health-care in particular) infrastructures of the country. As a consequence, while political participation was curtailed, the economy flourished. For the duration of this study (2011–2019), when groups, principally organized along ethnic lines, demanded more political openness, they were met with a strong arm from the government. Many rallies were forcibly squelched, journalists and political activists were imprisoned, sometimes by the thousands, and a general sense of uncertainty and unease reigned over the country. The government grew increasingly repressive and showed signs of becoming a veritable dictatorship. Ethiopia concurrently experienced significant political and social upheaval. Thus, the government's lack of openness, extending even to political repression, led to people "voting with their feet."[54] People questioned when the exodus would end.[55] Increased repression led to increased public demonstrations in many parts of the country. More recently, between November 2020 and December 2022, a civil conflict broke out in the northern part of the country, pitting the national government and its allies against the TPLF (Tigray People's Liberation Front),[56] which had been in power since 1991.

As of 2024, an estimated two to three million Ethiopians were living outside their homelands.[57] Solomon Addis Getahun estimates that the Ethiopian diaspora (including both the first and second generations) in North America alone surpasses one million, although reliable global estimates are unavailable.[58] Ethiopia's diaspora emanates mostly from migration since 1974, and it comprises a refugee population, among others. Ethiopians employed migration as a tool to deal with various crises the country experienced, such as famines, civil conflict, political repression, economic downturns, and high levels of unemployment.[59]

There are currently three main areas of settlement for Ethiopian migrants: the Global North, including countries in North America, Australia, and northern and Western Europe (this is the focus of this study); the Arabian Peninsula or Gulf States; and South Africa. These geographies invariably become the source regions for returnees. While migrants can generally gain legal long-term residency and even citizenship in the Global North, the same does not necessarily hold true for the other two regions.

As Ethiopian migrants were crossing international borders in search of better livelihoods and opportunities, a visible return migration was occurring simultaneously. Therefore, while return from any of these regions can be undertaken voluntarily, return from the Arabian Peninsula and South Africa is often compelled by expulsion or deportation.[60] Regardless, the experiences, reception, and integration of returnees from these geographic locations is vastly different depending on levels of preparation, volition (forced or voluntary), accumulated savings, and connections to the homeland.

Statistical data would have helped contextualize the larger flows against which returnees are positioned. Moreover, positioning the size and prominence of returnees and repeat migrants against the backdrop of larger groups of migrants and non-migrants is important. However, statistical data outlining the size of the diaspora settled in different geographies (in Africa, the Global North, and the Arabian Peninsula) is unfortunately unavailable.[61] Moreover, we have little data on African return and repeat migrants in general, and Ethiopia is no exception. The Ethiopian government does not keep data on returnees or repeat migrants because these categories are not officially recognized. This lack of statistical data prohibits us from mapping out the migration of the population. Yet, starting from the late 1990s and continuing in the 2000s, there was a documented wave of returnees resettling back in their home nation because of improvements in the socioeconomic and political situations.[62] Although the cases of return migration have garnered attention from both academic researchers and policymakers, they have yet to be qualitatively investigated in depth.

Political and economic upheavals in the homeland undoubtedly affect non-migrants, returnees, and members of the diaspora, engendering specific migra-emotions. Migration may look more attractive to non-migrants because of constant upheavals in the home country. Migrants settled in different parts of the world may alternatively look on the homeland with hope and trepidation. Some returnees may question or even regret resettling back in their home nation because of ongoing political instabilities. Finally, repeat migrants may feel discontent with the homeland. Nonetheless, this background of constant economic, social, and political changes invariably shaped my respondents' experiences as non-migrants, returnees, and repeat migrants.

Ethiopia experienced an economic boom between 2010 and 2019, and as an emerging economy, Ethiopia offered unrivaled opportunities for those poised to take advantage.[63] At the same time, the economic prosperity did not necessarily translate into a better lifestyle for everyone. The economic boom failed to keep up with the population rise, leading to high rates of unemployment in both rural and urban areas. Increasing inequalities are often associated with growing economies. In fact, the majority of the population is still poor and contends with harsh economic realities.[64] Even though our understanding of migration pressures has evolved over the years, economic motivations persist as a central force that generates labor migration.

This is sadly illustrated by the scores of Ethiopians who regularly die attempting to reach the shores of Europe by crossing the Mediterranean Sea. African migrants, a large number of them from countries such as Ethiopia, Eritrea, and Somalia, engage in dangerous crossings of the Sahara to reach the supposed dreamland of Europe. Others cross the Sinai desert and the Red Sea in search of better opportunities in the Gulf States. Recently, East African migrants crossing the Red Sea have inadvertently ended up in the middle of the Yemeni civil war (2014–present) or similar harsh conditions. All these different streams of irregular migration are fraught with challenges, including starvation, human trafficking, prostitution, dehydration, and ultimately death.[65] A lucky few successfully make it to the shores of Europe or the Arabian Peninsula, and thus begins another chapter of their migration ordeal.

Currently, Ethiopia is in a unique position where it continues to experience both massive emigration and also return migration. One of the first documented and renowned Ethiopian returnees at the turn of the twentieth century was *Hakim* Workeneh Eshete (1864–1952), the first Western-educated medical doctor.[66] Similarly, Tekle Hawariat Tekle Mariyam (1884–1977), the father of modern Ethiopian theater, spent twenty-plus years of his life in Russia.[67] These two historical figures exemplify some of the first returnees in Ethiopian modern history. Considered to be leaders of modernization, the few Ethiopian migrants at the turn of the twentieth century were lauded for their contributions to society.

The Janus face of Ethiopian migration indicates the duality of in- and out-migration.[68] Additionally, Ethiopia is a big regional destination primarily for (forced) migrants from Eritrea, Somalia, and South Sudan. According to the United Nations High Commissioner for Refugees, in 2019 there were at least a million refugees and migrants from the neighboring countries of Eritrea, Somalia, and South Sudan settled in Ethiopia.[69] The confluence of massive out-migration and return migrations indicates a society in flux. These changes in the Ethiopian migration landscape inspired this research. Ethiopia is no longer just a migrant-sending nation; it is ushering in a new historical period where members of its diaspora are returning to resettle in noteworthy ways. Although most would see a contradiction in the practice of Ethiopian migration, exit and return form two sides of the same coin. The findings of this study have to be understood within this context. Massive exit can engender return, and return can incite further emigration. This brief background on the historical, political, and socioeconomic facets of the homeland serves as a starting point for a discussion of the socio-ecology of migration.

Ethiopian migrants provide a fertile case study for the investigation of counterstreams in migration movements for three main reasons. First, Ethiopian history is marked by internal and cross-border migration.[70] Second, Ethiopia has a significant contemporary diaspora settled in the Global North, particularly in North America, and this diaspora can serve as a potential source for return migration. Ethiopian migrants have been increasingly relocating voluntarily back to their home nation because of the improving socioeconomic and political situations. Third, just as initial migration leads to streams of return, this return invariably engenders streams of repeat migration.

Study Design

In this book, I present an academically rigorous, evidence-based research rooted in qualitative methodologies.[71] I interviewed a total of ninety-four Ethiopian migrants with the following breakdown: sixty-two returnees, sixteen non-migrant kin, and sixteen repeat migrants. I used a nonprobability snowball sampling method to solicit interviews using several different entry points into the population. In addition to the interviews, over the course of almost a decade (2011–2019), I carried out a total of twenty months of ethnographic participant observation in Addis Ababa, Ethiopia. This book depicts a brief moment in time, a span of a decade in which simultaneous and contradictory processes of migration took place.[72]

While there is insufficient quantitative data to map out Ethiopians' overall pattern of return and repeat migration, qualitative studies allow an exploration of the nuances involved in the migration experience, with an emphasis on the meanings migrants attach to events and processes in their lives.[73] Personal accounts of migration and intricate life stories tell us a great deal about the larger picture. Qualitative methods help disentangle nuances in attitude and behavior and their ensuing effects, providing a depth of understanding.

My initial questions and focus morphed into an examination of the emotional lives of migrants. How do non-migrants, returnees, and repeat migrants feel about their migration status? How do they perceive and live migration? Are there emotions specific to migration? How do (non)migrants measure their life satisfaction? With a reading attuned to the emotional lives of my respondents, I started to pay attention to the dialectic between respondents' emotional processing of their circumstance and the decisions they made.

For the data analysis, I employed grounded theory, an inductive methodology that allows the generation of theory rooted in observation and systematic research.[74] Grounded theory goes beyond the accurate description of the phenomenon at hand to enable the researcher to generate concepts that capture the concerns and lived realities of the respondents.[75]

As knowledge is socially constructed, it is important to explicate my social position and identity vis-à-vis the research.[76] This research was not impersonal for me, nor did I approach it with clinical detachment. Instead, my family's experience with (return) migration highly influenced my perspective.[77] My academic research interests are deeply intertwined with my lived experiences, and at times those two areas are hard to detangle, not that I necessarily want to extricate one from the other. For the most part, my respondents considered me an "insider" since I am a first-generation Ethiopian immigrant currently residing in the United States. At the same time, I was an "outsider" to this group as an academician carrying out research on this important topic. My insider-outsider status helped me gain keen insight into the lives and motivations of Ethiopian return migrants.[78] I also provide an autoethnography using my personal experience to explicate larger sociological realities and an account of different spaces imbued with meaning for migrants. As a method, autoethnography recognizes that there is no such thing as a purely objective perspective. In fact, this methodology incorporates and celebrates personal perspectives as an important aspect of the research.

Finally, I do not want my writing to alienate those outside of academia and thus render this important work inaccessible. I do not want to tell these stories of migration in a dispassionate, third-person, seemingly objective way, with my authority legitimized by the letters after my name and the strength of my citations. Rather, I employ storying as praxis, as methodology, and as a form of resistance. I am interested in telling the untold stories of African migration, reclaiming our narratives.

It behooves us to remember that storying is connected to power—who can tell stories, how many, when, and under what circumstances. The father of African literature, Chinua Achebe, highlights the importance of "a balance of stories where every people will be able to contribute to a definition of themselves, where we are not victims of other people's accounts."[79] In her 2009 TED Talk (which at last count has garnered over forty million views on Ted.com and fourteen million views on YouTube), Chimamanda Adichie warns against the dangers of a "single story."[80] She cautions that a single story flattens, creates stereotypes, robs people of their dignity, and makes the recognition of our equal humanity difficult. Building on this admonition and the practice of African writers, my narratives aim to counter one-dimensional representations that flatten. Rather, I aim to disrupt broad narratives of the African migrant, providing an opportunity to reframe this representation. I hope this work contributes in some small way to the restorying of African migration to better reflect the diversity of perspectives and experiences.

Limitations of This Study

As it is impossible to address every possible topic in a single volume, every study comes with its own limitations. Accordingly, several shortcomings of this study must be acknowledged: First, its focus on privileged migrants by definition excludes other types of migrants. Second, the lack of statistical data impedes the ideal of showing the scale of counterstream movements within and outside of the African continent.

This book primarily focuses on relatively well-off Ethiopian (non)migrants and examines the back-and-forth movements between Ethiopia and the Global North. The book therefore does not address the experiences of less privileged or forced migrants, although some of my interlocutors might have started out as such. The types of overlapping multiple mobilities I discuss in this book are enabled by the relative privilege of the migrants, including (but not limited to) their socioeconomic and documentation status. My interlocutors are typically wealthier and highly educated, and many have gained citizenship or residency permits from Global North countries. Their positionality within this global structural hierarchal matrix has imbued them with certain privileges that other migrants do not possess. Without these relative privileges, their ability to move, return, and engage in circular migration would be significantly curtailed. However, these privileges must be understood within a larger intersectional system of migration advantages and disadvantages revealed through a comparative analysis. In other words, these are relative privileges that need to be located within larger global and unequal social relations. These relative privileges allow space for potential migrants to choose to stay, migrate, return, or engage in circular migration and accordingly lead to a rich and fruitful discussion of migra-emotions. Therefore, the respondents in this study are ideally situated to consider the forces that weigh on the decision-making processes, allowing for a discussion of multidirectional and overlapping migration movements. Given the specific focus on relatively privileged types of migrants (and the justification behind the choice), other types of migrants (less privileged, undocumented, or forced migrants, for example) have consequently been excluded from this study.

The second major limitation of this study is the unavailability of statistical data to properly contextualize the size and scale of return and repeat migration. The paucity of the available statistical data and lack of a unified definition of return and repeat migration pose a significant impediment to researchers. Migrant-sending and migrant-receiving governments do not always levy data on the significant phenomena of return and repeat migration. Even if some governments do collect this data, they differ in their definitions and therefore do not enable a comparative analysis. As a result, the global volume and regional characteristics of return and repeat migration are not well known or understood. To enact any migration policy, the source or destination country must first map out the scale and frequency of the phenomenon. Although this research contributes to our qualitative understanding of the intricacies of immobility, return, and repeat migration, we need large-scale quantitative data to get a better sense of these specific forms of migration at the global level. Furthermore, quantitative data would enable researchers and policymakers to identify long-term trends in return and repeat migration.

Overview of Upcoming Chapters

Counterstreams consists of a total of seven chapters, including the Introduction and Conclusion. The discussion of returnee motivations and experiences in Chapters 2, 3, and 4 is encased in an analysis of two comparative groups sitting at the bookends of a migration life cycle—non-migrant kin and repeat migrants—discussed in Chapter 1 and Chapter 5, respectively. *Counterstreams* covers the forces and motivations behind less visible aspects of migration, experienced by non-migrants, returnees, and repeat migrants. None of these migration stages can be taken for granted as "natural"—I label them to make better sense of the changes over a life in transit—but together they can elucidate the benefits, pitfalls, and overall experiences of geographic mobility. *Counterstreams* thus offers a groundbreaking 360-degree view of migration from an African migrant-sending nation's perspective, building on the inherent idea that mobility is a dynamic process and not a one-time event.

This study illustrates the complexity of the shifts in migration motivation, illuminating the affective landscape concerning migration that people assess and reassess over a life course. This illustration emerges primarily through interview data. However, my own positionality informs my theorization throughout this study. I too am an Ethiopian migrant. I foreground my subjects' voices in these chapters. But seeing that my own perspective can likewise illustrate the emotional landscape I theorize as weighing on migration and migrants, I set aside space for reflexive explorations of my own confrontations with my emotional landscape as I navigate spaces and moments that are particularly weighted with meaning for an Ethiopian migrant. I do this in short passages between the book's chapters, in the interludes. I focus my interlude reflections on portions of the city of Addis Ababa, including but not limited to Bolé International Airport and the ethnoscape in the Washington, DC, metropolitan area, where there is a large concentration of the Ethiopian diaspora to illustrate how different geographies and artifacts unlock the interior calculus of motivations and meanings of one migrant: me. These distinct urban spaces are filled with significance and symbolism for Ethiopian migrants. I highlight the complex relationships between objects, people, places, and spaces, centralizing how communities are continuously (re-)created, articulated, and experienced. A reflexive reading of these different geographies imbued with emotional meaning provides further insight into the conflicting values weighed by my subjects.

Chapter 1, "Migration from the Vantage Point of Non-migrants," charts non-migrants' perspectives on Ethiopian migration and questions of belonging and identity. Rather than discount non-migrants as most of the migration scholarship tends to do, I make non-migrants a central focus of my work. I highlight that immobility can be an active state and that non-migrants are deeply entangled in migratory movements although they have never left their homelands. On the basis of interviews with non-migrant kin, I identify a set of conflicting emotions non-migrants develop toward migration: indignant patriotism, hope, and ambivalence. The perspectives of non-migrant kin are particularly important as their experiences demonstrate that migration is a transformative force even for those who have not migrated. It is paramount to fully grasp the background of the home country and non-migrants before delving into the particulars of return and repeat migration.

Interlude 1 focuses on Bolé Airport, the only international airport in Ethiopia. This transient space, the threshold between in and out, is imbued with its own unvoiced stratification, which is visible in the destinations and the interactions between travelers and airport staff. As an emotive, economic, and political space where different dreams and agendas are on full display for the initiated, Bolé Airport provides a glimpse into the different streams of Ethiopian mobilities.

Chapter 2, "Beyond the Myth of Return," focuses on the factors that motivate and enable Ethiopian returnees to realize their dream of returning. Migrants hold on to the deep-seated belief that they will return to their homelands if and when circumstances allow. Because this individual and collective desire to return is often not realized, it is known as the "myth of return." I delve into the factors that have enabled Ethiopian returnees to go from myth to reality, exploring economic and financial factors as well as family dynamics, stages in the life course, and other pertinent sociocultural considerations. But beyond the structural, returnees may prioritize more personal, emotional, indelible ideas of home, the disappointment of burnout and dissatisfaction, retirement, the hope of economic investments, the prioritization of caregiving, family dynamics, and disgust with racism. I end the chapter with a push-pull analysis of return migration as understanding the motivations of return migration requires a dyadic consideration of the situations in both host and home nations.

In Interlude 2, I focus on a single object with deep significance for migrants: the passport, a seemingly innocuous object that can shed light on global hierarchies. I highlight how passports, as instruments of migration, are imbued with ingrained hierarchies that can determine a person's international mobility.

Chapter 3, "The Joys and Frustrations of Return," discusses the pros and cons of return as returnees experience it affectively. Homecomings prove to be complex, ambivalent, incomplete, and subjective. Ethiopian returnees engage in what is known as lifestyle migration as they search for a better quality of life. Class-based privileges influence migration and return in a time of economic boom. Relatively affluent individuals express (as in commanding the labor of others) and contest (particularly in gendered ways) the many privileges of Ethiopian returnees.

In Interlude 3, I offer an ethnography of the Ethiopian capital city of Addis Ababa, a city affected by migration. I foreground how migration is inscribed on the cityscape, emphasizing various emotive responses to the spaces described.

Chapter 4, "Saviorism and Returnee Belonging," offers an analysis of the relationships between returnees and non-migrants. I explore some of the cultural disconnect that returnees face upon their return and compare this with how non-migrants rate returnee belonging. I also offer a critique of many returnees' mindset of "saviorism" and their tendency to fetishize all things Western. This chapter also sets the stage for the next one by laying the groundwork to explain how returnees may become repeat migrants.

The last interlude, Interlude 4, reflects on Ethiopian migrants who have settled in the greater Washington, DC, area and serves as a comparative lens for the earlier ethnography of Addis Ababa. While returnees and aspiring migrants in Addis Ababa adorn their businesses with names from the Global North, in contrast, Ethiopian ethnic businesses in the Washington, DC, area are christened with monikers from the homeland. These experiences are in conversation with one another, not necessarily by design but through a migrant's individual agentic decisions.

Chapter 5, "Repeat Migration," shifts the attention to Ethiopian repeat migrants, highlighting the impermanence of return (migration). While the returnees and their non-migrant kin in this study are residents of Addis

Ababa, Ethiopia, all the repeat migrants were living in the United States at the time of the interview. Scholars often view repeat or circular migration optimistically as a triple win, benefiting the host country, the home country, and the migrants themselves. Circularity has been praised for increasing flows of financial, human, and social capital between different geographies, particularly as relating to socioeconomic development and technology exchanges. However, the optimistic "win-win-win" discourse needs to be tempered with discussions of the many downsides involved in repeat migration. A variety of emotional landscapes may confront repeat migrants, depending on the flows of their lives that led them back to their destination and on their status as young professional, retiree, disillusioned, or inadvertent returnees. These various positionalities and their attendant values and trajectories help make sense of the different motivations, experiences, and lifestyles of Ethiopian repeat migrants. This level of detail further enables us to interrogate belonging, privilege, and inequality in a circular system of social and economic relationships between the Global North and the Global South.

The Conclusion briefly summarizes the central theoretical contributions of this work. While most migration studies focus on migration and processes of assimilation as a one-way flow, my distinct perspective, informed by focusing on a sending country, grants a fuller picture of the streams and counterstreams between origin and destination and the shifting landscapes that bring individuals into those flows. I expound on how migra-emotions influence non-migrants, returnees, and repeat migrants within the larger socio-ecology of migration. Additionally, in the Conclusion, I tie the four different interludes together, summarizing how migrants and non-migrants simultaneously transform and are transformed by these transnational spaces. Finally, I discuss suggestions for future research.

CHAPTER 1

Migration from the Vantage Point of Non-migrants

As I lounged in the outdoor seating area of the Starbucks knockoff café *Kaldis Coffee*, Ethiopia's largest coffee shop chain, sipping my *macchiato*, I was joined by Yosef (M, 55), a local resident and businessman who has family living abroad. He was introduced to me by a mutual acquaintance who believed he would provide key information for my research and facilitate introductions, as Yosef works with a lot of returnees. After some small talk while we shared numerous cups of aromatic macchiato, our conversation invariably turned to the appeal of migration. According to the Gregorian calendar, it was January 6, 2015, Christmas Eve in Ethiopia. The fragrant aroma of the fresh coffee roasting in the background wafted through the café. The floor of *Kaldis* was covered in *ketema*, the long grass scattered on festive occasions. A group of traditional dancers called *tewezawajz* were entertaining customers and onlookers from the street. The constant takeoffs and landings from the not too far off Bolé International Airport were faintly audible. The couple sitting next to us was discussing their recent flight from London, expertly switching from British-accented English to Amharic, one of the most widely spoken languages in Ethiopia. The *tewezawajz* wore traditional garb representing the different ethnic groups that populate the country. Amid this mixture of foreign and familiar, a lanky, dark-skinned man dressed as Santa Claus walked onto the makeshift stage. The tall Black Santa saluted the crowd, which, with the exception of a few children, did not pay him much attention. He made a few flimsy attempts at the iconic "Ho ho ho," holding his nonexistent paunch. He then casually walked over to the traditional dancers and joined them in the rhythms of *Gurage* dance. In the warm heat of the East African sun, a skinny Black Santa Claus was expertly dancing a traditional Ethiopian dance, and none of the audience was batting an eye. With this fascinating cultural amalgamation as our background, Yosef and I continued our discussion of the pros and cons of staying versus leaving.

I am always curious to hear non-migrants' opinions about what is and is not attractive about migration. We discussed Yosef's family members' experiences with migration. He told me he was always encouraging and enticing them to return to their homeland. While he intended to send his two teenage daughters to college in the United States, he did not want them to settle there permanently. He stated, "I want them to experience it [life abroad]. I want them to get their education there [in the United States], one, because of the higher quality and that it would make them globally competitive but, two, because I want them to see they are not missing out on anything. They can live a comfortable life here among their family, their own people, contributing to the growth and development of their own country. They can build on the family business if they want or strike out on their own. Either way, I want their futures to be here [in Ethiopia]." As Yosef discussed his hopes and dreams for his progeny, he spoke out of a sense of responsibility and love for his country. While acknowledging the interrelated political and economic problems that persisted in the country, he warned that no country is without challenges and that it is up to each citizen to either be part of the solution or at the very least carve out a life for themselves despite the challenges. Taking a quip at me and the Ethiopian diaspora more generally, he jokingly stated, "We can't all leave, you know. Some of us have to stay."

As the conversation continued, Yosef became quite animated. He stated, "We need to have pride in our country and use our abilities to build it up, our country, not somebody else's." He exhibited a sense of national pride and dignity, as he espoused ideas of self-sufficiency and love for the country. Yosef was squarely against migration, particularly the perilous irregular migration often depicted in the news. He believed that through hard work any Ethiopian has the opportunity to succeed in the homeland without ever resorting to living in someone else's country. In his own words, he explained:

> Consider for instance where we are sitting, Kaldis. Everybody knows Kaldis with so many branches everywhere in Addis and throughout the country. Everybody knows the story of how Tseday Asrat [founder and managing director of Kaldis] got started and how large her enterprise grew in such a short amount of time. This is a locally

grown business with local money, local know-how, and has nothing to do with migration. This is a successful business by a woman who is local. She is a good example of making it without having to leave the country. I am not saying that everyone can do what she does, but she shows us what is possible. It shows us that you can dream big and achieve great heights without migration. It can be done.

In this short response, Yosef repeats the word "local" several times to emphasize that migration is not the only, best, or even preferable method of achieving success. Yosef is emphatic that Ethiopians unequivocally belong in Ethiopia. Faced with the specter of migration, of all the possible reactions, Yosef responded with an *indignant patriotism*.

Why Non-migrants?

A short note on terminology is warranted before we move forward. Various terms have been used to refer to those who do not migrate, each carrying different positive, negative, or neutral connotations: "immobile," "non-migrant," "stayee," "left-behind."[1] The choice of terminology is determined partially by the researcher, and in many cases the individuals would not describe themselves in the same way. The most commonly used term, "non-migrant," defines this group by what they are not rather than what they are, seemingly adopting a deficit model. However, as we are comparing this group with migrants, it is the most appropriate term. While some argue that "non-migrant" diminishes the agency of this group, the term positions their choice as an apt counterpart to that of migrants. Describing non-migrants as such does not take away or diminish their agency. In fact, while it is important to distinguish between voluntary and involuntary non-migrants, immobility is an active state. In this chapter, I employ the neutral term "non-migrant" to refer to an individual who has not migrated internationally.

So why start a book on migration with non-migrants? Why begin stories of movement and displacement with those who have stayed put? What is the logic of including non-migrants in this work on counterstreams? It may seem illogical to start a book on migration with a discussion of immobility, yet to get an all-encompassing view, there is no better place to start discussing Ethiopian migration than with non-migrants—for two main reasons.

First, non-migrants warrant investigation in their own right. Within migration studies, migrants are taken for granted as the focal point or unit of analysis, and not enough attention is accorded to non-migrants. Because of the mobility bias, migration studies accord more attention to migrants, an infinitesimally smaller population than non-migrants.[2] This perspective takes sedentary life as the norm and migration as an anomaly requiring explanation. However, this shift of perspective with a focus on non-migrants (centering migration as the norm and sedentary life as one requiring explanation) not only disrupts this taken-for-granted outlook but also serves as an appropriate place to start a 360-degree view of migration. Every individual in the world is confronted with the quintessential question of whether to live where they are born or to leave. Instead of focusing on the reasons people leave, this shift in perspective helps us shed light on the reasons people stay. Examining the causes and consequences of the opposite side of migration helps us to understand mobility motivations, processes, and outcomes in a new way. Although we cannot equate staying and leaving—migration generally requires more resources than staying—both are possible choices that require equal attention. Considering the immense economic inequalities across the globe, we would expect more people to actually engage in migration. However, this is not the case, and therefore nonmigratory behavior demands an explanation. Moreover, we cannot assume that overall (migration) preferences are constant across societies and over time. People's socioeconomic status, education, exposure, personal life aspirations, home culture, and perceptions of migration may influence their viewpoints. As we probe the reasons that people stay in their home countries, it is important to distinguish between being forced to stay (involuntary immobility) and choosing to stay (voluntary immobility).[3] The academic literature often presents non-migrants as individuals with little or no agency. However, this is an erroneous and even problematic understanding. In this work, I argue that a focus on non-migrants is also a focus on agency as choosing to stay is agentic as long as a real choice is present.

The perspectives of non-migrants can shed light on selectivity factors in migration (voluntary versus involuntary non-migrants). Since there are scores of non-migrants for every single migrant, we can examine the factors that lead individuals to choose not to migrate, if indeed it is a choice. Migration researchers have looked at the decision-making process in migrating but not necessarily in staying, although it similarly warrants close scrutiny and cannot be taken for granted. How do the considerations of those who decide to migrate differ from those who have not (yet) made such a commitment? Is it a matter of circumstance or of meanings and values? How do the meanings and values of one who has not yet migrated persist into migration—and return? What is the role of migra-emotions in the decision-making process of non-migrants? By exploring the differences in opinion and in positionality between migrants and non-migrants in countries of origin, we can glean more information about the factors that motivate some to leave and others to stay.

Second, as either external to or part of the premigration stage, non-migrants can shed light on initial migration, return, and repeat migration experiences. Non-migrants serve as a comparative stage in the life course of migration. The benefits of comparative social science research are widely recognized, multifold, and well documented; they are useful for analyzing similarities and differences across groups and broadening our insights and perspectives.[4] Because the non-migrants included in this study have some type of close relationship with returnees and other migrants, their perspectives provide useful insights into questions of belonging and integration in a 360-degree view of migration. Moreover, as Aida's account in the Introduction amply demonstrates, non-migrants are deeply affected by migration trends and cultural diffusion, even if they never physically migrate. Finally, this comparative framework enables an exploration of the prevailing social inequalities between returnees and non-migrants. In sum, the study of non-migrants serves a double purpose: while they are worthy of investigation in their own right, they also allow a comparative analysis with returnees and repeat migrants.

This chapter charts specific factors that determine an individual's desire to migrate or to stay, motivating them or deterring them. It investigates migra-emotions in light of the socio-ecology of migration—larger structural factors that enable or inhibit migration. This chapter draws mostly from interviews with friends and family members of returnees conducted in Ethiopia from 2014 to 2019. As I spent time with returnees as part of my immersive data collection, I inevitably interacted with their kin. The shared social space invariably led to conversations about their perceptions of migration. I was consequently interested in soliciting non-migrants' viewpoints of people intimately acquainted with the lives of migrants and returnees. While our conversations generally started with our common acquaintance, the returnee who facilitated the introduction, we would discuss a range of topics related to migration. I asked non-migrants three main sets of questions: First, I gathered their general views on Ethiopian migration, whether they found migration and the lives of migrants to be (un)desirable, (un)enviable, or something in between. Second, I inquired about their own personal desire (or lack thereof) to migrate. I pointedly asked, "Ideally, if you had the opportunity, would you like to move permanently to another country, or would you prefer to continue living in Ethiopia?" Just as migration scholars probe the reasons and motivations enticing migrants to migrate, I questioned how those factors affect non-migrants such that they are not enticed. I looked at economic, political, sociocultural, environmental, and psychological reasons to stay. Third, I solicited their opinions on whether returnees belong and integrate well in the home country, a question that is covered in Chapter 4. While I had the opportunity to interact with dozens of non-migrant kin over the years, I only formally interviewed sixteen individuals, and these interviews form the basis of this chapter. Since I focus on non-migrant kin, this chapter highlights the transformative force of migration even for those who have not migrated. Non-migrant kin and other non-migrants, in both the home and host societies, are invariably transformed by the migration experience. I investigate non-migrants as a group deeply affected by migration despite the fact that they have never lived outside the borders of their home country.

Emotions Affecting Non-migrants

Through interviews and ethnographic observations with friends and family members of returnees, I encountered among non-migrants a competing set of values and emotions shaping their consideration: indignant patriotism, hopefulness, and ambivalence (each discussed in detail in the sections that follow). Adopting a more deterministic nomenclature, one might label the non-migrant whose reaction is dominated by indignant patriotism and pride as a voluntary non-migrant, the non-migrant who views migration predominantly with hope and eagerness as an involuntary non-migrant, and the non-migrant whose emotional ambivalence gives way to pragmatic inaction as an incidental non-migrant. Although these three types of migra-emotions do not represent the totality of perspectives, they each echoed prominently among the subjects in this study and serve to highlight the nuances that exist in perceptions of migration.[5]

Indignant Patriotism

One of the most poignant things Negussu (M, 64) said to me upon our first introduction was "Tell them all to come back home!" He was referring to diasporic Ethiopians. Negussu is the brother of one of the returnees interviewed for this project. His sister invited me to talk to him, explaining, "He has interesting views on migration." She said he was the reason she ended up returning and resettling in Ethiopia. After his sister and I jointly explained my research project, he agreed to talk to me. Negussu stated, "*Ye sew hager nuro ayasekeberem*" (One is not respected living in someone else's country). "Is there anything remotely like your own country?" he asked rhetorically, not really expecting me to answer. This promised to be the genesis of an interesting conversation. He continued his soliloquy:

> I would never want to live outside of Ethiopia. This is where I belong. This is where I can walk down the street *be mulu leb* [with a full heart]. People would greet me with *gashe*,[6] and my gray hair brings me respect. I speak my own language and not be ridiculed for struggling with another man's tongue. I am proud of being *Habesha*.[7]

Don't forget we are *kuru hizb* [a proud people]. We fought off the Italians and sent them off with their tails between their legs. We were not colonized then, and now do you think that I am gonna go cower and beg in their country? [Huffs]

Negussu was adamant about Ethiopians belonging in Ethiopia and saw migration as an undesirable displacement, a deplorable condition even, to be avoided at all costs. He historicized his views on migration by referencing often-retold stories about dignitaries refusing to leave for posts as ambassadors in foreign countries during Haile Selassie's regime. The dignitaries would apparently beg the emperor not to banish them from the country, not to deny them the pleasure and privilege of living among kin.[8] Although the post would generally be perceived as a great promotion in most situations, nobility in the Ethiopian imperial regime in the twentieth century interpreted it as a form of punishment—banishment from the homeland. Migration is historically often portrayed as exile, an unwelcome, contemptible condition in Ethiopian society.[9] There is a deep-rooted (and perhaps no longer justifiable) shame associated with migration in Ethiopian cultural history. For most of the country's modern history, migration has been perceived as something utterly negative, akin to exile and banishment from the homeland. Although the sociopolitical and economic circumstances have drastically changed in the past fifty to one hundred years, the prevailing story about migration has not significantly changed for some, particularly elders in the society. Negussu continued:

I understand that during the Derg [socialist military junta that ruled the country from 1974 until 1991], most people did not have a choice. They had to flee. It was either that or death. But now, now? Even if things are not perfect, this [Ethiopia, the home country] is where we belong. You do not abandon your mother because she is poor! You stay and help your mother when she is suffering. You do not abandon her. We all ate and drank her milk and honey. How can we turn our backs on her? We stay and make it a better place for the next generation.

Negussu emphasizes civic duty and uses the metaphor of the homeland as a maternal figure. In his impassioned speech, he relates the socioeconomic problems of Ethiopia with a suffering mother who needs her children's support to survive and thrive. He highlights the responsibility each citizen should feel toward their country: the duty to "stay and make it a better place." Negussu's words indicate that he views himself as a patriot and a responsible citizen.

Negussu speaks to a common political and cultural sentiment among Ethiopians confronting migration, one that weighs even on those who decide to leave. This antimigration line of thought espouses strong nationalist sentiment and loyalist feelings for the home country. It constructs migration as an undesirable condition to be avoided at all costs. It can manifest as grieving another life or the loss of possibility. It carries a sense of social or moral superiority over migrants. On the other side of the coin, the pride Ethiopians feel about staying in the homeland accompanies a shame, sadness, and perhaps even collective guilt associated with migration. However, Negussu neglects to acknowledge his privileged position as a male elder from the upper class.

My exchange with *Eteye* Etagu (F, 68), the mother of one of my respondents, was just as enlightening.[10] When I asked whether she would consider migrating to Canada, where most of her children live, her reaction made me smile: "*Wey, men arekush leje?* [What have I done to you, my child, to wish me such a thing?]" She explained:

> I visited my children once. I stayed there for four months, rotating between each of them. They all wanted me to stay, but I could not wait to come back. I could not walk to my local church to kiss the door; I had no one to drink coffee with. . . . That damn box [the TV] was my only companion. The children were at school all day and the adults at work. What was I supposed to do?

Eteye Etagu talked about wanting to spend more time with her grandchildren but lamented the fact that the children never learned Amharic or Tigrigna, two of her native languages. She could not overcome the language barrier as she did not speak English or French as her grandchildren did. She was overjoyed when one of her children chose to relocate back to Addis and live close to her. Her answer reflects an emphasis on the importance of social networks and belonging, particularly for a woman her age. She explained, "Despite all the material comforts of Canada, nothing equates with home." For emphasis, she added, "*Ager, ager eko new.* [Your country is always your country.] *Ager yaskeberal.* [You are respected and can be proud in your own country.] *Agere kiberugn.* [Bury me in my country.]" Ethiopians commonly express a desire to be buried in their homeland, the last vestige of belonging that trumps everything else.[11] Being buried in somebody else's land is akin to an eternal curse. In his inaugural speech on April 2, 2018, Prime Minister Abiy Ahmed, who was later awarded the Nobel Peace Prize, famously said, "When we are born, we are Ethiopian, and when we die, we are Ethiopia."[12] This often-quoted line, which came as Prime Minister Abiy made an emotional call for the diaspora to return and resettle back in the home country, signifies that upon passing our bodies decompose to become soil and therefore become part of the homeland. He is implying that all Ethiopians should benefit the home country as it is part of their blood and they will all be reintegrated as part of its soil. This call for responsibility for community is targeted toward the diaspora and fills an important part of the emotional and value landscape of Ethiopians considering migration.

My exchanges with Negussu and *Eteye* Etagu remind me so much of my own late father-in-law's constant blessing every time we talked on the phone or visited in person: "*Lageratchehu yabkachehu*. May the Lord bless you with return. May the Lord bring you back safely among kin. May the Lord bless you with a life among your own people." A deeply religious man, he rained this most prominent blessing down on us without fail. The two times we convinced him to visit us in the United States, he complained for the entirety of his stay. He lamented the fact that his son, a medical professional, and his family lived so far away from kin. The comfortable life we had built in the United States as highly educated professionals could not, in my father-in-law's eyes, compensate for living outside our homeland. Upon his last return to Addis, my father-in-law could not contain his joy when the plane finally landed at Bolé Airport. He cried loudly, got down on his knees, and kissed the tarmac several times. Although we often laugh about this incident in the family, I have included this synopsis to show a particular understanding of migration that is still pervasive among Ethiopians, particularly those of the older generation. My father-in-law's perspective and behavior are not particularly unique for a man of his generation, as the concept of *sidet*, migration or exile, is saturated with negative connotations. After this incident, my father-in-law refused to visit us in the United States again, but he held onto the hope that, one day, his descendants, those of us who settled in faraway lands, would return to and resettle in our homelands.

Negussu, *Eteye* Etagu, and my father-in-law are all part of a generation who still see migration negatively, but they are not the only ones. Zemenaye (F, 38) worked with numerous returnees and even held several short-term positions in North America and Europe. While most people in her situation would have found a way to extend their stay in lucrative positions abroad, she was adamant about returning to Ethiopia at the end of each contract. Her job in the nonprofit sector enabled her to travel widely while maintaining Addis Ababa as her primary residence. When I inquired about her stance on permanently relocating outside of Ethiopia, she laughed as she referenced Teddy Afro's song "Alhed Ale."[13] In this widely known song, one of the most famous Ethiopian songwriters and performers debates whether to migrate or not. Translated literally, the title means "My feet refuse to move." In the last refrain, Teddy sings, "In the early morning I say I will go unequivocally / Yet I vacillate, I am afraid, I am of two hearts / Who is like my own country?

My own river? My own neighborhood?" These words underline the artist's hesitation and internal struggle over the question of migration. Teddy refuses to migrate as nothing compares to the homeland. He would rather succeed in the homeland without migrating. By referencing this song, Zemenaye indicates that it artistically resonates with her own lack of desire to leave her home country.

Yosef (M, 55), the wealthy businessman introduced at the beginning of the chapter, ran several companies that combined had at least one hundred employees. "This is home. This is where my life is. Why leave when I can achieve anything I want in my own country?" he stated self-assuredly. In general, I found that homeland success correlates negatively with the desire to migrate and leads respondents to develop more hopeful and warmer views of their homeland. Yosef explained, "As long as we have peace, I do not see myself going anywhere." Here, "peace" describes not the structural state of Ethiopia but the tranquility with which Yosef views his life there. He said that only intractable threats to his peace, safety, and security would prompt him to leave the homeland.

These respondents' discussions of migration clearly place indignant patriotism within their migra-emotional landscape. Their love for their country, national pride, strong notions of home, embeddedness, and sense of responsibility to their homeland provide strong motivations to stay, disdain migration, and even pity migrants. This affinity for the homeland, or cultural "home preference," indicates a high level of embeddedness and community attachment, which helps explain non-migrants' lack of desire to migrate, or more aptly their desire to stay in the home country, as well as the eventual appeal of return for those who do migrate.

Individuals' socioeconomic positions significantly inform their opinions, values, and ability to make meaning in different aspects of their lives, as lived experiences and social positioning inform our views and perspectives on every aspect of life. Indignant patriotism comes more easily to older people and those with a higher socioeconomic status.[14] Age and socioeconomic status significantly inform people's perception of migration and, later, the level of integration of returnees in the home society. *Indignant patriotism* holds greater meaning for those who are well off; as their wealth may afford them the privilege of holding the opinions they do. They highlight their ability to work and earn a decent living without leaving the country. They are generally economically well positioned, involved in lucrative businesses or gainfully employed in well-paid fields. Their comfortable socioeconomic positioning allows them to view migration with disdain and look down on or pity migrants. Many of those most moved by *indignant patriotism* could migrate if they so desire; some have even dabbled in short stays abroad but have chosen the homeland. The freedom to choose affords certain non-migrants the ability to attach a moral value to the decision to stay. In a way, their indignation would be less salient if they could not migrate themselves. It is meaningless to talk about choosing to stay when you do not have the option to leave. Staying is only a real choice when one is able to live a dignified life at home or when leaving is truly a viable option. In certain circumstances—settings with large-scale out-migration, cultures of migration, situations of oppression, and conflict, such as Ethiopia—choosing to stay requires more explanation than migrating. Staying may represent a statement of commitment, may challenge social expectations, and may even require the most agency and resources. It would be interesting to explore in future research how indignant patriotism manifests in other contexts outside of Ethiopia.

Hopefulness

Some non-migrants have positive views of migration and would like to migrate themselves. This reaction is perhaps the most straightforward and the most widely represented in the academic literature.[15] Although sensationalistic newspaper articles give the sometimes-unwarranted impression that everyone from the Global South is trying to leave their own country, there is some truth to this perception.[16] According to the Gallup World Poll, sub-Saharan Africans had the highest desire to migrate compared to other regions of the world between 2011 and 2023. In 2023, 16 percent of adults worldwide expressed a desire to migrate given the opportunity, compared to 37 percent of sub-Saharan Africans.[17] These numbers are much higher than the number of actual migrants globally (about 3 percent). Therefore, the idea of escape has broad appeal, featuring in the emotional landscape of those who choose to migrate. Jørgen Carling and Kerilyn Schewel argue that we live in an "age of involuntary immobility" rather than an "age of migration."[18] Some even believe that unfulfilled desire represents the majority of African youths' perspectives on migration. Charles Piot designates this desire as "fantasies of exile" created by a combination of poverty and failed political leadership.[19] Within the Ethiopian context, the perception of migration shifted in a few short decades from disapproval to the celebration of migrants, even projecting the migrant as a role model. The explicit (historical) antiemigration sentiment in Ethiopia coexists with a fresh discourse that has taken a 180-degree turn.

Simon (M, 28) explained his position this way: "I applied for a U.S. visa six different times and got denied each time. My sister tried to arrange a sham marriage with one of her friends, but that fell through. I have also applied for the DV [Diversity Visa] Program religiously since I turned eighteen. Right now, I'm just waiting for my sister's sponsorship to come through." At twenty-eight, Simon had been dreaming of migrating to the United States for at least a full decade. While he was economically privileged compared to his age-mates, his dreams and aspirations were squarely centered on migration. Simon was disenchanted with life in Ethiopia and desperately wanted a way out. He described the many ways he had tried to achieve his dream, including repeatedly applying for the U.S. Diversity Visa Program, without success. The Diversity Visa Program has become an attractive escape valve for Africans seeking to migrate and has created its own culture across the continent.[20] Many non-migrants emotionally invest in migration as the solution to a slew of real or imagined problems. It provides an escape from what is perceived to be an untenable political and economic situation in the homeland.

Although Aida (F, 26), introduced in one of the three vignettes in the Introduction, had traveled on vacation to Dubai and neighboring Kenya, she said she would not be satisfied until she lived in Europe, North America, or Australia for at least a year. She also did not necessarily envision a permanent relocation but "want[ed] to scratch that itch." As she explained, most of her friends lived in foreign lands, and she "just [didn't] want to be left out":

> You haven't really lived if you haven't traveled. My sisters, friends I grew up with, most are no longer here [in Ethiopia]. They are all over the place, Europe, Canada, Australia. I check their Facebook and Insta[gram] feed every day. All the places they get to experience. But here I am, still living in the same place I was born. How boring! I am tired of waiting, anticipating, planning, imagining what my life would be like once I finally move to the U.S.

As a young non-migrant, Aida described boredom with her home country, contrasting it with the hope and eagerness she felt when anticipating life as a migrant. She said she was tired of playing host to all the diaspora visitors, feeling they had a greater prominence, of which she was jealous: "I want to be the one they come to greet at the airport. I want to be invited to all my friends' places as a diaspora guest. That's the life, I tell you!" Although her material needs were well met, as she came from a wealthy family, had a good job, and did not need to worry about rent, one of the biggest expenses in a booming city like Addis Ababa, she viewed migration as a desirable adventure that would fulfill a lifelong dream. For Aida, migration was not a survival strategy, as it has been for countless others; rather, given her privileged background, her imagination was captivated by the potential for adventure living in a foreign country.

Similar to Simon and Aida, Adonias (M, 22) can be classified as a hopeful non-migrant. He quipped: "Are you kidding me? Heck yeah, I want to live in the U.S. I don't know why this idiot [his cousin] came back, when the rest of us desperately want to leave!" It is interesting that he did not further interrogate this disconnect; he seemed to assume that his circumstantial and emotional perspective would be shared by others in a similar position. When I asked him to elaborate, he stated that he saw a lot more opportunities in the United States. Adonias saw migration not only as a way out of unfavorable economic and political conditions in his home country but as an adventure, even a rite of passage that people need to undertake in their lifetime. It is therefore not just the lack of opportunities in the home country that fosters this desire to migrate among some of the youth; staying in the home country is interpreted as failure in itself, a powerful motivator. Adonias put it simply: "You haven't really lived if you have never left Ethiopia." He was not alone in expressing this sentiment.

The perception of migration as adventure and the lure of a lifestyle figure prominently in the hope with which many invest in the idea. Take for instance Miky (M, 19), the younger brother of one of the return migrants I interviewed for this project. In our conversation about his desire to migrate, Miky said, "U.S. life, that's what I want. That's the gangsta life, that's living!" I was not particularly surprised at his Americanism in terms of use of language, attire, and overall behavior. Non-migrants who view migration with hope can create a social identity premised on foreign experience. The resulting hybrid identity is sometimes coveted and other times scorned by peers in the homeland. Yet, for somebody who had never left Ethiopia, Miky could easily be mistaken for a young Black New Yorker or Angeleno. Miky's understanding and admiration of what he terms the "gangsta life" came from Hollywood, and more specifically hip-hop music videos depicting decadent abodes, fast cars, and lavish lifestyles. He dreamed of migrating to the United States, and from his migrant kin's descriptions and media depictions, he developed an idea of how an American acts and tried to emulate that while in Ethiopia. Miky transformed his identity performance through association with another country without personally experiencing migration. The large and ever-growing Ethiopian diaspora has engendered a significant deep-seated yearning for migration in some, particularly young folks. Not only the images projected by Hollywood but also the social remittances of the Ethiopian diaspora fuel this desire to migrate.[21]

One of the most enlightening exchanges I have had on this topic was with Nega (M, 26), who claimed he feels like he belongs in the West rather than in his own home country. This is an excerpt from our exchange:

NEGA: I don't belong here.
HG: Where?
NEGA: In Ethiopia.

HG: You were born here.
NEGA: So?
HG: You are Ethiopian.
NEGA: But I am not meant to live here.
HG: Where are you meant to live then?
NEGA: In the States, in Canada, in Europe, anywhere but in Africa!

Nega, a non-migrant, felt such a strong draw toward the idea of migration that he did not feel he actually belonged in the society where he was born and where the majority of his family lived. He thought he was destined to migrate to North America or Europe. His narrative adds an interesting twist to the story of belonging in a society where migration holds such sway. He discussed his discontent with his life in Addis, despite his relatively privileged position. Nega also appeared to take belonging as a Black immigrant in a Western nation for granted.

As Chimamanda Adichie aptly described in her 2013 novel *Americanah*, African youth are conditioned to look to other countries for the solution to their problems. Daniel Mains, in his study of young men in the town of Jimma, Ethiopia, found similar patterns where his respondents, dissatisfied with their lives, constantly dreamed of life in the United States.[22] He discusses the high unemployment rate in Ethiopia, even among college degree holders. In addition to the nation's chronic lack of jobs, my respondents also expressed distress at what they identified as its rampant corruption. Many, facing that uncertainty and lack of control, thought the odds of success would be stacked against them if they stayed in Ethiopia. Some even wanted to metaphorically burn everything to the ground and leave because they were so discontented with their situation in the home country. They viewed migration, or voting with their feet, as a good solution to the multitudes of problems in the home country.[23] Because of their tendency to seek opportunity elsewhere, young Ethiopians have earned the label of the "exit generation."[24]

While more non-migrant respondents might have expressed hopeful emotions toward migration if I had interviewed other, less privileged segments of the population, it is very telling that young people of the middle and upper classes equally desire to migrate at such high rates.[25] Although the hopeful non-migrants in this study self-reported their unlikeliness to attempt clandestine migration, they would all jump at a (safe) opportunity to leave for greener pastures. Globally, it is rarely the poorest of the poor who migrate; the middle and upper classes are more likely to have the significant social and economic resources required to make the journey and resettle.[26]

Aside from their socioeconomic status, my interlocutors' gender and age should be highlighted. Five of the seven respondents who viewed migration hopefully were male. An older gentleman once affirmed to me that "migration is a young man's game"; this idea resonated with me as I spent time with the young respondents who viewed the prospect of migration with such hope. As these respondents took stock of their feelings toward migration, the patriotism of their older family members and even the negative experiences of their migrant acquaintances did little to change their certainty that life must be better elsewhere. On the contrary, these respondents saw migration as a positive step in life, particularly in economic terms. The people who felt this way tended to be young, in their teens and twenties, and could be seen as involuntary non-migrants.

The migra-emotions that draw these non-migrants toward the notion of migration include hope, ambition, adventure, and dissatisfaction. Yet the desire to migrate is constrained within the socio-ecology of migration, as most have repeatedly attempted to migrate but failed. They still continued to try different means and routes of migration to exit the home country and resettle in the West. While the hopefuls reported wanting to migrate primarily to find better economic opportunities, they also often mentioned other matters, such as lifestyle choices and access to abundant goods and services. Respondents with strong hopes described in detail how they imagined life in these places would look. Perhaps the relative privilege of their socioeconomic class allows the hopefuls to view migration as something more than an economic survival strategy and to emphasize the lifestyle and adventure aspects. Regardless, we need to understand push-pull reasons for migration not just in economic terms—real or projected—but also in terms of social aspects such as lifestyle aspirations.

Generally, the United States, Canada, and the United Kingdom ranked as the top three countries among those imagining a better life in the diaspora. Ideas of racial hierarchies have seeped into Ethiopian migrants' choice of destination countries, and Western nations such as the United States and United Kingdom are preferred, whereas migrants going to other African nations (notably South Africa) and the Gulf States are looked down on. In what Milena Belloni terms the "cosmologies of destinations," migrants internalize a ranking of most desirable and least desirable destinations.[27] The varied valorization of migrants based on destination country can be seen as a by-product of a global racial system.[28] In a global migration-scape, potential migrants perceive Western nations as desirable destinations, while the rest are less enviable. Western nations in particular are thought to offer an abundance of choice. Respondents generally ranked these locations high in the hierarchies of global migrant destinations, but their migrant kin also often resided in these countries. The correlation highlights the importance of social networks.

Ambivalence

Not all respondents had such clear hope or disgust in the notion of migration; this highlights the complexity of the competing emotions and values at play in how Ethiopians who have not migrated consider migration. Those expressing a more ambivalent reaction, neither decidedly for or against migration, were a more eclectic group with no clear-cut delineation based on gender, age, or socioeconomic status. They oscillated quite often between positive and negative representations of migration in their emotional landscapes. While they recognized some of the potential benefits of migration, valuing and esteeming the pursuit of educational and economic opportunities, for instance, they also expressed apprehension about some of the existing routes and realities of living as (Black) immigrants in the Global North, where their educational credentials and skill sets would be, for the most part, devalued.

One respondent, Dereje (M, 53), reasoned, "I have in the past [thought about migrating]. Especially when a lot of your friends leave, you have to wonder, but the older I get, I see more wisdom in staying, but I am not totally discounting the possibility." He continued: "One of my friends once asked jokingly, 'If you all leave, then who is going to stay?' It's a joke, but don't we have a responsibility, particularly as the educated, to build a better world? When I think about it as an individual, I think I might be better off in the U.K. or U.S., especially financially, but at the larger level, at the country level, I am not convinced." Dereje contrasted the benefits and drawbacks of migration when thinking about it as an individual and at the societal level. This micro-versus-macro contrast contributed to his ambivalence. The possibility of individual glory competed in Dereje's emotions against a pride in the role he played in his social world. What may be good at the individual level is not necessarily good at the macro level, and vice versa.

Another respondent, Haile (M, 37), reasoned:

> Do I see the benefits of living in the U.S. or Canada? Yes, but I also know the problems. The world is not closed anymore; information goes out, spreads everywhere.... I know the types of jobs Ethiopians [immigrants] do in these places, menial jobs they would never do if they were still living here [in Ethiopia] and all the problems that come from being a refugee, an immigrant, like the Somalis or the Sudanese here, looked down upon and pitied.

Haile compared the fate and reception of Ethiopian migrants in North America or Europe with the migrant populations he knew locally: the Somalis and the Sudanese. He stated that migrants are not always in enviable positions. Just as Somalis and Sudanese migrants, mostly refugees in Ethiopia, are subjected to xenophobia and relegated to low-paying jobs, low-skill Ethiopian migrants in other parts of the world are treated just as poorly. Haile weighed the value that Somali and Sudanese migrants hold in the Ethiopian imagination and, with clear apprehension, applied it to his perception of how destination countries would treat him.

Given the mixed, uncertain feelings of a complex emotional landscape, it can be difficult to arrive at the requisite resolution to migrate. Dereje stated, "I guess it works for some, somebody like you, for instance, who speaks the language well, who is educated, who is equally comfortable here or there, who can be equally successful either way." He was using me as an example of a successful migrant "equally comfortable here or there," but he wondered if he had the qualities necessary for success.

Similarly, Teferi (M, 43) stated:

> I guess there is always a good and bad to everything. I understand the things that can be frustrating about living in Ethiopia: the cost of living, the politics, the traffic jams, the unreliable infrastructure, water, electricity, etc.; the list goes on. I understand why people leave in such large numbers, but I do not think that's for me.

Teferi described a rich landscape of concerns that motivated him toward exit but found they did not overcome his apprehension about the prospect. He said he saw large-scale migration as a state failure. Yet he emphasized the individual choice in making the most of one's opportunity, whether in Ethiopia or abroad, perhaps rationalizing his satisfaction should he not be able to migrate. He further explained:

> I've filled out the DV application the same way you buy a lottery, knowing the very high unlikelihood that you get it. But since everybody else is doing it.... If I do win the DV, I guess I will have to try it out [living in the United States], but I know too many people who have returned, who have given back their green cards [to the U.S. government], so they must know something I don't.

In contrast to the more hopeful respondents, Teferi was influenced by the counterstreams back to Ethiopia, recognizing that there were pushes and pulls affecting his peers. Another respondent, Marda (F, 29), stated, "I don't think you can solve your problems by running away, but sometimes running away is so attractive!" She highlighted that migration is a response to uncertainty and precarity in the home country. At the same time, she knew that while migration can be an escape, it can also be an unsatisfactory response to the problems of the homeland.

These respondents expressed discomfort with the possibilities of migration. They had profound misgivings about the migration of Ethiopians outside their homeland, particularly in light of the increasingly risky and dangerous clandestine movements. For the most part, their misgivings were about the journey and the associated monetary, physical, and emotional cost rather than the final resettlement. A few individuals in this group wondered if people who reached the shores of Europe or North America through clandestine means would be emotionally and mentally undamaged afterward or experience lifelong mental and emotional scars. Because of their misgivings about clandestine migration, non-migrants who responded ambivalently to the prospect of migration sometimes made competing claims. Their statements reveal a deep sense of conflict and nebulous sentiments among their considerations. At times, respondents even sounded as if they were equivocating.

Migration posed an ideological dilemma for respondents who expressed conflicting ideas and competing emotions about migration. Publicly, most individuals in prominent positions offer an unadulterated critique of migration, as perhaps they see it as their responsibility to quell the flow of clandestine migration. In contrast to the public outcry, my respondents' ambivalence and reluctance to either support or oppose the project of migration reflect private musings. The emotional attachment to an idealized narrative of the Ethiopian homeland exhibited by the indignant patriots was less prevalent in the more ambivalent respondents, who were more pragmatic and less moralistic in their approach. At the same time, their arguments were infused with concerns that emerged from competing moral imperatives and dilemmas, including a sense of concern for the well-being of the homeland, just not in the same terms as the more patriotic responses. Many Ethiopian non-migrants seem to be caught between two generational perspectives: the long-standing historical stance that migration is undesirable, a view held mostly by the older generation, and the impatience of particularly younger folks to migrate to greener foreign pastures. The ages of the ambivalents ranged from their twenties to their fifties; however, the largest concentration was people in their late thirties and early forties. In a way, their views emanated from their generational positionality. Many raised safety as their primary concern, a concern born of an increasing awareness of the dangers of clandestine migration and the disheartening realization that the flow will continue for the foreseeable future. Many employed equity, social justice, and ethics terminology to explain their positions.

One young professional non-migrant woman, Tsehai (F, 41), explained herself in this way: "I keep working, my husband also works, but nothing. We are not able to make significant changes in our lives. I know we are better than the multitudes that are unemployed, but you always compare yourself up, not down, right?" For her, the question of migration was a question of her deservingness and individual merits, weighed against the deservingness of others, and she wondered who migration is for. She explained how some people had used migration as a shortcut to more wealth and a better socioeconomic standing. Tsehai further explained that she had applied to the Canadian government as part of their Federal Skilled Workers Express Entry Program. While waiting to hear back, she reevaluated her choice: "I am not sure I want it for me anymore, but I think about the opportunities my children will have there compared to here. But I also do not want them [her children] to grow up disconnected from their culture, not knowing their language, as I see a lot of diaspora kids." Tsehai highlighted what she saw as the positive and negative aspects of migration for the entire family unit. Another respondent, Teferi (M, 43), a government employee, adopted a more comparative approach to assessing the desirability of migration, interrogating how race changes the meanings of migration: "I work with a lot of development folks, mostly white, of course, and I see that they look down upon us. They come here and enjoy the benefits of their education and inflated salaries. Yet, if I was living in their country, doing exactly what they do here, I would be viewed with suspicion. Their presence is not viewed with hostility here, but ours in their country is.... How is that fair?" Teferi highlighted a global dissonance in discussions of migration and explained that the migration of Africans is perceived globally as different from the migration of Europeans. His response illustrates a keen sense of global hierarchies. Both Tsehai and Teferi externalized the question of migration's desirability and meaning to them into a question of migration's desirability socially on a broad scale. These questions reflect a consciousness of the broader trends in how migration is understood and presented as a concept.

"Migrant" is an umbrella term for any person who moves away from their original home or residence to live and work either temporarily or permanently in a new territory.[29] For the most part, the term "migrant" evokes people of color, while white migrants are generally referred to as expatriates or transplants.[30] In other words, the term "migrant" rarely connotes white and privileged migrants. The dichotomy between "migrant" and "expatriate" indicates the racialization of migration terminology.[31] That racialization appears not only in the labels but also in the policing of migrants, oppressive border controls, hierarchical visa systems, and other problematic practices. This obvious, blatant, and racist Western bias in migrant classifications reveals a coded statement about global racial hierarchies. We therefore need to question the nature of racial stratification in migration. What makes migrants "migrants"?

My more ambivalent respondents were also critical of the potential destination countries, such as the United States. Some were particularly uneasy about race relations in the United States. Teferi said, "I guess the English-speaking countries will be the easiest [to integrate in] in a way. The U.S. is the land of opportunity, right? But why do the police keep killing African American men?" This question led to an interesting conversation about U.S. race relations. At the time of this interview, the Ferguson protests were in high gear after the fatal shooting of eighteen-year-old Michael Brown by police (August 2014) and those officers' subsequent acquittal (November 2014). In 2015, the city of Baltimore erupted after the death of Freddie Gray at the hands of police. Once again, the police officers were acquitted and cleared of all wrongdoing. In 2016, the world witnessed the Charlotte riots in the wake of the shooting of Keith Lamont Scott, and 2017 ushered in a new divisive U.S. president who flamed racial tension and anti-Black sentiments. A couple of years later, the Black Lives Matter movement took on renewed energy after the killing of George Floyd in May 2020 in the midst of a global pandemic. While there have also been Black women victims of police brutality,[32] my respondents perceived that Black *men* have experienced the brunt of this state-sanctioned violence that has resulted in mass protests.

At the time of my field research in 2015, quite a few return migrants even half jokingly asked, "Are you sure you don't want to move back [to Ethiopia]?" While the more patriotic and the more hopeful non-migrant respondents also mentioned race in the United States, those who were most ambivalent in their feelings about immigration were also the most analytical.

Theorizing ambivalence is no easy task, but it is an empirically and ethnographically rich area of inquiry.[33] Ambivalence is often defined as mercuriality, disharmony, fence-sitting, vacillation, doubt, or antipathy. Ambivalence is holding conflicting, contradictory, and fluctuating views and opinions on a matter or person. Many non-migrants have a love-hate relationship with migration, in which both emotions coexist without displacing each other. In the Ethiopian context where migration is a pervasive force, it is important to tease out ambivalence, as it provides useful sociological insight. The ambivalent respondents in this study highlight that migration is both desirable and lamentable. It is something to both aspire to and look down on. These non-migrants oscillated between pragmatic and idealistic responses. Although it highlights a double consciousness within Ethiopian culture and its understanding of migration,[34] I find ambivalence less reflected in academic or journalistic writings on Ethiopian migration. People generally hold negative views of ambivalence, yet those expressing ambivalence in this study were measured in their responses and reasoning.

In general, as humans we are uncomfortable with ambivalence, and we try to resolve it by asserting some form of certainty and decisiveness. Yet there are benefits to ambivalence. In this scenario, ambivalence highlights that migration presents a significant societal challenge; it also informs us that a clear-cut answer is not readily available, nor can it be taken for granted. We must investigate where ambivalence comes from, as it generally points to conflicting and intersecting moral imperatives. Rather than dismissing it as maladjustment, we have to question the sociological and political significance of ambivalence. There is no reason that ambivalence and dissonance should not be accorded the same level of weight and legitimacy as more clear-cut responses. Moreover, ambivalence is not necessarily a mental state that needs to be overcome and conquered. Rather than dismissing this last group as one with inconsistent stances and beliefs, it is more fruitful to lean into the simultaneous existence of attraction and dislike, of love and hate, of an embrace and rejection of migration. Ambivalence is the antithesis of unilinear logic and serves as a commentary on the limitation of available choices. Ambivalent non-migrants clearly identify the many costs of migration, politically, culturally, and socially. They express solidarity with both migrants and non-migrants alike.

Spectrum of Non-migrant Migra-emotions

In this chapter, I focused on non-migrants' views and perceptions of migration. Table 1.1 depicts non-migrants and their prevalent migra-emotions. Since this book focuses on the less studied aspects of migration, it is of paramount importance to start the discussion with the attitudes and feelings of non-migrants, as this group sets the stage for our subsequent discussions of returnees and repeat migrants. They help us understand the lay of the land even before individuals become mobile and migrate from their homelands. Non-migrants can be subdivided into (1) involuntary non-migrants, who aspire to migrate but lack the ability to do so; (2) voluntary non-migrants, who remain in the homeland because they believe that staying put is preferable to migrating; and (3) ambivalent non-migrants, who are more measured in their approach. While the ambivalent non-migrants are content staying in the homeland, they may be open to migration under the right set of circumstances. The overriding emotions facing non-migrants illustrated in this chapter—indignant patriotism, hopefulness, and ambivalence—help us question and contextualize ingrained assumptions about (African) non-migrants. Migra-emotions have proved a defining variable in the socio-ecology of migration.

While indignant patriotism fuels a nostalgia for a bygone era (and loyalty to an idealized version of the homeland) and hopefulness leads respondents to dream of an idealized imagined elsewhere, respondents expressing ambivalence are more pragmatic in their approach and assessment. On the question of race, while the indignant patriots used it as a reason to dismiss

TABLE 1.1. NON-MIGRANTS AND THEIR PREVALENT MIGRA-EMOTIONS

	Spectrum of volition	Personal desire to migrate	Prevalent migra-emotions
Indignant patriotism	Voluntary non-migrant	Low	Pride, indignation, shame
Hopefulness	Involuntary non-migrant	High	Eagerness, despair
Ambivalence	Incidental non-migrant	Mixed	Pragmatism, apprehension, deservingness, responsibility, social concern

migrating to the United States ("Why would you want to live in a place where your skin color makes you a target?"), the hopefuls dismissed it as an inconsequential factor in their decision making, and the ambivalents once again took a more measured approach stating that the division of powerful and powerless is present everywhere in different forms ("the Agazi [federal police][35] beat up people here for no reason too"). In general, ambivalents question what the end goal of migration is and whether migration is the only means to achieve it. They discuss their dreams and goals, employing a philosophy akin to Maslow's hierarchy of needs, starting from physiological needs and progressing to safety, love and belonging, esteem, and self-actualization. They question whether, once the basic physiological and safety needs are met, migration will truly enable them to meet their higher needs. At the same time, people do not necessarily aspire to migrate for the sake of migration; rather, they may aspire to the benefits they associate with migration. The important distinction between migration as a means to an end and migration as an end in its own right can help explain how hopefulness can overwhelm one non-migrant or be contrasted with apprehension in another. At the same time, we can posit the desire to migrate or lack thereof as an adaptive preference in the face of limited migration ability. Moreover, by subconsciously repressing their migration aspirations, ambivalent respondents are employing a valuable psychological defense mechanism. They are therefore highly cognizant of restrictions within the socio-ecology of migration. They have significant misgivings about the project of migration and are keenly aware of the dangers and discomforts associated with it.

INTERLUDE 1

Ode to Bolé Airport

After the long transatlantic flight, with a transit stop in London, my family arrived at John F. Kennedy Airport on a nondescript afternoon. Born in relative privilege in Addis Ababa, I was to call New York City home for the next couple of decades. But first I had to pass through immigration control. It was October 1997, and this was my first entry in the United States. After standing in the line marked "alien" for what seemed like hours, I presented my dark navy blue Ethiopian passport to the American immigration officer sitting behind the glass. After nothing more than a brief glance at my passport, he declared, self-assuredly, "You must be happy to be away from famine and poverty." At the time, I instinctively sensed in my body, rather than comprehending mentally, that this interaction was prejudicial. I was too young and completely unaware of American racial dynamics to fully comprehend the significance of this interaction. I could not grasp why the immigration officer, an official representative of the U.S. government, would associate me with famine and poverty, when I had never experienced either. My passport was stamped with a G-4 dependent visa, which, according to the U.S. Citizenship and Immigration Services, is a nonimmigrant visa reserved for "International Organizations officers or employees, and members of immediate family"—essentially a privileged category providing temporary residence, with no indication of a refugee or forced migrant background. Yet, somehow, my Ethiopian nationality, my indelible Africanness, my indisputable foreignness, my coco-lathered dark skin had all equated me with misery, suffering, and victimhood in the minds of the U.S. immigration office. Although at the time I did not have the words to articulate anti-Black racism, I have reflected on this interaction with my first American border control agent countless times over the years. It was an eye-opening moment when I first became aware of the racialization of Black bodies and the way my beloved homeland fits in the American imagination. I wrote about this encounter in my college entrance essay, and it subsequently became a springboard for my research interest in African migration. As I reflect on this moment, I wonder about the different types of encounters individuals have at airports.

My transnational journey, however, began, not at John F. Kennedy Airport, but rather thousands of miles away, on the other side of the world, at Bolé (pronounced "bo-lay") Airport in Addis Ababa, Ethiopia. I was born and spent the first fifteen years of my life in Addis, not too far from Ethiopia's only international airport at the time. A three-pronged stela reminiscent of the obelisks from the fourth-century Axumite Empire greets passengers upon their arrival at Bolé International Airport. Three columns form the support for a large horizontal signpost with multilingual inscriptions: Passengers and their companions are greeted with "መልካም ጉዞ —Bon Voyage" as they enter they airport and with "እንኳን ደህና መጡ —Welcome" as they exit the airport and are swallowed up by the labyrinth that is the city of Addis. The understated concrete Axumite arches serve as a literal and figurative gateway, symbolizing Ethiopia's incorporation into the global on her own terms. The inside of the terminal is peppered with the ubiquitous logo of the mighty Ethiopian Airlines, adorned with the Pan-African green, yellow, and red. Outside of the airline branding and the floating decor, large-scale replicas of traditional *tilet* Ethiopian wear, there are only the barest suggestions of the airport's specific location, as airports are generally interchangeable, with only minimal proof of their locality.

Let's be honest: little about airports is romantic. They are uncomfortable spaces of containment, septic petri dishes with excruciating security checkpoints, missed connections, mind-numbingly long layovers, jostling, and incomprehension. Yet airports are also places of possibilities and faraway destinations. They represent a transitory microcosm of civilization brimming with diversity. Airports are transient places of constant flows and dislocation.[1] Global and transnational connections are inadvertently articulated within them. The airport is a stage where different actors make their entrances and exits, where one can witness hectic, nonstop comings and goings. The centrality of airports in the global movement of people is undeniable; they are both an origin and a destination. They are emblematic of migration and the interchange between the local, regional, and global, and they inhabit and transcend all of these levels, ensuring the continuity of flow. They provide an ephemeral space for passengers, a space for inclusion and exclusion, a local site where the global is front and center, reified with the flow of mobile people. It is important for travelers and researchers to consider certain temporalities, as airports are places in constant flux and motion.

Bolé Airport is one of the largest hubs in Africa, with the capacity to accommodate twenty-two million passengers a year as of 2019.[2] The airline industry is like a cybernetic organism with thousands of tentacles spread out to the far reaches of the world, swallowing up millions of passengers on one end before spewing them out on the other. As facilitating the mobility of people is fundamental to participation in the global service economy, Bolé Airport positions Ethiopia among its international peers. It signals the country's openness to the rest of the world, enabling global connections and time-space compression. While Ethiopian Airlines was founded more than three-quarters of a century ago (in 1945), the current location of the airport was inaugurated in the early 1960s.[3] Since its founding, it has undergone several renovations, the most recent funded by China to the tune of $363 million in yet another example of China's penetration into every aspect of African economies. When considering airports and the aviation industry in general, we have to be cognizant of their economic impacts, political importance, negative environmental externalities, and sociocultural significance.

Bolé Airport is a city within a city, a citadel, if you will. It is a place with its own social order, separate yet implicated in the larger social world. The awkward power imbalance and socioeconomic divide between travelers and enablers (cogs in the air transport machine) lead to fascinating power dynamics. Which way does the power imbalance lean? Although airline employees and customs officials at Bolé Airport are bestowed with the authority to delay or even deny mobility, most could never afford the cost of an international flight or secure the coveted visa. On the flip side, travelers, who have access to freer mobility, while envied and scorned, are still at the mercy of the airport staff. Legal requirements are implemented and subverted with equal competence. Border controls are an apt testament that mobility does not dilute territory. In fact, border control testifies to the importance of place and situated mobility. Questions of national sovereignty, citizenship, and access to mobility all invariably arise in this context, where individual, national, and supranational agendas diverge. Travelers encounter the full force of the power of the state as it polices entry and exit from its territory. The (necessary) bureaucracy around border control, regulating the movement of bodies, is acted out like a well-rehearsed play, replicated in countless border controls around the world.

With an estimated two to three million Ethiopians living outside the country, the revolving doors of Bolé signify the changes and intensification that are shaping Ethiopian migration. We can position Bolé Airport as a defining feature of Ethiopian migration. It is a particular geographic location, critically important to our understanding of the dynamics of migration. A place that is mundane to some and inaccessible to many, it excludes a significant portion of the Ethiopian population, who will never see beyond the Axumite arches at the entrance. Ingrained socioeconomic hierarchies are clearly visible in travelers' circumstances: Are they traveling toward the coveted West or the rest? As a tourist or as a migrant? As a well-paid, skilled worker basking in the spoils of globalization or as a low-skilled laborer toiling in slave-like conditions? It is not hard to imagine which type of migration dominates. Yet, in a common scene in Bolé Airport in the last decade, lines upon lines of young women are being shipped to places like Saudi Arabia to work mostly in pink-collar jobs as maids and nannies. Bolé is emblematic of people leaving through legal, regulated migration, unlike the countless less privileged people who leave through different means.

Exit through Bolé Airport hides behind it a more insidious form of exit: that of irregular migration. As an exit strategy, Bolé is often contrasted with Balé (pronounced "ba-lay"), a region in the South of Ethiopia that migrants historically crossed to seek refuge in the neighboring country of Kenya. Bolé and Balé mark the exit strategies of migrants: they leave by air or by foot. While Bolé symbolizes legality or regular migration, Balé indicates irregular or undocumented migration. Migration through Balé evokes a long and arduous journey, most likely by foot through inhospitable regions with the threat of violence and death always looming overhead. The means of exit through Bolé or Balé, although one syllable apart, can mean a world of difference. This marks the first of a multitude of deep-seated hierarchies within Ethiopian migration.

My personal recollections of Bolé Airport are at times painful and at times ecstatic. They are memories of departure and return, of separation and reunion, of loss and gain, of belonging and exclusion. Most times, they contain a little bit of all of the above. As a child, I would revel at my father's passport, a magical booklet filled with mysterious stamps in a multitude of foreign languages and scripts. My young heart invariably ached when he had to fly out to numerous exotic locations—Abuja, Johannesburg, Kinshasa, Lusaka, Maputo, New York, Seychelles, Zanzibar—only to be overjoyed when I saw him again a few days or weeks later. Throughout most of my childhood, Bolé represented separation from and eventual reunion with my father. However, in due course, my family, just like so many others, was swept up in the throes of transnational migration in my teenage years. While Addis Ababa is where my umbilical cord is buried,[4] as the colloquial Amharic saying goes, I am now part of the multitude of voluntary and involuntary Ethiopian migrants living outside of my homeland, forever transformed by migration.

As a member of the Ethiopian diaspora living outside of my homeland, I have crossed the Axumite arches more times than I can count. Despite the passing of two decades—and repeated takeoffs and touchdowns, countless entries and exits—since my initial migration, Bolé Airport, for me, remains an emotive site of loss and reunion undiminished by the inevitable passing of time. I disremember the specifics of each joyful or forlorn tear shed, as these lifetime periods of exit and reentry bleed into one another. Yet Bolé still holds an evocative place in my psyche. Whenever I see the arches, they always engender some strong feeling in me. They are either the last hurdle before leaving the country or the first welcome sign upon arrival. I am either leaving for some time or returning after a long stay elsewhere.

Bolé Airport is an emotive site holding within it multiple and contradictory forces, a liminal site for both exit and entry, the last threshold between in and out. This is the allure for the observant social scientist. While airports are not customary sites for social research, the ethnographic glimpse into this transient space marks a fuzzy boundary between those who depart and those who arrive. Within this frontier of migration, the keen social scientist can participate in this space and observe the ways in which people on the move create social and cultural contexts.[5] As a sociologist, I am conditioned to always see individual behavior as constrained within specific historical, socioeconomic, political, and cultural contexts. This miniature ethnography of Bolé Airport as one emotive geography in the socio-ecology of migration provides a glimpse into different facets of Ethiopian mobilities and their embedded inequalities.

CHAPTER 2

Beyond the Myth of Return

Exploring Returnees' Motivations

Home is home is home. There is no way around that. There is no escape from it. No matter how far you travel, it always calls you back. It is not always easy to get all your ducks in a row and answer that call [to return home]. I know so many people who keep postponing their return saying next year, next year, next year . . . but as I said, home is home. *Emama* Ethiopia beckons.—Gizaw (M, 66)

Gizaw seemed somewhat surprised that I would ask him what motivated him to return to his homeland after living in the United States for a number of years. His response "Home is home is home" indicates that he took this idea for granted. Despite his many years abroad, his idea of "home" was still his birthplace, and he considered wanting to return a no-brainer. "Home" for Gizaw meant his social embeddedness in and emotional connection to his birthplace, which he took for granted. According to his words, time and distance did not dilute his connection to his homeland. Gizaw returned to Ethiopia after his retirement in the United States. Highly educated with decades of experience, Gizaw worked for an intergovernmental organization, which enabled his family's initial migration to the United States. His wife, Nigist, who had trained as an accountant in Ethiopia, switched careers a few times in the United States, alternating between being a full-time homemaker and working for different small nonprofit organizations. They had initially moved to the United States with the intention of returning to their homeland after a period of years. Gizaw in particular was adamant that he would not spend his retirement age in a foreign land. They ensured that their children benefited from the educational opportunities available in the United States and were well settled before they relocated to Ethiopia. While living in the United States for over a decade, Gizaw and Nigist maintained their property in Addis, renting it out for the majority of that time. They also returned regularly to visit family and reconnect with their friend groups. Both Gizaw and Nigist maintained a strong sense of home and saw themselves as only temporary migrants biding their time until their children attained their educational credentials and became independent. Gizaw and his wife of thirty years resettled in their homeland, leaving their two grown children behind in the United States. Gizaw and his wife have actualized their desire to return, while scores of migrants living outside their homelands dream of one day returning.

Notions of home and homeland remain strong in the diaspora, and return has often been conceptualized as "homecoming."[1] Migrants residing outside their home countries are thought to hold on to a belief that, under the right conditions (sufficient accumulated savings, educational attainments, safety and security in the homeland, etc.), they would return to their homelands. The emotional tie to the homeland and this long-held belief (regardless of feasibility), labeled as the "myth of return," has both individualistic and collective elements where the desire is normalized within certain diaspora communities.[2] Migrants uphold the idea of return if and when circumstances optimally align, allowing such relocation. Migrants' idea of the homeland is rooted in sociocultural and geographical territories as well as affective notions of home. While some contend that migrants' yearning to return to their homeland indicates a deep-seated need to reconnect or a dissatisfaction with their lives in the host country, others allege that migrants maintain an idealistic and romanticized view of the homeland colored by the hazy lens of distance and that return is a hallowed desire seldom realized.[3] The longing for return is a dream, a cherished ambition, a fantasy, a myth, or a mirage.[4] By envisioning return, migrants can shield themselves from the psychological and emotional dissonance that accompanies migration.[5] Envisioning return can therefore be a psychosocial strategy in integration, a sort of meaning making in a new land filled with uncertainties.

Migrants' continued ties to the homeland are maintained through regular visits, remittances, and other transnational activities. Therefore, this "myth of return" requires further scrutiny. Just as initially migrating out of one's country of origin requires a high level of investment, returning to one's own country is a costly endeavor. Migrants often cite their lack of accumulated savings as a reason not to return to their home nations. Their intention of returning is hampered by insufficient funds (real or perceived), among other factors, leading to the "myth of return."[6] This chapter discusses when myth becomes reality.

Typologies of Return

Return migration is a complicated phenomenon. In one of the earlier works on return migration, Francesco P. Cerase put forth an often-cited typology of return that can be used as an introduction to different types of returns.[7] Cerase identified the return of failure, of conservatism, of innovation, and of retirement. Russell King expanded on this typology by adding a temporal scale (seasonal, permanent, etc.) and elaborating on spontaneous and planned return.[8] Dino Cinel further added to Cerase's typology by identifying ambivalent returnees, those without a clear goal before migration or after return.[9] While Cerase's, Cinel's and King's works are foundational and can serve as a springboard for further discussion, the field of return migration has grown significantly since the 1990s.

While these are important typologies, we still need better differentiation between categories and a better theoretical understanding of return. Return is not a one-size-fits-all phenomenon. We can identify a number of different types of return. In addition to the distinctions I highlight in the Introduction between lifetime and diasporic return and between voluntary and involuntary return, we can further distinguish between a physical and metaphysical return. In a physical return, an individual embarks on a corporeal journey back to the homeland. It is an embodied experience in which they have to pack their belongings in the host country, plan out the means of transportation, find lodgings in the home country, and so forth. In contrast, a metaphysical return is more intellectual and spiritual in nature. In addition, we can differentiate between permanent and temporary return. Although for the sake of clarity we can contrast these two temporalities, in reality, we should posit temporary and permanent return on a spectrum rather than conceive of them as distinct categories. Potential returnees often start planning their longer-term return by embarking on shorter-term home visits where they contemplate what a more permanent relocation would look like. Similarly, individuals who initially planned a permanent return may end up relocating to the host country or a third country for a number of reasons (such as the ones discussed in Chapter 5). While I acknowledge the multiplicity of return, in this study, I investigate the experiences of corporeal lifetime voluntary return.

Table 2.1 provides a classification of different types of return, differentiated on the basis of volution (voluntary or coerced), temporality (temporary or permanent), generation (first or later generations) and corporality (corporeal or metaphysical). Each of these different categories can be conceptu-

TABLE 2.1. TYPES OF RETURN MIGRATION		
Category	Type	Description
Temporal scale	Temporary	Return for a limited time; can include short-term visits or seasonal migration
	Permanent	Return without the intention of emigrating again
Voluntary vs. forced	Voluntary	Return based on one's own choice, without compulsion
	Coerced	Forced return, most often through deportation or expulsion from the host country
Corporeal vs. metaphysical	Corporeal	Physical, embodied return
	Metaphysical	Mental, cultural, spiritual reconnection to the homeland
Generation	First	Return of first-generation migrants in their own lifetime
	Second or later	Return of second or later generation, also known as diasporic return or return to roots

alized as a continuum rather than a set of discrete divisions. The difference between voluntary and coerced can be best seen through a legal lens, where voluntary returnees have a legal right to live in the host country but choose to return to the homeland. Alternatively, coerced returnees are either deportees or those who are no longer able to live in the host nation. Coerced return can also be compelled by other factors, such as health or unemployment. This is the reason I advocate thinking about coerced-voluntary return on a continuum. Similarly, the repatriation of migrants' bodies for burial complicates the dichotomy between corporeal and metaphysical return.[10]

In addition to the classification in Table 2.1, I propose adapting the long-established push-pull framework to explain return migration. The push-pull framework of migration has roots in Ernest George Ravenstein's ambitious "laws of migration" and has been refined by Everett Lee's comprehensive theory of migration.[11] The framework identifies the personal needs and societal structures that motivate people to leave and enter different countries. It explicates the reasons for migration on the basis of people's aim of improving their living conditions, allowing for intervening obstacles that could impede their mobility. I adapt this well-known theory to explain the reasons behind return migration. Thus, this chapter introduces a new framework to contemplate the main reasons leading returnees to leave and return to their homelands.

This chapter focuses on the factors that motivate and enable Ethiopian returnees to realize their dream of returning. It explores economic and financial factors as well as family dynamics, stages in the life course, and other pertinent sociocultural considerations. While later chapters examine whether or not the hopes and dreams of returnees have indeed been fulfilled, this chapter focuses on the expectations, motivations, and reasoning behind return migration. It discusses the many layers of motivations for returnees, explicating the simultaneous conditions in the home and host nations that enable return. These motivations range from the achievement of stated goals in the host nation (such as educational goals or savings targets) to an improvement in the political and socioeconomic conditions in the home country. Oftentimes, instead of a single motivating factor, returnees will present a confluence of motivations that prompted and enabled their relocation to their homeland. These motivations can include personal circumstances, family needs, economic conditions, and sociocultural considerations.

In the following sections, I organize returnees' motivations in three main categories: economically motivated return, sociopolitically and culturally motivated return, and return motivated by health factors, family dynamics, and life stages. Each of these categories is internally subdivided between push and pull factors. While I present returnees' motivations in thematically organized categories for the purposes of clarity, there is not always a clear-cut line between categories in the minds of returnees. Within the socio-ecology of migration, migrants have to contend with different moving parts and structural limitations and navigate the landscape of both the host and home country simultaneously.

Economically Motivated Return

> Wouldn't you want to be the biggest fish in a small pond or the tallest midget? [*Laughs.*] Why do you think so many are returning? Take my field, for instance, fashion. It is really hard to break into the fashion industry in the U.S.; you need the name, the connections, ridiculous amounts of dough [money] . . . but here [in Ethiopia] I can easily open my business and start my line. I won't need to work like eighty to ninety hours a week; I can have my social life, be surrounded with friends and family. . . . It is the best of both worlds, financial success, and the time to enjoy it. . . . I'm telling you I can be a tall midget!—Samrawit (F, 37)

Samrawit and I were sitting on the shaded veranda of her retired parents' villa in one of the new gated communities that had proliferated in Addis Ababa since the early 2000s. New buildings were rising up like mushrooms in the city center, and residential areas were eating up the nearby farmers' lands. While the gardener-cum-security guard tended to the roses on the far end of the vast compound, the smiling maid brought us freshly squeezed orange juice and homemade snacks to chew on as we chatted. Samrawit was explaining to me why she thought most members of the Ethiopian diaspora returned to live or work in their home country. Using the colorful and even highly offensive language of the "biggest fish in a small pond" or the "tallest midget," Samrawit underscored a common sentiment among my respondents: Whatever they did in Ethiopia, they would have a big impact and could easily make a name for themselves. She used her own field of fashion to illustrate the benefits of starting a new line in Ethiopia rather than the United States. It would not require as much investment, nor would she need as many connections. She claimed that she would not have to work as hard to succeed. Moreover, she figured that while building the success of her fashion line, she could also enjoy a less stressful life in Ethiopia, surrounded by friends and family. She presented Ethiopia as "the best of both worlds," where returnees could achieve financial success and the accompanying leisure time and lifestyle. Samrawit was one of the many returnees interviewed for this study who saw Ethiopia as a place to both make money and enjoy relaxed lifestyles.

The promise of development, coupled with Ethiopia's double-digit economic growth and its palatable hunger for investment and new ideas, draws Ethiopians from the diaspora to return to their homeland.[12] The pull of economic growth and the promise of greener pastures, coupled with relative political stability, render Ethiopia attractive to potential returnees. The development fervor is palpable in the capital city of Ethiopia, Addis Ababa, where the majority of returnees tend to congregate. For those poised to take advantage, an emerging economy such as Ethiopia offers unparalleled advantage. Just as non-migrants use migration as a means to achieve a higher socioeconomic status,[13] Ethiopian returnees use return as a pathway to economic improvement and social mobility.

Both economic success and financial failure can prompt migrants to leave the host country and return to the home nation. Economic success can be interpreted as migrants having achieved their savings goal or earned their desired educational credentials. Economic struggles, such as the lack of employment, can also lead a migrant to seek a return to the country of origin. Within the socio-ecology of migration, potential returnees have to consider the economic landscape of the homeland and their own earning potential in both the host and home country.

Minilik (M, 35) left a lucrative limousine rental business in the United States to relocate his family to Ethiopia at the height of Ethiopia's economic growth. Together with his wife, he opened a large restaurant business. Minilik expressed a common sentiment among the respondents: Ethiopia provides an unsaturated frontier market for new ideas and investments. He can see himself making more money and more of an impact in Ethiopia than in the United States:

> You know the market is saturated in the U.S., it has all been done, your profit margin is very low, there is not much new that you can

do there, while here [in Ethiopia], there is a thirst for new ideas, a thirst for investment, for development, you can make money, and you can make it fast.

In the economic analysis of returnees, the comparison between the "virginal" market of Ethiopia and the "saturated" one in the West is paramount. Time and time again, returnees contrasted the Ethiopian markets with those they had left behind in the West, as well as the opportunities offered in both settings. Minilik, like many of the respondents in this study, portrayed Western markets as stagnant or slow growing, while indicating that Ethiopia's economy has not yet peaked. The returnees thus sought to take advantage of the possibilities of rapid development growth. Minilik, like many other respondents, quoted to me the double-digit growth the country had been experiencing for several years.[14] This growth has been a rallying cry since the early 2010s as the state tries to move the country from an agriculture-based to a manufacturing-based economy.

Returnees see vast opportunities in the emerging economy of Ethiopia as compared to Western markets. They characterize the Ethiopian economy as "unsaturated," "untapped markets," a "land of opportunities" with a "human resource gap" and a "thirst for investment."

> You have to understand what the government is trying to do and position yourself to take advantage. We [Ethiopia] are growing at a faster rate than anywhere else, so being an entrepreneur at this time in our history is exciting. We [members of the diaspora] have the skills, the know-how, the connections to make a real impact and make real money . . . and the time is now! Not five years or ten years from now, but now!—Ezana (M, 35)

As a young entrepreneur, Ezana saw himself as poised to take advantage of the growing private sector in Ethiopia. Upon his return from Canada with a degree in computer science, Ezana went into agribusiness with his father, where he was responsible for attracting and managing foreign investments. Ethiopia has long been an agricultural society, but most of the food processing (where most of the value is added), packaging, marketing, and distribution was exported from the nation. As Ethiopia was shifting most of the processing and packaging internally, Ezana's family business aligned with the expressed development plans of the government. Moreover, Ezana painted the economic landscape of Ethiopia as "virginal" and named it a "greenfield." He stated, "This is a greenfield. I can start anything here. I really won't have much competition. All I see is opportunities everywhere, and it is exciting." Ezana explained that a greenfield is a market that has yet to be commercially exploited, where one gets to define the market on one's own terms. Moreover, Ezana explained that his investments were time sensitive, and it was easy to note the sense of urgency in his tone.

According to returnees, one of the biggest needs of a growing economy such as Ethiopia is a thirst for skill sets and human resources. Both Ezana and Minilik contrasted their skills and expertise in their host nations of Canada and the United States, respectively, with Ethiopia. Both thought their contributions were much more needed and appreciated in Ethiopia than in the United States or Canada. As Ezana explained:

> They don't need us there [Canada]. They have plenty of educated people doing what needs to be done, contributing to the system, but here, we're actually the ones developing the system; anything you do here goes a long way! In our factory, for instance, we hired over fifty people with nothing more than a high school degree who would have remained unemployed otherwise. We trained them in the use of the machines, and now they are able to support their families.

The argument thus becomes not just making money and benefiting from investments but rather significantly contributing to the economy by creating jobs and spreading much-needed technical knowledge. Ezana, for example, disclosed that his family investment had resulted in the creation of over fifty jobs. Returnees thus feel that they are needed and their skill sets (together with their investments) valued in Ethiopia.

Ethiopia is the ostensible poster child for the "Africa Rising" narrative, where the continent is poised to outgrow and outperform other regions in the world.[15] Between 2010 and 2020, Ethiopia enacted two separate five-year Growth and Transformation Plans (GTP-5 and GTP-II), each active as a guide to its development mandate. These plans outlined the country's priorities for sustainable means of economic, social, and environmental development and were partly intended to strengthen the manufacturing sector of the country as Ethiopia emerged as a manufacturing hub in the region. Some of the major changes or development projects the country undertook in in that time include the construction of the Grand Ethiopian Renaissance Dam on the Blue Nile and other hydroelectric dams designed to serve the needs of East Africa,[16] the first electric passenger railway in the capital Addis Ababa, and another one linking Addis Ababa to the port in the neighboring country of Djibouti, improving the transportation infrastructure of the two nations.[17] These major development projects are but a few examples of the changes in Ethiopia's economy and infrastructure undertaken under the auspices of the Ministry of Finance and Economic Development. Ethiopia's government sees itself as a "development state" emulating the example of countries such as China and the so-called East Asian Tigers, where the state aggressively directs the growth of the economy.[18] While this has yet to be achieved, the Ethiopian government planned to transform the country into a middle-income nation by 2025. Nonetheless, Ethiopia has earned the privilege of inclusion in what is known as the PINE countries, emerging countries including the Philippines, Indonesia, Nigeria, and Ethiopia.[19] Moreover, as of January 2024, Ethiopia joined the BRICS (Brazil, Russia, India, China, and South Africa), a notable occasion of geopolitical and economic importance, marking a major significant shift in the country's status on the global scale.

As the Ethiopian government seeks to engage its diaspora and attract their investment, Ethiopian returnees are for the most part investing in small and medium-scale businesses.[20] Some of the economic sectors that returnees have invested in include small businesses in the hotel and tourism sector, such as restaurants, cafés, and tour companies. They infuse a Western-style customer service perspective in the tourism sector, which has proved to be lucrative. A large number of returnees have also invested in agribusinesses such as poultry and livestock farming intended for local consumption and export. Within the booming construction sector, returnees have invested in machinery import and rental. In the medical services, returnees dominate the high-end clinics and hospital services, as well as specialized services such as physiotherapy and dialysis. In terms of large-scale industries, the most famous example is in agroforestry, with the sustainable Bamboo Star corporation.[21] While most of the country's economic sectors are open to investment from foreign nationals and Ethiopians with foreign passports, until recently the Ethiopian government chose to protect certain sectors such as banking and finance.[22]

While the unprecedented growth in Ethiopia's economy has attracted members of the Ethiopian diaspora, there is also the perception that this is a gold rush where returnees are hastening to Ethiopia in search of untold riches. The promise of fast money has brought in returnees in unprecedented numbers intent on capitalizing on Ethiopia's economic potential. They compare themselves with their compatriots who have never migrated, explaining that non-migrants have done so much better financially. Because of the high return on investment, non-migrants have swiftly "shot up" (using local terminology) on the basis of small amounts of investment. Returnees would also like to reap the benefits of the growing economy and get a piece of the economic pie, in a manner of speaking. My respondents often repeated this need to benefit "before it is too late" in different forms. Minilik (M, 35) expressed the same sentiment as he tried to entice me to return and resettle back in Ethiopia:

Come now, start your business, buy your land, build your house, get your investment in before the floodgates open, before it is too late, before everybody else does it and you find that Ethiopia's market has become saturated or entry becomes impossible, too expensive. Come now!

Returnees thus see that the return migration is time sensitive, and Ethiopia is optimally primed for the investments and technical expertise of members of the diaspora. As Minilik admonished, members of the diaspora should return "before it is too late." Again, the urgency is palpable and the fear that the present situation will not last unambiguous. In fact, some respondents felt so strongly about the time sensitivity of return that they packed their bags and resettled in Addis Ababa without securing jobs or having clear and well-thought-out plans for investment. From a migra-emotions lens, returnees reported feeling hope in the homeland's economic outlook, which motivated their return. Moreover, their self-interest and eagerness were apparent in their responses. Economic concerns, however, although important, do not constitute all the drivers of return migration. Although financial concerns and family dynamics are paramount, return migration is not possible without some political stability (i.e., relative peace) in the home country. Moreover, factors such as health (both physical and psychological) and sociopolitical and cultural landscapes also affect the decision-making processes of returnees.

Sociopolitically and Culturally Motivated Return

Within the socio-ecology of migration, we have to simultaneously consider the perceived landscape of the home and host nations to understand migrants' motivations for return. In addition to the economic reasons previously described, individual feelings about the social, political, and cultural landscapes, all of which are extrinsic to the migrant, can greatly influence their decision-making. For instance, experiences of racism and xenophobia, dissatisfaction, and burnout can serve as explanatory variables. Each of the experiences I describe in the following sections can bring about different migra-emotions, such as anger and disaffection as push factors and sense of belonging as a pull factor.

Racism and Xenophobia

Zechariah (M, 32) is a young Ethiopian American man who voluntarily returned to Ethiopia at the age of twenty-six for a combination of work and family reasons. While living in the United States for most of his teenage years and early twenties, he experienced the confluence of racism and xenophobia because of his status as a Black immigrant man in a white-dominated society. He explained:

> Not only are you Black in the U.S., but you're African, which comes with its own baggage. They think you're uncivilized, that you live in trees and keep lions as pets. . . . I always felt targeted because of my race. I was always on guard. It is no way to live. I am glad I don't have to deal with that anymore.

His experiences are not unique as at least half of my sample reported experiencing racism or xenophobia while residing in the Global North. While in the host nations, Black immigrants are marked for both their migration status and their racial identities. It is important to note the intersection of race and gender. Zechariah argued that being male and Black in a predominantly white society constitutes a "double strike." In particular, he mentioned encounters with the police for DWB—driving while Black: a form of racial profiling that disproportionately affects Black men.[23] He explained, "I was refused access, followed around in stores, arrested for DWB, all the things I went through as a Black man in the South." It is not surprising that the phenomenon of DWB was repeatedly referenced by the male respondents who resided in the United States, as this is an unfortunate feature of American society. It is important to highlight the intersectionality between gender (in this case masculinity) and race (Blackness) in the experiences of DWB and overall violence against Black men in the United States. Zechariah's experiences echo those of other males in my sample, particularly those who lived in the United States during their migration years.

Similar to Zechariah, Sammy (M, 29) was motivated to return to Ethiopia partially by the racism he encountered during his migration years. He spent his early years in various African nations, then lived in Europe for a number of years before moving to the United States for college. The only person with mixed heritage (Ethiopian and white) in the sample, Sammy grew up battling race issues for most of his teenage life. Marked as "nonwhite," he was the victim of racially motivated bullying. He stated:

> We lived in Germany with my family when I was a teenager, and that was my first encounter with neo-Nazis, who once told me that "Your mom is a n***** and we're gonna slap her and spit on her." I had such an identity crisis as a teenager because in Germany I was rejected because of who I am. I was called a "wigger," a white n*****, and I internalized it, which made me bitter and a very angry person. My

mom told me over and over again that I was hurting them [his parents] and myself as I was lashing out at home, constantly, constantly, constantly.... I had to find my Black identity. I had such hatred for white people.... I was battling the race issue for so long while growing up. I wanted to be in a place where I am accepted, where my race is not questioned. This [Ethiopia] is where I belong without question.

Despite his mixed background, Sammy felt that he belonged in Ethiopia more than he had in any of the other countries where he lived. He said he grappled with his racial and national identity for so long but belonged in Ethiopia "without question." Although from a mixed parentage, he self-identified as a Habesha.[24]

While Zechariah and Sammy are relatively young men, older age does not necessarily protect migrants from racist encounters, as experienced by *Gash* Kebede (M, 77). Having relocated to the United States in his fifties, *Gash* Kebede had a hard time incorporating into American society. While he came from a hardworking middle-class background, he felt that he was constantly discriminated against and ridiculed in the United States because of his age, his accent, his immigrant background, and his Black skin. He felt constantly disrespected, undervalued, and generally treated as less than. Whenever he had such an encounter at work or in public spaces, he would remind himself that he had his own country where he could live in peace. *Gash* Kebede did not initially migrate because of financial need or his political leanings, as so many other Ethiopians had in the past. Instead, he migrated out of a vague sense that life in the United States would somehow be better than his life in Ethiopia. He regretted his migration years as wasted time spent chasing a pipe dream that was never realized. *Gash* Kebede vehemently stated, "I was tired of living my life as the white man's slave. I would rather be thrown amongst the refuse of *Merkato* [the largest open-air market in Ethiopia] than live there [in the United States] one more day." He entreated, "Bury me in my country among my people."

While some returnees encountered overt racism, others reported more nuanced experiences such as exoticization in the host countries. For instance, Wubit (F, 27) felt she was marked as different even though she did not feel like the victim of direct racism. She explained, "It was subtle in the sense that they were surprised at the texture of my hair, or they assumed a certain socioeconomic background, where they assumed that we [her family] could not be educated and not poor." Similarly, Beza (F, 32) reported experiencing subtle racism. She asked, "Can ignorance be called racist? [*Laughs.*] I was asked 'Who is the president of Africa?' more times than I care to remember! I was asked other very dumb questions, like 'Did you live in trees?' type questions.... It is frustrating to see how Africans are perceived the world over. I'm so over it." The microaggressions that Wubit and Beza experienced also included a gendered layer where they felt they were sexualized for their Africanness and Black skin. They often received unwelcome sexual propositions from white men in particular, seeking to expand their sexual repertoire by bedding a Black woman. Both women reported embarking on a journey of return migration to be among people who look like them, in a place where they would not be constantly exoticized and othered because of their African heritage. As Beza aptly put it, both were "so over it."

Respondents' experiences varied greatly from ignorance of the racial layout of the land in the host nation to experiences with direct racism, animosity with other Black groups, and more subtle forms of racism, such as exoticization. Respondents also understood that racism intersected with gender and that race was not the only possible or even major axis of difference in the host nation. These respondents' struggles with racism in Europe or the United States contributed to their reasons for returning to Ethiopia, a place where they knew they would no longer be judged by the color of their skin. They felt racially profiled, and this took a toll on their family lives and mental health. They constantly felt unwelcome in the host nations and preferred to live among kin in their Ethiopian homeland. In the host nation, the returnees were disenfranchised because of their race, and they believed that they could best achieve equality and a sense of belonging back in the home country. Return can therefore sometimes be a way to reclaim some of the racial dignity lost during the migration years.[25]

Migration is highly racialized, and the salience of race for immigrants is undeniable.[26] As Black immigrants, Ethiopians experience different forms of racism, xenophobia, and othering in the host nations. Racism is the process whereby social groups categorize others as different and inferior on the basis of phenotypic differences or cultural markers. Xenophobia and othering are related concepts whereby the other is marked as different (and subsequently less than) on the basis of migration status or a number of other factors. The process of racialization or othering implies the social construction of a specific group as a problem. Sometimes these processes of racism, xenophobia, and othering can constitute a reason to leave for migrants. We can therefore posit racism in the Global North as a push factor for returnees. From a migra-emotions perspective, a sense of belonging is an important pull factor for returnees. We thus have to consider the different identities of the migrants themselves (e.g., race as Black migrants) to elucidate their motivations for return to the home country. Moreover, as discussed in the beginning of the chapter, ideas of home and belonging strongly influence the return of migrants to their homeland. Although a sense of belonging is an emotive reason that is hard to quantify, its importance to returnees is paramount.

Dissatisfaction and Burnout

Regardless of their initial intention before migration, some returnees became increasingly dissatisfied with their lives in the West. They contemplate their dissatisfaction vis-à-vis their work, their family life, and their overall sense of belonging in the host nation. Consider, for instance, Alemneh (M, 47), first introduced in one of the three vignettes in the Introduction. Alemneh was a highly educated medical professional who upended his lucrative practice in California before relocating to Addis Ababa. He explained:

> I was so busy with work, committed to the rat race of accumulating, accumulating, with no time for family. I was close to burnout like I have seen so many of my colleagues. My marriage was deteriorating. My wife was alone raising the kids with no support system. Our kids were not doing so well as the only token Black kids in a mostly white environment. It all just compounded. It became unsustainable. We needed a drastic change. This was honestly the best decision we could have ever made for the entire family. I don't know what took us so long.

Alemneh discussed how every member of the family benefited from the relocation. Both he and his wife found the trappings of an upper-middle-class lifestyle in the United States suffocating. They felt they were part of a rat race trying to constantly outdo their neighbors at the risk of their family and mental well-being. They relocated to Ethiopia in search of a slower-paced life that would allow them to reconnect with each other, their extended families, and their cultural roots.

Like Alemneh, Redeit (F, 28) is an individual who found life in the United States unsatisfying. She stated:

> The U.S. messes you up if you ain't careful. You get into ridiculous debt to pay for school, loan after loan, then it traps you with the fancy cars, shiny gadgets, and other material stuff that you somehow just can't live without. Loans, debt, more loans, more debt. And once you get a mortgage, you're done. You are finished with. It never ends. They tell you you need to upgrade the kitchen. So you rip out a perfectly fine, functioning kitchen to install a new one with fancier gadgets, only to replace it again in a few years. You have to keep up with

the Joneses. You are f***ed for life. You become a slave to the system. I had to leave before it swallowed me whole.

A nurse by training, Redeit was at the beginning of her career, with the potential for upward mobility. However, she found that the U.S. medical sector was more interested in making profits from people's pain and ailments than in truly healing the sick. She felt restricted in her role and impeded in her ability to connect with and care for her patients at a deeper level. She also felt she was getting "sucked into" a system that valued keeping up with the Joneses more than anything else. Although she had a financially rewarding career ahead of her, she thought it best to extract herself from the system before she became entangled in it even further.

Hiyawit (F, 38) echoed Redeit's perspective that the capitalist culture of the United States is antithetical to Ethiopia's. After finishing her business degree, Hiyawit was not motivated to settle long term in the United States. In addition to being dissatisfied with her potential career, Hiyawit felt that her skill sets were not truly valued and her presence as a Black immigrant woman was tokenized in corporate America. She explained:

Living my life in the West is a waste of time. They don't want us there, and honestly, we don't want to be there. If things were better here [in the home country], if we can live in safety and can earn a comparable living, why live in somebody else's country, speaking their language, adhering to their norms? We have our own language and culture, which is far more superior than theirs.

Hiyawit was adamant that the economic benefits of living and working in the West did not outweigh the social and emotional costs that it incurred. While she might have been earning a good income in the United States, she felt increasingly dissatisfied with her life and ultimately decided to relocate. Part of her dissatisfaction was directly related to the sexual harassment she experienced at work. Thwarting her boss's unwelcome advances and the calculated inaction of the company's Human Resources Department had left a bad taste. Her experiences preceded the #MeToo movement,[27] and she felt a lack of solidarity from her coworkers and a hostile work environment.

Respondents such as Alemneh, Redeit, and Hiyawit additionally emphasized how underappreciated and undervalued they felt in the host nation. They reported that, despite the financial benefits of living in the West, their skill sets and overall presence were not respected the way they were in the home nation. Therefore, dissatisfaction on one end (push factor) and a sense of accomplishment on the other (pull factor) can explain return in some cases. Although economic factors matter, they are not the only considerations for migrants.

Return Motivated by Health Factors, Family Dynamics, and Life Stages

Family reasons (such as taking care of elderly parents or raising children) constitute a leading motivation for engaging in return migration. Let us consider the case of Birhan (F, 65), a divorcee and mother of two who lived in New York City for over twenty-five years. Despite her long-term settlement in the United States, when her father suddenly died and her mother fell ill, Birhan took an early retirement package and relocated to Ethiopia. At this point in her life, her children were adults leading their own lives in the United States and thus did not hinder the relocation. She elaborated on her position:

> My mother is old, my father has already died, and I couldn't be there for him, so at least I can be there for her. I mean, I don't expect her to live forever, but if she passes now, at least I know I fulfilled my duties as a daughter. I am nursing her in her old age. I am her companion. She wouldn't have to face death by herself. It broke my heart when my father died while I was still living in the U.S. I can't imagine letting that happen again with my mother. I came back here to be with her.

Birhan understood taking care of elderly parents as the role of a dutiful daughter, no matter her own age. She had the freedom and financial means to uproot herself from her job and life in the United States to fulfill this role. At the time of the interview, Birhan had been back living with and nursing her mother for four years. She was glad to have been able to spend the precious last years of her mother's life with her, and she looked forward to however many years they had left together. She occasionally traveled to the United States to see her children and her friends, but for the most part, she stayed grounded in Addis Ababa, close to her mother. Birhan's example provides an insight into migrants returning to their home nations to fill a primary caretaker role: in her case, taking care of an aging mother.

Ashenafi (M, 34), in a similar situation, explained:

> I was living a comfortable life in the U.S. I had my MBA, my apartment, my social circle. It was good . . . I was good, predictable. I knew what was expected of me . . . but then both my parents passed away,

and that changed everything. I have an autistic brother, you see, and he had no one to take care of him with my parents gone. He was all alone, and it is hard in a society that does not understand autism. There was also the family business, a business my parents built over a lifetime. Now somebody had to run it, and this is not something you can delegate, even if it is someone related to you somehow. All my siblings were in the U.S. with me, I mean different states, but you get it . . . it was easier for me to return than any of them . . . so here I am running the family business and taking care of my little brother.

Ashenafi posited two main reasons for his return to Ethiopia, both prompted by the death of his parents. First, he felt responsible for his younger autistic brother, who no longer had his primary caretakers. Second, Ashenafi needed to take over the family business (a combination of real estate and import-export). This joint role of family member and business caretaker prompted his relocation to Addis Ababa, Ethiopia.

It is important to note that in both of these cases (Birhan and Ashenafi), the respondents had the economic means to uproot their lives in the host nation to take on the role of caretaker. Birhan cashed in her generous retirement packet, while Ashenafi exchanged his corporate American job for a lucrative family business in Ethiopia. Caregiving is thus enabled by the respondent's socioeconomic class.

For migrant families, care can be a momentous issue that can lead to return migration.[28] Instead of caring from a distance, returnees uproot their lives in their host countries to become primary caregivers to ailing family members or elder parents. From a gendered perspective, my respondents indicate that men and women are equally likely to return to take care of an elderly parent or another family member (an ailing sibling, for instance) regardless of age. This is surprising considering that the literature cites that women, and particularly young women, are generally designated as caretakers within the family dynamics.[29] This study, however, shows that the role of the caretaker is negotiated within the family, and caretaking is not necessarily assigned to one gender.

Retirement and Other Life Stages

Postretirement returnees are motivated partly by their life stage and partly by the consideration that with their retirement funds they can afford a better, more relaxed lifestyle in the home country, where the cost of living may be considerably lower. As Demekech (F, 61) explained, "We have been looking forward to our retirement for the longest time. Time to leave the hectic lives we led in the States and finally reconnect with our families and loved ones here [in Ethiopia]. It also does not hurt that our retirement savings goes a long way here than it did in California." In addition to their ability to stretch their retirement income further in the homeland, some postretirement returnees also consider the overall respect accorded to elders in Ethiopia compared to the host nation. They lament the prevalence of ageism in Western nations, where a competitive capitalist system values the labor or consumption of individuals and where the elderly are "put to pasture," as one respondent put it. Mebratu (M, 71) declared, "Why would I want to live in the U.S. once I am retired? What am I gonna do there? Stare at a TV all day long or wait until my children send me to a retirement home? Have you seen those places? It is so depressing. I feel bad for all those elders who are put to pasture like that." Maaza (F, 66) never felt embedded in the social fabric of the host nation outside of her role as worker or consumer. The older she got, the more disenchanted she became with American-style consumerism. She stated, "I would rather live in a place where I am valued for just being me. [In the United States] you are either a worker or a consumer; otherwise you don't matter. Your humanity doesn't count for anything."

Retiree returnees reap another advantage: the respect elders receive in the home country compared to the ageism they see prevalent in Western societies. Elelta (F, 72) stated, "They just throw out their old. They have no respect for elders. They just sit them out to pasture in horrible care homes where their children don't go to visit them or nothing. I do not understand how they can do that." They interpret the American social norms around eldercare as a lack of strong familial connection and lament what they see as a lack of respect or an abandonment of the elderly in Western society. Even though Mengesha (M, 68) confessed that the social norms in Ethiopia, particularly in a metropolitan city like Addis Ababa, had changed, becoming more "cutthroat," he thought elders were generally accorded more respect in Ethiopia than in the United States: "It might not be what it was when I was young, Addis [Ababa] has changed in that respect, but we [Ethiopians] still respect our elders. It is not like there [the United States]." As we can see from this discussion, the lower cost of living and postretirement financial incentives, coupled with the sociocultural practices of elder respect and belonging, can serve as a powerful incentive to engage in return migration.

As an important life stage, retirement allows a reevaluation of migrants' priorities. Retirees dislike the prospect of retirement in the Global North, disconnected from social network, cultural embeddedness, and social support (push factors). At the same time, they are drawn to the home nation, where they feel a stronger sense of belonging (pull factors). Retirees therefore engage in a cost-benefit analysis of where to live the remainder of their lives.

Similar to Gizaw, introduced at the beginning of this chapter, some returnees maintain that they always saw their sojourn in Western nations as temporary and invariably envisioned a return migration once they achieved their savings or educational goal in the host nation. For instance, Fatima (F, 32) explained that her primary motivation in emigration was getting an education and work experience. Once she achieved her stated goals, she could not wait to relocate to her home country to embark on the next stage:

> Look, I went there [to Europe] to get my degrees. Then I worked for a few years to gain work experience and provide myself some financial cushion. I never saw myself settling there long term. I don't know how others do it, live most of their lives in foreign lands. This [Ethiopia] is home. This is where I belong. This is where I am respected. This is where my family is. This is where I can make an impact. This is home.

Fatima underscored that she always saw her migration as temporary, motivated primarily by educational opportunities. She repeated that, for her, Ethiopia was home and she never envisioned living long term outside her home country. She also equated the home country with respect and belonging: "This is our home. These are our people. I know we have our share of problems here [in Ethiopia], but they are our problems. We need to be the ones to solve them." While acknowledging the deep-seated structural and political problems that exist within the home country, Fatima emphatically argued that she preferred for her and her family to live in Ethiopia. She listed a number of problems her family encountered while living as Black immigrants in Europe, including racism, Islamophobia, homesickness, and declining mental health. These different factors came together to cement her motivation to return after over a decade abroad.

Similarly, Abigail (F, 32) stated, "I was always going to return. There was no question about that. I never saw myself living long term, getting married, raising my children, etc. in France. I knew I was going to come back at some point. I did not know when, but I knew it was going to happen." Abigail initially migrated to France because of a scholarship opportunity after graduating from the sole French lycée in Addis Ababa. She migrated to a small city in southern France with some other students from her high school. After earning two degrees in engineering and spending a decade in France, she relocated to Addis Ababa to open a restaurant. Although this was a complete career change for her, she had felt increasingly dissatisfied with her work and unwelcome in France and desired to live close to her family in Ethiopia. Therefore, for Abigail, her sojourn in France was always meant to be temporary.

Marriage Dynamics and Return Migration

Abebech (F, 74), a mother to seven children and grandmother to ten, first migrated to the United States with her husband when they were both in their mid to late fifties. Four of their children lived in the United States, United Kingdom, and Canada, while the other three lived in Ethiopia. Abebech and her husband initially migrated to California, to be near two of their children. While the husband worked outside the home, the wife took care of the household. This separation between the wife in the home, or private sphere, and the husband at work, in the public sphere, highly influenced their integration into U.S. society. While Abebech's husband reported experiencing significant amounts of racism and xenophobia, Abebech herself did not have a hard time integrating into U.S. society. Their differing experiences during their seven years in California led to divergent conclusions about their overall stay. The husband insisted on returning back to his home country to resettle, while the wife would have preferred to live out the remainder of her life in California. They ended up relocating to Ethiopia even though Abebech was highly reluctant to make the trip back to Addis Ababa. She begrudgingly returned with her husband to keep her marriage of fifty years intact:

> What can I do? Tell me, what can I do? It was either come back with him [her husband] or stay there by myself. He wouldn't hear of staying. He constantly talked about coming back; he constantly nagged. He would complain every day about life in the U.S. while I was out enjoying myself window-shopping or watching TV. Life in America was great, but he hated it. After years of nagging, I had to make a choice, and I chose my marriage. You don't give up on fifty years.

Abebech's case demonstrates that not all migration undertaken by women is autonomous. Abebech had the choice to remain in the United States, but she opted to return to her home nation for the sake of staying with her husband and maintaining the integrity of her family. Although she was able to delay the process, she could not stop or completely avoid the return trip. In fact, the majority of the literature posits women as subordinate to men's migration, as women are sometimes compelled to migrate to appease spouses or other family members under situations of social pressure or obligation.[30] Abebech somewhat fit the stereotypical "trailing wife" picture prevalent in older migration analysis.[31] She migrated under a situation of social pressure or obligation. Yet Abebech was part of an older cohort and, compared to some of the younger couples in this study, subscribed to a very different gender dynamic within married life.

The stereotype of the "trailing wife" is by no means representative of most women in my sample. The following case demonstrates that women can be the proponents and initiators of return migration. Beza (F, 32) and her husband, Abtew (M, 37), moved to Addis Ababa in the spring of 2005. Abtew explained:

> My wife was really the one who pushed for us to move to Ethiopia. Although my parents are Habesha, I have never been to Ethiopia prior to moving here! But my wife is a force unto herself. She knew what she wanted, and she made it happen.

Abtew was an assistant pastor and a founding member of a major church established by a group of close friends and family members, all of whom had returned from the United States. After the couple had lived in the Washington, DC, area for fourteen years, their Christian faith led them back to Ethiopia to establish a ministry. Beza had initially entered her marriage with the agreement that they would live and raise their family in Ethiopia. Beza, part of a younger cohort (aged forty and below), was the main factor behind her family's return migration. The return proved to be more of a challenge for her husband since although he was Ethiopian by descent, he was born and grew up in the United States. He had never even traveled or visited his parents' homeland before packing up and moving to settle permanently in Ethiopia. This, of course, led to challenges in Abtew's integration in Ethiopia. Beza explained:

> [Abtew] was a good sport about the whole thing. He has heard stories about Ethiopia from his parents, but he has never been, so it must have been challenging to wrap his mind around a lot of things. He just had the right personality I guess since he laughed off all the cultural shock he experienced, and we had fun with it . . . I wouldn't have it any other way.

This example shows that the gender dynamics in the family cannot always be assumed to be patriarchal as Beza was the deciding force in the move. Even though after relocation she predominantly focused on her role as a mother and homemaker, the fact that she convinced her husband to move to a country he had never even seen indicates the gender dynamics within the household for younger families.

The relationship between marriage and return migration is complicated. Return migration can test marriage dynamics. One spouse (generally the wife) may refuse to return to the homeland or reluctantly engage in return migration, or the marriage may even dissolve as a result of return. My study demonstrates that the relationship between marriage and return migration is not straightforward or clear cut. While return migration can alleviate existing tensions within a marriage (for instance, related to the household division of work), it can also create new sources of tension, particularly if one partner has a harder time readjusting to the home country.

It's (Not) about the Children

Netsanet (F, 27) felt she had hit a wall in her corporate job in Toronto and was looking to expand her horizons. She was utterly bored with the "mediocrity of life" in Canada, where the primary preoccupation seemed to be making ends meet and, if possible, accumulating wealth:

> I know why you are looking at me like this when I tell you this . . . [*laughs*] you think I'm so young, I shouldn't have been bored with my work so early in my career, but I just couldn't see myself doing the same thing over and over again for the next decade! Oh my God, I would have died! . . . This is the perfect age to make such a drastic change in my life. I think if I was older, I probably wouldn't have done it because if you have a mortgage, married with kids, who is likely to just up and move like this?

Netsanet thus decided to venture to her parents' homeland, a part of the world she had left as a child. She moved to the city of Addis Ababa seeking work opportunities to relieve some of the angst she had felt in Canada. She credited her adventurous return to her singleness, youth, and lack of financial and other responsibilities. At the time of the interview, Netsanet had been back living in Addis Ababa for a little more than a year. She explained that if she were a bit older, married with kids, she would have been less likely to engage in return migration.

While Netsanet followed a career opportunity in the same field she had worked in while in Canada, Abigail (F, 32) opted for a complete career change. Abigail had trained as an engineer in France and held several well-paid positions over the previous decade; however, she wanted to open a restaurant in the heart of Bolé, the upscale business area of Addis Ababa. Her small-scale market research proved that the food service industry was underserved and that restaurants were a lucrative business in the growing metropolitan city. With the help and support of her family, she opened a Western-style bistro and lounge. She explained, "But why not? This would be the time for me to do this if ever there was a time. I am young, unattached, no kids, so this is the perfect time." She emphasized that the timing of events helped guide her to make the return journey. The fact that she was young, unattached, and childfree contributed to her decision-making process. The autonomous migration of Netsanet and Abigail demonstrates that lack of attachment (not having children) can contribute to the decision-making process of young adults.

Women were not the only ones who engaged in return migration for work or investment opportunities and cited being single and childfree as an added justification. Melkamu (M, 31) returned from the United States to open an agribusiness, a field in which he had no prior experience. He explained:

> Look, I am telling you, this is prime time to return to Ethiopia. The economy is growing; new industries are opening up. This is the time to invest, and yes, it comes with risks, but it is just me, I do not have any kids, I am not married; this is the perfect time to start a new life, embark on a new adventure. I do not have anybody who depends on me for their livelihood. Even if I fail, at least I would have tried my luck. Besides, I did not want to settle down in the U.S. It was just not for me.

Melkamu posited his investment as a gamble, far from a sure thing. He admitted he would have been less likely to gamble with his life savings if he was responsible for a family, particularly if he was a parent. But, as a single person, he felt freer to choose a riskier path with a higher potential for reward.

Netsanet, Abigail, and Melkamu all emphasized that being young and child-free can make it easier to engage in return migration. They saw this age as allowing more freedom because of a lack of significant attachments; of financial responsibility, such as a mortgage; and of parental responsibility. This freedom and their taste for adventure led them to resettle back in their home nation. Age thus is a factor in understanding return migration. Being single (unmarried) and child-free allows individuals to be adventurous in their quest for career advancement and investment opportunities. It is also important to note that there is no significant difference between the men's and women's narratives around parenthood.

Alternatively, Nigist (F, 62), an empty nester, engaged in return migration after her children were grown and her husband retired. Her family lived in the United States for ten years. She mostly worked for a small nonprofit before resettling in Ethiopia in 2008. Nigist returned to Ethiopia after her husband retired, even though she had not reached her own age of retirement. She relocated from New York City to Addis Ababa and opened a minimart in a busy part of the city. Since a very young age, she had dreamed of owning a small business, and she saw her golden years as the perfect time to fulfill her dreams. Nigist explained:

> This was something I've wanted to do for the longest time, I mean ever since I can remember . . . owning a business, being my own boss . . .

> but life got in the way. I was busy working, raising children, taking care of a household, my husband's career . . . there just was no time or capital for that matter. But now that my kids are grown, and have kids of their own, my husband is retired, I thought it is finally time.

Nigist no longer felt encumbered by her family life as her children were independent adults and her husband was retired. Although she was primarily motivated by an investment opportunity, family reasons (her husband's retirement) provided the catalyst for her return migration.

In the cases discussed in this chapter, we can see that the absence of minor children significantly affects both men's and women's motivations for return migration. While some respondents explained that children added a layer of responsibility that they did not want to consider upon return migration, others, those with young children, engaged in return migration specifically because of their roles as parents and their desire to raise their children with a sense of cultural belonging and with some distance from racialized societies. Parents were concerned about raising children in a highly racialized society where they would be marked by their skin color. They preferred their children to grow up in a nonracialized society with a strong sense of Ethiopian identity.

Makeda (F, 41) explained that her decision-making about migration was heavily colored by her role as a mother and her experiences of growing up as a Black teenager in the United States:

> There was no way I would have my daughters living in that environment. . . . I was a scared child, not understanding what it meant to be Black in the U.S. . . . in LA in the 1990s, go figure! I did not want that influence on my beautiful girls. . . . It was so cliquish, you had to stick to your own kind, and when you are not sure who or where that is, it makes for a lonely childhood. . . . The Black folks don't really consider you truly Black because of our light skin and my accent. . . . They ostracized me because I was African! Imagine the Black folks playing the Africa card! Ouch! . . . And they would tell me, "Go back to Africa," so I did!

Makeda migrated to Los Angeles, California, with her parents and siblings in the late 1970s. Her family was part of the wave of migrants who moved to the United States out of fear of religious persecution by the Derg communist regime in Ethiopia, which lasted for seventeen years (1974–1991). Even though the family enjoyed a middle-class income and religious freedom, the racial tension in California after the Rodney King incident heavily affected Makeda and her siblings.[32] In the predominantly white suburbs of Los Angeles, Makeda felt like an outcast. She felt alienated from her classmates and confused by the racial cliques in her middle and high schools. Friends she normally spent time with in the neighborhood or one-on-one would pretend not to know her at school. She felt discriminated against by both white and Black people and consequently had a hard time fitting in anywhere. She felt scarred and did not want a repeat of this experience for her own daughters. She strongly desired her daughters to spend their formative years in Ethiopia developing a strong sense of self and culture. Her decision to return resulted from her status both as a mother and as a Black person in the United States.

The experience of another respondent similarly demonstrates how children's experiences of racism can incite the relocation of an entire family. *Gash* Bogale (M, 62) reported that his kids experienced racism growing up in an all-white neighborhood:

> Other kids would touch their hair and exclaim "How kinky!" and run away. My boy, who was an excellent soccer player, couldn't play with the other kids because they didn't want him. . . . What parent wants to see this? I did not want my kids growing up thinking that they are inferior, thinking that they have no history.

He said his children were constantly ostracized and made to feel that they did not belong. He explained that his main reason for wanting to move back to Ethiopia was to raise his children where "they would not be made to feel inferior for their skin color." As a result, *Gash* Bogale ended up relocating his family mostly out of concern for his children. In the cases of Makeda and *Gash* Bogale, we can see that concerns for children growing up in highly racialized societies such as the United States can incite family relocation. Makeda and *Gash* Bogale did not want their children to feel inadequate because of their race. Instead, they wanted their children to grow up within Ethiopian society, where they could reconnect with their family roots. Although the categories of fleeing racism and xenophobia, on the one hand, and reconnecting with cultural background, on the other, are not exactly the same, they do tend to overlap. Some returnees were motivated by the racism they or their progeny experienced in the host country. They wanted to live and bring up their children in a racially homogeneous society where they would not have to be constantly on guard because of their skin color. While the previous examples discuss returnees who relocated in the interest of their progeny, others were motivated by their own encounters with different forms of racism, as previously discussed.

Despite the prevalent argument in the literature,[33] the presence or absence of children was not a good indicator of whether an individual was likely to return. While there are not many studies of return migration that focus on the presence of children, either as return migrants themselves or as the children of migrants,[34] the literature in general indicates that individuals with children are less likely to return as they have to consider the children's education, assimilation, and adjustment in the parent's home nation. Nevertheless, in my study, the presence of children was sometimes used as a justification for engaging in return migration. In a seemingly contradictory manner, those with children indicated that they returned because of their children, while those without children declared that they returned because they did not have children and claimed that they would have been less likely to return if they were parents.

Family dynamics are therefore a significant factor that affects the motivations of returnees. Caregiving (e.g., taking care of elderly parents), important life stages such as retirement, marriage dynamics (e.g., search for a partner or dissolution of marriage), and the presence or absence of children differently influence the motivations of returnees. Their love or sense of responsibility and, to some extent, perhaps guilt all influence their decision-making processes.

Return Migration through a Push-Pull Framework

> You have to understand that both places [the home and host nations] have their own pros and cons. It is more a question of which one outweighs the other. Do you prefer to remain in the U.S. and live as an immigrant, or does the homeland pull at your heartstrings? The answer is not the same for everyone.—Tekle (M, 42)

Tekle had a succinct and pragmatic approach to return. While he employed a side-by-side comparison between the home and host nation, advocating for a cost-benefit analysis, he also employed emotional language, asking if the homeland "pull[s] at your heartstrings." His short description demonstrates a keen awareness of the emotional aspect of return, which figuratively pulls the migrant homeward.

As amply demonstrated in this chapter, understanding return migration motivations requires a dyadic consideration of the situations in both host and home nations. I propose applying the vastly popular push-pull models of migration to the study of return migration.[35] Push-pull models of migration have traditionally been applied to migrants' initial migration from their countries of origin.[36] Yet exploring the reasons that migrants leave the host nation and return to the home nation requires a two-way comparison of the conditions in the home and host societies. We must examine what makes the host nation unattractive and home nation appealing to returnees. Although the push-pull model of migration has seldom been applied to the study of return migration, it is possible to adapt it to explain the motivations for returnees.[37] This framework has the advantage of being a simple, straightforward, easy-to-understand model, adaptable to return migration and even repeat migration; however, it has often been criticized for being too simple as it fails to take into account the complexity of migrants' lived experiences. Moreover, the push-pull framework has been criticized for being shallow, neglecting the agency of migrants and paying insufficient attention to cultural norms in decision-making. Despite these valid critiques and seeming shortcomings, the push-pull framework is an intuitively intelligible, easily adaptable, and useful model to understand a wide range of migrant experiences, including return migration.

Although push-pull reasons provide a descriptive framework to capture the complex lived realities of migrant motivations, they do not constitute a prescriptive or full-fledged theory of migration. In addition, there are a number of other caveats to remember. First, while I focus on push factors that lead migrants to leave the host nation, it is important to underscore that not all migrants have negative experiences in the host nation. Similarly, when I discuss pull factors, I do not intend to paint an idealistic picture of the homeland. Rather, returnees' emotional landscape affects how they perceive and portray both the host and home nations in a dialogic approach. Second, adopting a push-pull framework of return migration does not dilute the emotional aspect of the decision-making process. Before embarking on a physical return, migrants engage in a mental calculation weighing the pros and cons. Similar to the significant emotional and other costs of initial migration, uprooting oneself and one's family from the host country to return to the homeland is no easy task. Among other things, it is an emotional process with deep psychological meaning and impact on the migrants.

Table 2.2 provides a push-pull overview of return migration, taking into consideration economic, family-related, health, and sociopolitical factors. It juxtaposes the conditions in the home and host countries to provide a simultaneous understanding of the considerations of (potential) returnees. The factors are listed alphabetically and not in order of importance. Moreover, not every possible push and pull factor for return is accounted for in this table or discussed in this chapter.

The push-pull factors are not necessarily discrete or independent categories, and they vary in potency. The discussion around return migrants' personal motivations reveals a confluence of factors affecting their decision-making processes. Even though I present returnees' motivations in separate categories for the sake of clarity, in reality motivations are not neatly packaged into two or three separate categories. In fact, respondents state a confluence of factors influencing their decision-making process. It is important

TABLE 2.2. PUSH-PULL REASONS FOR RETURN MIGRATION		
	Push factors: Reasons to leave the host nation	Pull factors: Reasons to return to the home nation
Economic / financial	Success: achievement of savings goals and wealth accumulation; educational goal attainment; retirement Failure: debt, unemployment / underemployment; financial dissatisfaction; high cost of living	Lower cost of living Demand for skill set Investment or job opportunity
Life stage and family dynamics	Retirement Marriage: search for partner, marriage, or divorce Maladjustment of children	Retirement Marriage: search for partner, marriage, or divorce Assistance in raising children
Physical and psychological health and well-being	Declining physical health (availability of caregiver and cost of care) Homesickness; psychosocial maladjustment (self or family member)	Declining mental or physical health (e.g., elderly parent) Availability (and cost) of care providers for ailing returnees
Sociopolitical	Anti-immigrant sentiment Racism, xenophobia, othering Loss of cultural identity; lack of sense of belonging Deportation;[1] undocumented status; forced repatriation	Return to roots Sense of belonging; emotional attachment to the homeland Peace and security

[1] Since this book is primarily concerned with voluntary return, no respondents in my sample were forcibly returned to Ethiopia, their home country, because of deportation or undocumented status. For a discussion of forcible repatriation, see Laura Hammond, *This Place Will Become Home: Refugee Repatriation to Ethiopia* (Cornell University Press, 2004).

to not seek out a single motivating factor but rather to take into account how these motivations work together to create the ideal conditions for return migration. Finally, some of the factors to leave and return bleed into one another. For instance, a lack of a sense of belonging is both a sociopolitical and a psychological factor. Similarly, retired returnees would fit under both the economic and life stage categories, as they are making a financial calculation and also relocating to a place that provides social support postretirement.

The emotional aspect is clearly visible through this push-pull framework. Negative emotions such as dissatisfaction, burnout, lack of a sense of belonging, and disenfranchisement (due to racism, xenophobia, and othering) can all compel migrants to leave the host country. On the other hand, positive emotions such as a strong sense of belonging, a positive sociocultural identification, excitement (at investment opportunities, for example), and a sense of family responsibility can alternatively create a yearning for return to the homeland. These nonmonetary, psychological, and emotive factors are negotiated within the larger structural factors such as socioeconomic development and political stability, which I call the socio-ecology of migration. We always need to contextualize returnees' migra-emotions within the context of the socio-ecology of migration that enables or prevents return. Moreover, just as the initial migration is fraught with uncertainty and discomfort, the return journey can similarly encompass unknown elements and precarity.

Finally, it is important to consider that the migrants (i.e., returnees) and the home country have likely undergone significant changes during the migration years. As the famous Greek philosopher Heraclitus, highlighting that things are in a constant state of flux, aptly stated, "One cannot step in the same river twice."[38] When we apply this principle to migration, Thomas Wolfe's statement "You can't go home again" is fitting as migrants' places of origin change during their absence.[39] Sometimes the change is for the better, sometimes for the worst, but the change is constant. While returnees once dreamed of returning "home," the place they dreamed of may, in fact, no longer exist anywhere but in their hearts and minds. In the next chapter, I discuss whether or not the dreams of returnees are realized, through the lens of the joys and frustrations of return.

INTERLUDE 2

Passports Tell a Story

When she invited me to guest lecture in her Introduction to Global Studies undergraduate class, a dear colleague once asked that I bring one physical item that epitomized my research as a starting point for class discussion. As a migration scholar, I thought the choice was obvious. I brought in my old Ethiopian passport, expired decades ago, as part of my show and tell. Passports are concrete objects, aspects of material culture, that we can explore as part of the histories of im/mobility. They contain their own socioeconomic and political histories. No other single portable object illustrates my research and my lived experience as much as this small booklet. I have had many adventures with this passport. It is the one I presented at my first crossing into the United States more than twenty years ago, when I had the racist interaction with the immigration officer. This is the same passport that drew the fascination of no less than six Singaporean immigration officers when I entered the country by bus from Malaysia while my travel companion crossed with her American passport without them batting an eye. It is the same passport I nonchalantly waved through internal checkpoints crossing between the West Bank and Israel to visit the beautiful city of Bethlehem, gaining mobility denied to some locals. It is the same passport that led a Norwegian visa officer in New York to interrogate me suspiciously before begrudgingly stamping it with a Schengen visa valid for less than a week, even though I was also a U.S. green card holder at the time. Passports can tell stories.

I asked the attentive undergraduate students to raise their hands if they owned a passport. Only about a third of the class did. This was not surprising as only 45 percent of Americans have passports, according to the U.S. Department of State.[1] I then asked the students to define a passport. They provided different answers but generally agreed that a passport is a government-issued official travel document certifying the beholder's identity and nationality. I proceeded to show them my blue passport with gold lettering spelling out "People's Democratic Republic of Ethiopia" in English and "የኢትዮጵያ ሕዝባዊ ዴሞክራሲያዊ ሪፐብሊክ" in Amharic on the top, the national coat of arms in the middle, and "ETHIOPIAN PASSPORT" and "የኢትዮጵያ ፓስፖርት" on the bottom. Before 1994, the interiors of Ethiopian passports were imprinted with "Valid for all countries EXCEPT South Africa," limiting the use of the official documents. This is particularly interesting in light of the fact that Nelson Mandela (1918–2013) once traveled under an Ethiopian passport. In 1962 Emperor Haile Selassie provided the South African antiapartheid leader some freedom of movement with an Ethiopian passport furnished under the name of David Motsamayi; it listed his profession as a journalist in what is now an archaic practice. Nelson Mandela had to be smuggled out of South Africa under a pseudonym, and he chose the name of one of his former clients. Mandela then traveled to Ethiopia for secret military and political training, a journey he documents in his six-hundred-page memoir *Long Walk to Freedom*.[2] Mandela did not have the opportunity to use his Ethiopian passport for long as he was imprisoned soon after returning to South Africa. Between 1962 and 1990, he languished in various institutions, most notably on Robben Island.[3] Mandela's first South African passport was issued to him in 1990, days after his release from his twenty-seven-year prison sentence. Passports are not equally available to everyone.

In a similar talk in a different classroom, I displayed various Ethiopian passports, from the era of Emperor Haile Selassie, from the Derg regime, and from the Ethiopian People's Revolutionary Democratic Front (EPRDF), ranging in color from gray to blue and maroon. You can buy some of these vintage Ethiopian passports on Etsy and other sites as pieces of history. The current machine-readable biometric passports many nations provide to their citizens are a modern iteration of an ancient tradition. Historical records from different geographies show letters stamped with an official seal asking permission for the safe passage or movement of individuals, particularly those tasked with official business. However, before the First World War, the average person was not necessarily required to have a passport to travel. As crossing borders was much less bureaucratic and more straightforward than in our present day, few people had passports. The League of Nations in the 1920s was one of the first to attempt to standardize passports on a global level, and they developed the general booklet design. After the Second World War, as the system of independent nation-states replaced empires, governments started closely monitoring their borders, and individuals crossing these geopolitical borders came under increased scrutiny. By the 1980s, it became imperative for nation-states to implement passport standardization protocols to facilitate global travel. Passports have their own histories.

Passports also reflect unequal mobility. A passport's mobility score is based on the number of countries that allow visa-free or similarly hassle-free entries (such as with visas on arrival and e-visas with fast processing times). According to Passport Index, which calculates the mobility score of close to two hundred national passports across the globe, some of the strongest passports in the world are from Singapore, the United Arab Emirates, and various Western European nations. Unsurprisingly, some of the weakest passports in the world emanate from African nations and war-torn nations such as Afghanistan and Syria. The value of a weak passport is intimately felt by the bearer, who must humbly apply for elusive visas and provide tons of documentation and assurances not required of holders of strong passports. For the Ethiopian passport, over the decades, not only have the colors changed but so has its value. Passport inequality is an extension of other forms of global inequality. Passports are not created equal.

Nicole Constable, in the preface of her book *Passport Entanglements*, writes, "Passports are endlessly fascinating, partly because they are full of contradictions. They both facilitate and prevent mobility. They represent the state's unity and equality but reinforce social inequality and differences. They are instruments of freedom and of control, of protection and exploitation. They represent modernity, rationality, and transparency, but they are entangled with murky and conspiratorial discourses of power, surveillance, and corruption."[4] Similarly, in her first nonfiction book, a collection of essays titled *Conditional Citizens*, the cover of which depicts a U.S. passport, the novelist Laila Lalami writes about American identity, citizenship, and the meaning of her American passport.[5] She discusses the difference between legal and sociocultural belonging, warning against erroneously equating the two. She, like many others, finds it challenging to live in a country that loves and hates immigrants at the same time.

Like Lalami, I remember taking the oath of allegiance during my swearing-in ceremony as I became a newly minted U.S. citizen in the early 2010s, more than twenty years after my initial arrival. I also remember studying for the citizenship exams, memorizing facts about U.S. history and the U.S. Constitution, questions I doubt most native-born Americans would be able to answer. The ceremony took place in a small courtroom in Brooklyn, packed with mostly brown and Black people from all over the globe. It was anticlimactic, more of a bureaucratic processing rather than the emotional moment I have heard other naturalized citizens recount. It was pragmatic, expedient, and efficient. Perhaps my lack of emotionality at the time was a protective measure, as I pondered whether I was betraying the country of my birth by pledging allegiance to my adopted country. Changing citizenships is a momentous life event for a migrant, warranting reflection.

Even now that I have lived more than half my life in the United States, my attachment to my homeland has not diluted. While I acknowledge that there is widespread inequality within the United States, based on axes of race, gender, and religion, among other things, my U.S. passport has opened unparalleled doors in terms of travel. Traveling on my U.S. passport means that I no longer worry about being allowed to enter a new country. Gone is the anxiety I used to feel at border crossings. I am now part of the privileged few who can travel without many restrictions, a freedom I savor. When I return to the United States from wherever I have been, I am now greeted with "Welcome home" rather than being questioned why I am here. This simple document makes a world of difference.

As the Ethiopian Constitution does not currently allow dual citizenship, I applied for the Ethiopia Origin Identity Card, colloquially referred to as the Yellow Card, after losing my Ethiopian citizenship.[6] Modeled after the Overseas Citizenship of India (OCI) Card, my Yellow Card accords me certain rights and privileges, such as entering without a visa, owning property, and legally securing employment without a work permit. One of the mains limitations is that the Yellow Card prohibits involvement in the political sphere; the holder cannot vote or hold public office. Alternatively seen as a consolation prize or a pragmatic response, the card serves as a political regulation tool for a government more interested in the pockets than in the political voice of its large diaspora.

While in this interlude I focus on passports and other documents as instruments of migration, as part of the bureaucracy migrants have to navigate, the other side of the story consists of those who cross geopolitical borders without any documentation. Passports, even weak ones, provide the bearer with a level of protection, compared to those who are forced to undertake perilous journeys without legal recognition, whether they be refugees fleeing conflict or devastation or irregular migrants risking their lives for freedom or opportunity. Stories about migrants who destroy their own passports or whose passports are coercively confiscated are not uncommon. There is a level of disenfranchisement that comes with dispossession of identity paperwork, particularly at border crossings. Within the 360-degree view of migration, it is important to recognize such nodes (such as airports) and instruments (such as passports) of migration.

CHAPTER 3

The Joys and Frustrations of Return

> I am enjoying life, I am telling you. I am so much more relaxed. I have time for myself, time with friends, time with family. I can hire somebody else to do my cooking, laundry, cleaning. I can outsource all of that cheaply and not be spread thin like I was back in the U.S.
> —Zinash (F, 50)

Zinash invited me to join her on one of her regular self-care days. We met in the early afternoon on a Thursday at a Boston Spa, one of the premier health and beauty facilities in Addis Ababa, a business started by a returnee from Boston and named accordingly. "I love this place. Their standards are unmatched," Zinash said. She was planning to get an exfoliating facial, a mani-pedi, and a blowout treatment for her hair. She explained, "I never had the time to do things like this when I was in the U.S. Even if I could afford it, there was just no time. Look at us! Would we be able to do this in the middle of the day if we were in the U.S.? No, absolutely not!" Shortly after her marriage ended in divorce, Zinash returned to Ethiopia after living in the United States for twenty-three years. It had only been a little more than a year since she returned when we first met. The mother of three children, she reported how unhappy she was in her marriage and overall life in the United States: "I waited until my last one [child] went to college to move back home. My marriage has been on the rocks for ages, so divorce plus no more kids at home meant I could finally come back home [to Ethiopia]." She contrasted her life in the United States—where she worked in a physically and emotionally draining job as a home health aide, performed never-ending household chores, took care of three young children, and dealt with an unhelpful and sometimes even abusive spouse—with her new life in Addis Ababa. She stated, "I can finally prioritize me instead of being pulled in a thousand different directions, meeting other people's needs at the expense of my sanity. Here I can prioritize my own happiness. What a world of difference from my life in the U.S." While she was still in the United States, Zinash had partnered with her siblings to build an apartment complex on a piece of land inherited from their parents. Each sibling owned two floors of an eight-story building in a desirable neighborhood in Addis. Zinash rented out three of the apartments and lived in the fourth one. With one of her siblings, she also ran a small café on the ground floor of the apartment complex. Between the rents she collected from the three apartments and the profits of the café, she was financially secure and had plenty of time to relax and enjoy herself.

Return migration holds the promise of a better lifestyle for those well positioned to take advantage. While migrants generally relocate with the expectation that a change in location will result in a better way of life, the particular type of migration undertaken by relatively affluent people in search of a better quality of life is known as lifestyle migration.[1] Lifestyle migration is about relative (rather than absolute) affluence and mobilizing privilege vis-à-vis local populations within destinations. Returnees, for the most part, have planned their journey and usually come armed with savings and a purpose, which enable them to enjoy a privileged lifestyle they could not obtain in the host nations.[2] Returnees generally enjoy a higher standard of living than they did before migration or in the host country.[3] Lifestyle migrants seek to take material advantage of lower costs of living and intangible benefits such as a slower pace of life, a more sociable culture, more leisure opportunities, and a better life for their children.[4] In the field of lifestyle migration, scholars have highlighted the inequalities and power differentials between sending and receiving societies. Lifestyle migrants are believed to generally originate from countries of the Global North and therefore they travel under the privileged passports of powerful nations.[5] These powerful passports enable them to be geographically mobile and relocate to their choice of desirable destinations globally.[6] The asymmetrical power dynamics between countries of the Global North and the Global South affect the privileges of migrants originating from those geographies. Even though the concept of lifestyle migration has been widely applied to individuals from developed nations moving semipermanently to warmer climates (for instance, North Americans moving to Panama or northern Europeans moving to southern coastal Europe),[7] I argue that the term is just as applicable here, where Ethiopian returnees are relocating to their home country in search of a better lifestyle. Ethiopian returnees from the Global North who hold foreign passports generally live like expats in their own birth country. They take advantage of the power asymmetries between their birth country and their former host countries (often their countries of naturalized citizenship) to access better services, earn better salaries (expat versus local rates), and generally enjoy the good life.

In Chapter 2, I discussed the multifold reasons for return, including pursuing economic advantages, escaping the rat race, and raising children in preferred locations. However, that is not the end of the story. This chapter examines whether those expectations were in fact realized. Here are the questions that animate this chapter: How do returnees experience their return? What are the joys and frustrations of return? How are returnees alternatively welcomed and rejected in their home societies? How do returnees negotiate the landscape of the home country? What migra-emotions does the process engender? And what privileges are returnees accorded within the socio-ecology of migration? As stated in the Introduction, I am heeding Laura Nader's call to "study up," to study the culture of power and affluence rather than a culture of powerlessness.[8] I intend to paint a picture of the relative privilege of returnees, the lifestyle they enjoy in Addis Ababa, which is not available to most, and the ways the local non-migrant population challenges their relative privilege.

The Joys of Return

> It is the best decision ever. I feel like I can finally breathe. I am home, amongst my people. . . . This is the good life.—Elizabeth (F, 38)

I had asked Elizabeth to assess her return, three years after relocating from Australia. She explained that she had intended to live abroad and never thought she would prefer living in her homeland again. However, after a series of financial and relationship mishaps, she was happy to be back. Elizabeth was reluctant to talk about the life she left behind in Australia, although she alluded to having lived through challenging times. Instead, she wanted to discuss the life she had built in Ethiopia postreturn. Elizabeth characterized her life postreturn as "the good life." Elizabeth stated, "I am surrounded by my family, my parents, aunties, and uncles, who never tire of taking care of me. I have a strong group of trusted friends. I belong." She emphasized the importance of her social network and her cultural embeddedness as the cornerstones of her well-being. These are some of the intangible benefits of return.

The Luxury of Time

> You come here because this is home, your family, your people, and all. But you also come here because you will have access to the things you did not have in the U.S. . . . Mostly the time to enjoy the fruits of your labor. Time to develop deep social bonds. Time to play with your kids. In the U.S., there is all this talk about quality time, and they say "quality time" because they don't have quantity time. It sounds funny, but it is true. If you only have a very limited time, two to three hours a week to spend with your family, you are going to squeeze the life out of those minutes. Here it's different; you can spend quantity, quality time with your loved ones. Time is the best luxury.—Mahlet (F, 37)

As a married mother of two children, Mahlet valued time, a commodity she did not have enough of in the United States but found in abundance in Ethiopia. By contrasting the restrictions on time in the Global North and in Ethiopia, Mahlet emphasized that return gave her more time to do the things she valued, like relaxing with family and friends. She posited time as a valuable resource available in different quantities in the two different locations.

Another respondent, Alemneh (M, 47), first introduced in one of the three vignettes in the Introduction, expressed the same sentiment more succinctly: "I told you I was tired of the rat race in the U.S. I appreciate having more freedom and time here [in Ethiopia]." Returnees defined the "good life" in the Addis Ababa context as the slow life, with time to smell the roses, so to speak. Similarly, Makeda (F, 41) explained:

> In the U.S., outside of work, a big portion of my time was spent at home, taking care of the household, washing, cooking, cleaning, or if I am outside, I am shopping, doing the groceries, or buying clothes for the kids, chauffeuring the kids here and there, but here [in Ethiopia] I have so much more time to indulge myself. I go to the hair salon weekly, at least twice a month for my massages or Morocco bath. I have regular lunches and dinners with friends. I take an hour-long macchiato break in the middle of the day. I chillax, girl! This is the place you can live *zena yale nuro* [a relaxed lifestyle].

Another respondent, Ashenafi (M, 34). explained the difference in his lifestyle in this way:

> I still work and earn a good living, but I am not working seventy-two hours a week or twelve-hour day shifts like I was doing in the U.S.

> Here, life goes at a much slower pace, and it suits me perfectly. Nobody will bat an eye if you take a one-hour coffee break in the middle of the day. I can still be productive minus the super structured minute-by-minute scheduling that gets ingrained in you in corporate America. No wonder people are stressed there. Here, you are human first and a worker second. It is an exact reversal of the norm there [in the U.S.].

Ashenafi hated the regimented structure that was externally imposed on his time. He appreciated the flexibility he had in Ethiopia, where he had a lot more freedom to schedule his day as he saw fit. Time is one of the luxuries returnees take advantage of in the homeland. They have more leisure time, more time to spend with family.

Commanding the Labor of Others

> I did a lot of menial, repetitive, mind-numbing jobs while trying to survive in the U.S., and on top of that I had to do the majority of the household chores, cleaning the house, the cooking, and I had two small children at the time. It was tough. But here [in Addis Ababa], and this is one of the beauties of being back, no more laundry, no more cooking or cleaning . . . I have people who can do that now, and I can spend time on things that I love.—Makeda (F, 41)

While Makeda was an hourly wage worker at Starbucks in the greater Washington DC area, in Ethiopia, she owned and operated a lucrative leather accessories business. She employed six full-time leatherworkers in her business and three to four household workers at a time, including a cook, a maid, a guard, and a part-time gardener. Employing the labor of others frees up time to enjoy leisurely activities. Returnee privilege becomes apparent within the asymmetrical employer-employee power dynamic. More specifically, commanding the labor of others, both within and outside of the household, is one of the most visible ways returnees and local elites express or display their privilege. Returnees can command a whole slew of servants, such as chauffeurs, housekeepers, and gardeners, because labor is relatively cheap in Ethiopia. For less than fifty dollars per month (a little over 2,000 birr,[9] according to exchange rates at the time of the research), one can easily hire any of these workers. For instance, Makeda (F, 41) explained, "Not having to do household chores is a big plus, even though sometimes the management of it can be challenging, but having household help is necessary." Most of my respondents did not have the privilege of employing other people's labor in the household while living in the Global North.

In Ethiopia, it is customary for the middle and upper classes to have household help, although the amount depends on the income and size of the family. Household help generally includes male gardeners, who most times double as security guards, and female housekeepers, nannies, cleaners, and cooks. Abtew (M, 37) explained, "Isn't that one of the biggest benefits of being back? Enjoying the fruits of all this cheap labor? You can hire your maid, your gardener, your cook without breaking the bank! Does that make me sound like a crass capitalist?" Similarly, Desta (M, 41) explained, "My wife no longer asks me to do the dishes, one major thing we do not fight about anymore." Gender dynamics are blatant in these short responses. First, domestic labor is gendered: while outdoor labor (gardening, security) is carried out mostly by men, indoor domestic duties and caretaking are almost exclusively relegated to women. Moreover, while women returnees appreciate not having to do household work themselves, some men are cognizant that they are no longer *asked* to carry out household chores.

Parents with small children interviewed for this project mentioned that they received assistance in the raising of their children in Ethiopia both from hired household help and from unpaid extended family members. Similarly to returnees in other parts of Africa,[10] Ethiopian returnees consider assistance with childcare a major bonus. Almaz (F, 33) explained:

> In Sweden, my kids had to go with me or their dad wherever we went, any event or a trip to the grocery store. Finding someone to babysit was always a hassle. Here, that's never an issue. There's always someone, either the [live-in] nanny, or I can drop the kids off at my sister's, or either of their grandparents, who love to have them anytime. You have no idea how much of a difference that makes in my life.

The assistance families receive extends from childcare to care for the sick and the elderly.

Returnees explained that hiring household help to take care of everyday chores allowed for freedoms they did not have previously. To the exception of one family, none of my respondents had any household help while living in Europe or North America. Birhan (F, 65), a well-to-do, high-skilled worker who migrated from New York, resisted the idea of hiring someone to do household work while she was living in the United States. She explained, "Yes, technically I had the means, but you know, in the U.S., I look like the people who get hired as the help." In her response, Birhan highlighted her racial perceptions of employer and housemaid, which made her uncomfortable. She further explained her position:

I know there are people who do that [hire household help in the United States], I mean, people who look like me [Black] and who do that, but isn't it kinda just weird? I remember walking into my building once dressed kinda shabby, hair a mess, I was living in Manhattan then, and I got stopped by the doorman in my building asking me who I worked for. I did not understand, so I told him I worked for the United Nations, and he gave me this look, and I understood he meant who did I work for in the building! It was a mostly white building, I mean the rent was expensive, and the doorman, a Latino guy I think, assumed that I could not live there but instead was there to clean someone's apartment.

In a few short words, Birhan summarized her discomfort with hiring household assistance in the United States, while in Ethiopia, she employed the services of two or three individuals at a time. She saw a racial component to hiring household help in the United States, but the same did not hold true in Ethiopia. As she explained, in Ethiopia "everybody [did] it," without a racial dichotomy between white and other. In Ethiopia, it was more of a class issue, which made it more acceptable from Brihan's perspective. Household chores thus get outsourced to poor working folks while returnees enjoy a more relaxed lifestyle. While some returnees attempt to overcome the glaring socioeconomic differences between employer and employee (for example, by eating meals together with their household staff), others view this as an insincere practice that does very little to change the socioeconomic status of the employees.

Some of the respondents did not see the employment of other people's labor as a form of luxury but as a necessity. As Mahlet (F, 37) explained:

Yes, in Ethiopia, you can hire plenty of servants, but it is less of a luxury and more of a necessity. In the U.S., housework is made easier with the abundance of technology. Here [in Ethiopia] most people cannot afford a dishwasher, I don't think I have actually seen one of those since I moved back, or a laundry machine, which is starting to become a little more popular. In the U.S., you can get help from your grocery store, where there is a lot of prepared food, prepeeled vegetables, chopped meat, etc. In the U.S., the difference might be in the brands you use, the size and the location of your living spaces, but the minimum is guaranteed. It is a whole different story here!

Mahlet's explanation of the need for numerous servants reveals her ingrained habits and dispositions due to her class position and migration experience. She was used to receiving assistance from the grocery store in terms of preprepared foods in the United States or, alternatively, household help to carry out the mundane everyday chores required for the maintenance of the body and household in Ethiopia. She argued that this is the natural order of things, rather than something learned and socially developed. The socialized expectation that somebody else will do household chores can lead to the justification of social inequalities. Although these are supposed necessities, the ability to employ a slew of servants is also a marker of class. Yet not everybody interviewed for this project had employed the labor of others within the household. Konjit (F, 40), a single woman, did not see the point in hiring household assistance:

> It's just me, and I live in a one-bedroom apartment. I have no place to house a live-in maid. Even *temelalash* [someone who comes in periodically] is not worth it because I can clean this small place easily, I cook my own food ... [*laughs*] well, that's not really true. I bring food from my mom's place most of the time, and before you ask, yes, she has a cook, a good one, so I just have to reheat the food.

Even Konjit, who rejected the idea of hiring household help, benefited from it by proxy, through the household help that existed in her parents' household.

Returnees justify their employment of a multitude of servants in several ways: First, they are creating much-needed employment. Second, employing servants is a necessity rather than a luxury as the household chores that returnees used to outsource to the grocery store (for prewashed greens, for instance) or mechanize (using food processors, for instance) are generally done at home, by hand, and thus are labor intensive. Therefore, they require multiple servants to carry out these types of time-consuming, mundane, and everyday household chores. Third, for Ethiopian urbanites, having household servants is an accepted norm rather than the exception. In reality, these types of class-based practices of commanding the labor of others are normalized within certain contexts; their habits become ingrained and consequently taken for granted.

I deploy the notion of privilege as a theoretical construct and an axis of stratification within multiple power hierarchies.[11] When discussing privilege, we have to be aware of the confluence of many facets of identity, including migration status and class position, as well as gender and age. These intersecting factors determine how returnees experience and negotiate their privilege. Privilege is thus not exclusively the product of class position or economic stratification. Consequently, I draw attention to returnees as embodied and multiply situated individuals who insert themselves into an existing hierarchical social structure. Finally, I discuss how returnees alternatively resist and reproduce the existing power structures. In general, the longer they stay in the home country, the more returnees become comfortable with and internalize their privilege. Returnees therefore become complicit in the perpetuation of inequality. Ultimately, returnees end up reifying and justifying class divisions within the home society.

The Frustrations of Return

While returnees enjoy a number of benefits (such as the luxury of time, social embeddedness, and the ability to command the labor of others), return is also accompanied by a number of challenges that can result in a sociocultural disconnect. Two main areas of frustration emerge from this study: the everyday challenges of living in a developing nation, and gendered frustrations that affect mostly women.

Living in a Developing Nation

> The poverty in the streets of Addis just assaults your senses. It is everywhere, and there is no escape from it while you are out and about in the city. I know poverty exists in Europe and the U.S. as well, but it is not so much in your face as it is here. Here, even if you hide out in your gated community or only frequent the luxury hotels, the minute you step out of these places, it is in your face.
> —Lydia (F, 30)

Returnees have to make some mental adjustments when relocating to live in Ethiopia, where the inequality is highly visible. Although the returnees lived in Ethiopia at some point in their lives, some have forgotten the level of inequality they left behind during their migration years. Lydia (F, 30), who used to live in Germany, explained that "for [her] own sanity," she had to accept the high levels of inequality (what she described as visual assault) after relocating to Ethiopia. Ashenafi (34, male), a returnee from the United States, echoed Lydia's sentiments:

> You walk out of your house, and you are struck with the misery of some of the people you see on the streets . . . a lot of haggard-looking beggars, mothers with very young children who look like they just walked from some rural area a week ago. You feel bad, you give something, a few birr, but it is not enough; it never seems enough.

Hiwot (F, 27) expressed her own feelings about living within a highly unequal society:

Accepting and living with the wealth disparity, the inequality, can be tough at first. It is in your face, but you get desensitized very quickly, which is sad. I remember when I first arrived about two years ago, I cried because I saw a beggar child in the street... hmm, I notice it less now; I guess it doesn't affect me as much anymore... Oh my God, what does that say about me? It is not like I am saying I should cry every time I see a beggar child, but, I don't know, it is always around you, and you can't help it.

Similarly, Meskerem (F, 45), the director of a midsize firm managing about seventy employees, explained:

One of the hardest things to stomach in Addis is the level of inequality. Let me give you an example: I was visiting the home of one of my employees for a *lekso* [the sitting period after the death of a loved one], and I could not believe the level of abject poverty this person, my employee, was living in! I had not seen that before, and this was a person who has some education and what is considered to be a good, a decent job.

Returnees have to account for the challenges of living with highly visible socioeconomic inequality and other inconveniences while benefiting from their relatively privileged positions. When I asked Alemneh (M, 47) about the challenges he had encountered since returning, he mentioned some drawbacks of living in a major African metropolitan city, including visible inequality and traffic. He explained: "I get that for most people [Ethiopians], Addis is an expensive city. It is hard for the average person to keep up with rising costs and the ridiculous inflation.... Sometimes, [extended] family can be too much, up in your business and stuff. It is hard to establish boundaries, but overall, it's good." He also briefly talked about the "minor inconveniences" of living in a developing country, such as "the nightmare of traffic" and the unreliable water, electricity, and internet connection. But he explained that these were to be expected and were easy to work around if you had the means. It is important to contextualize returnee privilege within the Global South, where the availability of water, electricity, and reliable internet cannot always be taken for granted. Returnees do not present the homeland as a bed of roses, where they do not experience any challenges. Rather, they are forthcoming about some of the challenges of living in a Global South nation and some of the everyday luxuries they no longer have access to upon their return. Consequently, we can discuss relative privilege, which is similar to the concept of relative deprivation.[12]

For some, the relationship to time in the homeland can be challenging. Although some returnees interpret the slower pace of life as a luxury, others are frustrated by it, particularly as it relates to work. Business-minded returnees do not always choose a slower pace of work; some structural factors are out of their control, and they are forced to be flexible. Minilik (M, 35), a business owner, encountered repeated delays in transactions due to structural factors. He reluctantly learned to accept that he would not always be able to accomplish everything he set out to do on his own timetable. He said, "Life is also so unpredictable, you have to learn to go with the flow. A product you expected might not materialize when you need it. A shipment might get delayed in Djibouti [port] for a month. You have to be adaptable. If you don't bend, you break." He learned that he had to adapt to the local culture of work and the structural limitations on his ambitions. When I asked Minilik (M, 35) how he dealt with these frustrations, he used an expression I often heard from returnees, emphatically stating, "TIA: This is Africa!" implying that you have to take the bad with the good.

Musse (M, 28) echoed the importance of adaptability, stating, "It is exciting being here. Life is unpredictable. Some hate the unpredictability. It is scary [for them] or whatever, but I cherish it. It reminds me that I am alive." He added, "I feel content, at peace. I set out to do something, and I did. There are a lot of ups and downs being back home, but I accomplished what I set out to do. How many people can say that?" Despite some challenges, Musse's overall assessment of his return was positive; he found the unpredictability of life in Addis energizing.

Returnees face another challenge in the homeland: the growing entrenchment of ethnic divisions. Those who left the homeland at very young ages (for the most part under ten years of age), in particular, were not fully aware of the salience of ethnicity as an organizing principle in the home nation. They were more in tune with global racial differences than subnational ethnic differences. For instance, Makeda (F, 41), introduced earlier, was "flabbergasted" by the ethnic division she encountered in her home country, especially as someone fleeing racism:

> I brought my children here to take them out of the race conundrum they would have faced in LA, but I feel like we took them out of the frying pan into the fire! I did not realize how divisive ethnicity has become here [in Ethiopia]. This is not how I remember it from my childhood. We live a very insular life, but I am not sure how much I can protect my children from it. Everywhere we go, in the media and whatnot, we're taught to value one ethnic group and hate another. It is so disheartening.

She used the colorful language "out of the frying pan into the fire" to describe her encounter with ethnic division in the homeland. She returned primarily for family reasons, to ensure that her children would grow up in a nonracial society, but she was confronted with a different set of hierarchical ordering. She felt completely unaware of the existing ethnic differences in the home country and unprepared to deal with them. Even during our exchange, she was uncomfortable discussing ethnicity. A number of topics, from the conception of time to the growing entrenchment of ethnicity as a marker of difference in the homeland, create some form of cultural disconnect. These challenges can lead to frustrations, which in turn can lead to discontent with return.

Gendered Frustrations

Gender needs to be taken up as a central analytical factor in the effort to understand the complexities of return migration.[13] Men's and women's return migrations are mediated through negotiations with spouses, parents, and larger kin groups and considerations such as children and the health of elderly parents. As migrants leave and return to gendered and variously stratified societies, it is necessary to expand the analysis of return migration to account for gendered axes of difference. In light of this discussion, it is important to keep in mind that the category of gender has been highly contested and challenged by African scholars who have argued that gender is a Western sociocultural construct.[14]

Gender comes up in many different ways for returnees, from frustrating encounters in the workplace to gender policing within the extended family and even sexual harassment in public spaces. The privilege that comes with being a returnee is checked by non-migrants in different arenas, such as the family unit, workplace, and city. Focusing on a few key events can help us elucidate expected gender roles and negotiations in postreturn experiences.

> I knew I made more money than most of the employees at my firm, by virtue of my foreignness, even though I am Habesha . . . to the exception of the executive director and maybe a few others . . . and I knew they resented me for it. They would say things like "Just because our degrees are not from Europe . . . ," and I understand, I completely understand. But just because the system is unfairly structured does not mean I should be a target, does it? The older men in particular try to undercut me at every step. They dismiss my input, anything that comes from me. I am constantly told, "Respect your elders." How is doing my job disrespectful to them? They

wouldn't be saying those things to me if I was a man. A man's opinion would be taken at face value. It is so frustrating!—Lydia (F, 30)

Lydia highlighted the intersection between her status as a returnee and her gender. While she enjoyed a certain class privilege due to her migration status, her input was devalued in the workplace because of her gender and young age. Although she had the necessary qualifications for her job, older male colleagues resented her for occupying her position. Many women in my sample lamented the fact that they had to fight to assert their presence within the workplace. For instance, Abigail (F, 32) did not think women got enough respect in the workplace. She recounted an incident that took place at the restaurant she owned and operated:

ABIGAIL: The male workers were the worst.... I had hired this one guy who completely refused to obey my orders. Anything I would tell him, he would refuse to do or pretend that he did not hear me. When [her then boyfriend] would tell him to do the same exact thing, he would rush to do it, which annoyed me to the utmost. I used to tell him, "I'm the one paying your salary! Me, no one else! I pay your salary," but he just would not listen. He made me want to pull out my hair.... He did not last very long, I fired him within two weeks, and even that is a story unto itself...
HG: What do you mean? Can you explain?
ABIGAIL: It was a day that [her boyfriend] was not there. I called the employee and told him that he was fired. But he refused to acknowledge me at first, as if I did not matter. It is my restaurant! Then I told him to leave the premises. He sat down as a guest and would not budge. We ended up calling the police to escort him out, and it was a huge, horrible scene ... but you know, it's *niket* [disrespect] because I am a woman, because I am young. He has a hard time stomaching the fact that his boss is a woman. I understand his poverty, but how is he going anywhere with that attitude?

Abigail attributed her trouble with the male employee primarily to gender but also explained that age and class were mitigating factors. Her employee's resentment toward her was due not just to her gender and returnee status but to her foreign experience, impressive credentials and mostly her higher socioeconomic status. From her perspective, a young male low-wage worker could not "stomach" having a young female boss and owner-operator of a large restaurant. She felt she had to assert herself in all her interactions with this particular employee, repeatedly stating that she was the one paying his salary and therefore demanding respect. She explained that the employee accorded more respect to her boyfriend, who had no ownership stake or say in the business.

Similarly to Abigail, Fatima (F, 32) realized she wasn't being taken seriously when out making business deals, so she resorted to letting her husband take over in most situations: having him make phone calls, negotiate prices, hire and fire employees, arrange business deals, and perform other tasks. Although she did not consider it an ideal situation, Fatima was willing to use a male proxy if it meant getting things done or having them run more smoothly. She explained:

> When I called to make arrangements for our business, they would give me the runaround, but when he [her husband] called and asked for the same exact thing, he would be able to get it done. After a while, I just gave up and let him take over.

Fatima was frustrated by her inability to conduct business the way she had while living in Britain. This type of complaint from young returnee women is even more pronounced in their dealings with older men. In Ethiopian society, there is a general expectation of deference to older people, particularly older men. Young women in the workplace are not seen as equal to their older, male counterparts. Therefore, the confluence of factors, being women and returnees, works to the disadvantage of these women. Mahlet (F, 37), a small business owner who relocated from the United States, explained:

> It is hard to know people's minds. I think being a woman is one thing that affects how people see you, especially in government office when you're trying to get something done, but if they also know that you are a diaspora woman, they want to doubly take advantage of you. It is crazy how easily you can be marked a target, and they will milk you for all your money.

Everywhere from the service industry to research institutes, gender-related workplace challenges seem to be similar. Even as an internationally respected researcher, scholar, and leader in her field, Dr. Maaza (F, 66) reported constantly being devalued among her male colleagues. She described her research think tank as a highly patriarchal environment where women were "patronized" and not judged by their merits. Particularly as a returnee, she was often told to "know her place," meaning to be differential to the male old guard. Dr. Maaza constantly had to assert that she held her position within her institution because of her many qualifications and not her status as a returnee woman. Hiwot (F, 27), another woman who described sexist experiences, reported being shocked by the level of sexism and sexual harassment she witnessed at a major university in Addis Ababa. As she was doing graduate-level research, she witnessed most of the male professors constantly asking for sexual favors to do the simplest things. She felt she was even more of a target as a returnee. While workplaces are common hosts to such incidents, they are far from the only locations where women encounter a barrage of restrictive gendered expectations.

Although privileged because of their return status, young women returnees have a particularly hard time readjusting to the home society. Their particular challenges can take on many forms, from the expectations of extended family members and coworkers to the presentation of self in public spaces. In private spaces, the young women experience gender policing from extended family members because of the combination of their gender and age. In public spaces, young women in my sample experienced chastising verbal attacks on the streets of Addis Ababa and confrontations behind the wheel. They interpreted these events as a loss of the freedoms they enjoyed in the host nation. Moreover, they interpreted these types of interactions as gendered checks curtailing their privilege as returnees. They painted the home nation as restrictive on the basis of the confluence of their age and gender.

For women, restrictive gendered expectations come into play particularly in three locations: within the family, at work, and in the city in general. Gender thus comes into play in private and public spaces. Within the household or extended families, gender dynamics can range from allocations of household chores to gender policing by elders. Managing the expectations of extended family members, particularly for young women who lived independently while in Europe or North America, can be a constant irritant. For instance, Aster (F, 29) explained:

> I miss my independence, especially as I was single when I first came back. I was staying with aunts and uncles, and they expected me to call and tell them where I was every day, especially if I stayed out late in the evening. I am not used to checking in like that. I missed my independence. Ironically, I have more independence now that I am married.

In Aster's description, we can see that well-meaning relatives' concern can be interpreted as gender policing. Aster valued her independence and ability to act without telling anyone where she was or what she was doing, but her aunts and uncles expected a daily accounting of her activities. Although they did not put any physical limitations on her movement, she resented their expectations. Similarly, Netsanet (F, 27) described the charade she put on for the benefit of her extended family, pretending she did not smoke. "You know they hate it when I smoke," she said as she took a puff of her cigarette while we were sitting in an outdoor café. She continued:

> I get weird looks everywhere I smoke, and it is annoying when I have to hide it from my aunts and uncles. I would brush my teeth, chew my gum, spray my perfume, air out my clothes . . . so much work to pretend I don't do something we all know I do . . . [*mimicking*] "It is not acceptable for a young lady to smoke." . . . Ugh!

Netsanet perceived her aunts' and uncles' admonishments about smoking as unnecessary gender policing. She thought that if she were male, her extended family would not care as much whether she smoked or not. She did not hide her irritation at being reprimanded for her smoking because of her gender and not for other reasons such as health.

Gendered interactions are not limited to the household or family unit. Gender comes into play many different ways in public spaces, although it is much more pronounced for women than for men. Driving in Addis Ababa can be challenging for the uninitiated, and some of the women in my sample believed the challenges take on a gendered meaning when a woman is behind the wheel. They attributed the problem in part to male drivers feeling they can take advantage of women drivers. Women are thus made to feel they do not belong on the road, where other, male drivers become very aggressive toward them. Some also think there is a class component, where male drivers seem to question whether a woman owns her car. Although this is not specific to returnees, the young women returnees interpreted it as a curtailment of their freedoms.

Meskerem (F, 39) explained, "I still get a lot of stares when I drive my big car, not that it is uncommon for women to drive in Addis, but I guess big SUVs are considered to be 'manly,' I don't know . . . I notice people staring at me though." Meskerem highlighted that her presence as a female driver and the type of car she drove led to people staring at her in the streets. Similarly, Almaz (F, 33) thought driving in Addis Ababa presented particular challenges to women. She recounted one incident where a male driver would not let her pass even when it was her turn. He blocked her way and expected her to back up for him. She backed up a little bit to let him pass, even though she didn't feel she had to do it, but he came nose to nose with her car and kept honking, expecting her to yield to him even more than she already had. She said she lost her temper at that point, so she just switched off her engine in the middle of the road and started talking on her phone to make him lose his patience. A traffic cop finally intervened, as neither of them would budge.

While driving a car can present its own set of challenges, some women feel that the setting of a private vehicle offers more protection than venturing out in town using public transportation. Women report being harassed on a regular basis riding in taxis and walking about the city on their own. Most of the comments have to do with their appearance—how they are dressed, how they comport themselves—and expectations of femininity. There is significant evidence that the sexual harassment of women in the street is a major problem in Addis. Although there are campaigns to discourage that—for example, a street sign that says "It is not OK to pinch" is part of a larger campaign targeted toward women's and girls' safety in public places—it is unclear how well the message is received by the intended audience. Street harassment is not as much a problem in affluent enclaves, but it is common out and about in the city, particularly on public transport. One young respondent explained that she no longer felt comfortable wearing shorts in public, as the response traumatized her, to use her own words:

> When I first came, I would wear shorts, skirts, and dresses, whatever pleased my fancy, but I would get the meanest comments in the taxis or just walking down the street. I would get propositioned. I would be called a whore for wearing shorts! I was traumatized within the first couple of months. I doubt I would ever wear shorts again in my life! You are laughing, but I am serious. I don't know how often you take taxis here, but you are not shielded the same way if you are driving your own car; this is the front lines.—Hiwot (F, 27)

Hiwot stated that gender and sexism were two of the biggest obstacles she encountered in her return experiences: She described the streets as a war zone and the taxis as the front lines. She became a lot more conscious about her dress style since her return and resettlement in Ethiopia. In general, there is significantly more attention to appearance in the homeland. Netsanet (F, 27) explained:

> People make certain assumptions about you because of your gender, that you should care about your appearance, that you care about certain things. . . . It is not that the gender dynamics we're talking about do not exist in Canada or the U.S.; it is just that it is much more pronounced here, it is in your face.

Netsanet discussed the expectation that women should care about their appearance (more so than men). She also emphasized that similar gender dynamics exist in countries in the Global North but said that people are more likely to make openly derogatory remarks in Ethiopia. More generally, verbal harassment is something (returnee) women encountered regularly.

Wubit (F, 27), yet another young woman returnee, explained the challenge she faced while on her way to her workplace:

> I walk twenty minutes to work every day, and I feel like I am in a battlefield when I do so, or a zoo where people just gawk at me. I'm the one in a cage on display, and when men are bored, women are their entertainment. That twenty-minute walk to work has made me super conscious of everything ... of the way I walk, the way I dress, even where I look while walking.... We live in a world where men can pee freely in the streets, but women can't ... can't eat or do anything! Catcalling is a form of violence, of harassment ... I constantly feel harassed! How can I live freely when I am filled with fear? I used to respond, but over time I learned to ignore it, at least outwardly. I learned not to smile in public, because how can I survive otherwise?

Wubit experienced the streets as a battlefield and harassment as a form of social control over women. She fervently talked about the harassment she experienced in her daily walk to her workplace. She compared catcalling to a form of violence against women and did not feel she could live freely or engage in the simple task of walking to work. Street harassment, a form of everyday gendered violence, indicates pervasive gender inequality and restricts women's sense of autonomy.[15] Unfortunately, Wubit's story is not unique. Many young women are treated in a sexualized way in public spaces. Women have to contend with a plethora of gendered expectations while working, driving, using public transportation, or just being out and about in the city. These types of gendered restrictions do not exist for men. Even though this gendered double standard is not specific to returnees, women returnees are constantly comparing their experiences to life in the Global North. Although they stand out in the society as privileged women, gender is one of the areas where their privilege is challenged. They might be returnees, but as women, they are still vulnerable to the insecurity and lack of autonomy that most young women in Ethiopia face. The overt sexism they encounter (e.g., the policing of their appearance) negatively affects women returnees' overall experiences.

Men's gender in public spaces has been muted or taken for granted. In my interviews with men, gender issues in public spaces came up spontaneously only once. Most men assume that gender issues are simply women's issues, and they do not understand that they are gendered beings as well. For instance, Dr. Caleb (M, 46) explained:

> I feel bad for women since I feel like they get the brunt of it ... for example, as a man, I can walk down the street and I am sheltered

from catcalling, I can do so freely, but I hear from my female friends how they dread such simple pleasures such as walking because of the verbal barrage they receive.

Like Dr. Caleb, Tiruneh (M, 29) sympathized with the challenges young women face in a patriarchal society:

I don't think most men understand the privileges that they have, like they don't get harassed when walking down the street, but women cannot take that for granted. We still have a long way to go in this society, just basic respect for a woman when she walks down the street.

Perhaps Samrawit (F, 37) best explained the effects of the restrictive double standard in gendered expectations:

I saw myself changing, almost to the point of no recognition . . . I was yelling at people, I mean at men, because they did not listen to me. I used a male standby to do almost everything related to my business. I had either my dad stand by me or speaking for me as I was dealing with construction workers. I had a male friend be my spokesperson when conducting business with whoever. . . . It is annoying, time consuming, degrading, and altogether ineffective.

Like Samrawit, Abigail (F, 32) claimed to feel her personality changing as a result of her return migration. She explained: "I feel like returning has changed my personality, I find myself becoming very aggressive. I feel like that is what I need in order to survive, not to be a doormat." Therefore, young women (those forty and below) can face unique challenges of return migration. The combination of their age and gender puts them at a particular disadvantage.

Young women returnees' range of emotions reflect the gender landscape in the homeland. The gendered restrictions these returnees face engender a range of negative emotions and frustrations. Young women are alternatively aggravated, annoyed, vexed, irritated, and angered by the disrespect they perceive from their daily interactions with non-migrant men in the society. Some of them report feeling harassed, dispirited, and bitter as a result.

Some women have pointed out that age can be a mitigating factor in gendered interactions. For instance, Birhan (F, 65) argued that gender does not matter much in Ethiopia. It could be argued that her age protected her from some of the catcalling and gender policing younger women undergo on a daily basis. Similarly to Birhan, Lydia (F, 30) considered age a more significant factor than gender. She explained:

> I think ageism is more prevalent than sexism here [in Ethiopia]. . . .
> Respect for the elders should not mean disrespect for the young,
> should it? . . . If I am seen questioning or disagreeing with an elder,
> they interpret it as disrespect, therefore problematic.

She referred to ageism to mean not prejudice or discrimination against elderly people, as it is generally used in the United States, but rather discrimination against the young. She argued that in a culture where respect for elders is paramount, the flip side is disregard for young people's opinions. She believed that in Europe (where she previously resided) people are judged on the basis of their own merits, not their age, but in Ethiopia, elders are held in such high respect that even disagreeing can seem disrespectful.

The rigid Western (colonial) construction of the gender category has at times been (erroneously) applied to African contexts to account for women's subordination and oppression without taking into account local particularities. Oyeronke Oyewumi has argued that "feminist researchers . . . assume that both the category 'woman' and her subordination are universal," when, in reality, African social categories are more fluid and situational, placing more emphasis on age and seniority as opposed to purely gender.[16] Thus, applying Western gender concepts is both limiting and misleading. Gendered understandings should take into consideration the local contexts, deployments, and contestations. Ethiopians place a strong emphasis on age and seniority, and gendered relationships can be highly situational.[17]

While the literature posits a reimposition of patriarchy (whereby men regain a lost masculinity and women lose the gender benefits they achieved in the host nation), my study shows that class and age are mitigating factors in African contexts. It is misleading to assume that the host nation is egalitarian and the home nation is patriarchal.[18] For older women, gender restrictions are minimal; they are respected for their elder status, and their gender almost disappears. As for younger women, they find the gender norms within the home country to be restrictive because of the combination of their gender and age. In both public and private spaces, younger women experience gender policing, which in extreme cases some interpret as a form of gender violence. Although younger women's privilege is checked and challenged more often upon return, stating that this is a reimposition of patriarchy, without contextualizing the ideas of gender in the home and host nations, is problematic. Rather, an intersectional analysis demonstrates that the experiences of gender in return and repeat migration are not straightforward. We therefore need to rethink the existing rather simplistic dichotomy of gender as dis/empowering for returnees.

Negotiated Privilege

In this chapter, I turn our gaze to a privileged group to highlight their lifestyle choices. I particularly tackle the questions of how privilege is localized or contextualized. I dissect how privilege is multiply contested by and negotiated with the local (non-migrant) population. This chapter therefore explores how returnees articulate and experience their multiple and embodied privileges. I offer a micro-level analysis of individual everyday practices to elucidate the embodiment of privilege and highlight multidimensional power relations. I explore how the group identity is formed, maintained, enacted, and displayed. I aim to highlight privilege as a multifaceted concept where it can mark both material inequality and differential social status.

I look at the returnees' narratives about the local inequalities to elucidate some notable areas of discomfort vis-à-vis their own privileged position within the home society. As privilege is generally taken for granted, I am interested in how returnees understand and experience their relative privilege postreturn. While some returnees (and more generally diasporans) are mindful and even self-conscious of their sense of entitlement, others do not share the same level of critical outlook, and some returnees are ambivalent about their privilege, sometimes denying its existence. Accordingly, I discuss returnees' awareness of their elevated positions of privilege vis-à-vis locals (non-migrants). In other words, I examine how returnees articulate, live, internalize, and negotiate privilege.

I evaluate whether returnees have in reality managed to live a more relaxed and privileged lifestyle upon return. I highlight returnees' articulation of privilege as lifestyle migrants. By focusing on what was and was not accessible to them previously, I elucidate the contrast in the lifestyles and relative affluence of returnees between the home and host nations. The contrast is most visible in returnees' command of labor both within and outside of the household. Given that the local context shapes how returnees live and articulate privilege, I look at the limits of returnees' privileges and the way they are contested by the local, non-migrant population. While I recognize that privilege is structural and systemic, I am interested in deconstructing the privileges of returnees and highlighting how these are negotiated with the local population.

I have argued that it is important to study the habits, cultures, and realities of the powerful just like the powerless. Returnees are, for the most part, aware of their positions of power in relation to local communities. Upon migration, lifestyle migrants do not necessarily become part of the local community but rather create their own social circles and congregate among themselves. They create a separate category, a class of their own premised on their otherness. Doing so reinforces existing class dynamics. The social identities of members of the diaspora and returnees reveal a sociocultural landscape based on difference. Returnees have created an identity at the same time coveted and scorned, depending on the perception of unbounded affluence and sociocultural capital based on migration or foreign experience. Nonetheless, returnees argue that they are making a positive contribution to the society and economy by returning to live and invest in Ethiopia.

Returnees, by virtue of their migration, are reckoned as a separate class or category of people. They share a common characteristic of migration, and upon return, they share similar socioeconomic, cultural, and even political positions. They both see themselves (internal ascription) and are seen by non-migrants (external ascription) as different from the overall society. Returnees have access to certain luxuries unavailable to them in host nations (such as household servants) but have to deal with the everyday challenges of living in a developing nation (such as unreliable electric power and internet access). Return migrants enact an upper-class identity through the use of a slew of domestic servants, ostentatious displays of wealth, and other practices.

As aptly demonstrated in this chapter, the processes and outcomes of return migration are far from gender neutral. I have shown that identities based on age, race, and class also matter for the migration experience. While men's gender seems to be muted or taken for granted in the home country, the combination of gender and age doubly disadvantages young women in Ethiopian society. Even though age can serve as an intervening factor (as older women are sheltered from the effects of sexism in a society where elders are respected), a certain level of patriarchy is reimposed on women returnees. The challenges include a wide range of issues such as gender harassment, gender policing, reverse ageism, and discrimination based on migration status. This analysis is not intended to perpetuate a false dichotomy of empowerment in the Global North and disempowerment in the Global South, as the different geographies present both opportunities and challenges differently for men and women. Return migration can be accompanied by freedom in some areas, while there might be a need for improvement in other areas.

Overall, returnees feel entitled to and take for granted a sense of belonging in the home nation. For the most part, returnees do not question their integration within the home society they left behind years or even decades ago. They take their belonging as a birthright, as a given not to be questioned. There is also an undertone indicating that they believe they deserve the luxuries available upon return from the Global North. Although returnees are aware of the high level of inequality that exists within the home nation, they are not necessarily cognizant of their roles within it.

INTERLUDE 3

Ode to Addis Ababa

The city of Addis Ababa, Ethiopia, is where my umbilical cord is buried, as the colloquial Amharic saying goes.[1] Addis Ababa was a settlement that began in 1886 with a few hundred people at the foothills of the Entoto Mountains. Empress Taytu apparently chose the name Addis Ababa, meaning "New Flower," to symbolize the promise of a new bloom after Emperor Minilik built his palace there and selected it as the capital city of his kingdom. It is now one of the biggest and most diverse urban centers in East Africa, with an estimated population of over five million. I am always happy to be back in my hometown Addis. (Locals affectionately say Addis, never employing its full, mouthful name, Addis Ababa.) I emigrated from my homeland as a teenager, but I always hark back to the Addis of my childhood, regardless of how many times I have been back and forth. I admit I am guilty of what Peggy Levitt calls the "ossification effect," where migrants often mentally preserve their homeland and do not cognitively accommodate for any changes that may have occurred since they migrated.[2] Ossified in my mind are the enduring white-and-blue Soviet-era Lada taxis that zigzag through the city, while the once ubiquitous monuments to Karl Marx, Friedrich Engels, and Vladimir Lenin have all been torn down.

The main landmarks of my childhood include Bolé MedhaneAlem Church; Abyot Adebabay, renamed Meskel Square after 1991; and Churchill Road, where my school was located. Churchill Road, named after former British Prime Minister Winston Churchill, one of the few roads in Addis popularly known by its official name, is a major thruway running straight from Legahar (an adulterated version of the French *La Gare*) train station, straight to the Italian addition, Piassa old city center. The British, French, and Italian influence is obvious in the names of the neighborhoods and streets. In fact, most of the major streets in Addis are named after African countries, perhaps to emphasize the importance of African politics to the symbolic identity of this city. Bolé MedhaneAlem Church, for instance, is located on the cross street between Djibouti and Cameroon Roads. The regional power of this African political medina is undeniable, in terms of both economic strength and political symbol. It is the seat of the African Union as well as the African headquarters of the United Nations, and as such, it attracts a multitude of nationalities and embassies. It forms an alphabet jungle, and deciphering the many acronyms (WB, IMF, AU, UNECA, etc.) becomes a daily challenge for the uninitiated. Although the major streets are named, none of the locals know or use these names, instead employing landmarks—churches, mosques, condominiums, government offices—to give directions.

This city for me is emblematized by the Amharic song "Addis Ababa Bete" from the 1990s by Alemayehu Eshete (1941–2021). It was a love song to a beloved neighborhood girl and to the city itself. Alemayehu, the contemporary of Bizunesh Bekele, Mahmood Ahmed, and Tilahun Gessesse, sporting 1970s-style bell-bottoms and the then-popular (and now antiquated) "Jontra" hairstyle inspired by the American actor John Travolta, used to belt out the unforgettable lyrics:

> *Addis Ababa Bete (x2)*
> *Shega Lej Konjo Lej, Aletch Gorebete . . .*
> *Ere Endyaw yemegnushal*
> *Bemegnot Yeqwatnu, Yet Yagegnushal . . .*
> *Piassa, Gulele, Merkatto Tchemero,*
> *Sefelegesh Meshe, Neyelegn Zendero.*
> *[Translation] Addis Ababa my home (x2)*
> *There is a beautiful girl in my neighborhood . . .*
> *Alas, they all desire you*
> *Let them burn with desire, they will never possess you . . .*
> *In Piassa, Gulele, Merkatto also*
> *Searched for you all day. Come to me shortly.*

This well-known song about an elusive love, a neighbor girl with whom everyone is infatuated but whom none can find or possess, is an apt metaphor for Addis, an enthralling city in constant metamorphosis that is hard to categorize. Addis Ababa does not constitute a cohesive urban space but is rather made up of a series of interconnected social, spatial, and cultural fragments. It is hard to describe this city, where so much contradiction resides. Destitute beggars are daily confronted with the lavish lifestyle of the rich, highlighting the stark inequality. Muslims and Christians, from the ubiquitous churches and mosques to the butcher shops clearly coded by a cross or crescent, fight for space and recognition. Different ethnic groups try to outshout one another, seeking to establish dominance, and the eighty-plus languages of the country all vie to be heard. Men and women try to one-up the other in an all-consuming constant gendered competition.

Gated communities of various sizes started popping up all over the city some twenty years ago, staffed by private security guards. Fortified enclaves, they are meant to keep undesirable elements out, protecting their inhabitants from outside violence, real or imagined. Insulated from the rest of the city, the enclosed neighborhoods designed to assuage the fears of the upper classes are increasingly becoming a standard of high-quality living providing dubious social prestige. This new form of urban planning based on residential segregation limits interactions between different classes of people outside of employer-employee dynamics. Similar housing structures, common in North America, are mushrooming in other geographies in the Global South, from South Asia to South Africa.

Inspired by global cities such as Dubai and Singapore, the speed of the urban renewal and beautification projects undertaken by Prime Minister Abiy's administration is dizzying. Massive projects such as Andent Friendship Park, Adwa Museum, Entoto Park, and the remodeled Jubilee Palace have all opened to the public since 2020. There is a brimming emphasis on parks, clean waterways, and beautiful landscapes. The constant complaint that Addis Ababa lacked green spaces is no longer true: in fact, it appears that the current administration has unequivocally vowed to upgrade the city to match its arboreal name: New Flower.

The unpredictability of life in Addis is both energizing (you never know what to expect) and terrifying (you never know what to expect). Every day can be a surprise as life is lived on the edge, electrifying those with a sense of adventure and distressing the rest. Forget the sanitized, clockwork predictable lifestyle of North America or Europe. The hustle and bustle of Addis Ababa is undeniable, leaving scores to grapple with its energy. The pace of life in Addis is simultaneously invigorating and exhausting, ever fueling an insatiable hunger for more: more wealth, more speed, more showy gaudiness. Addis has its own unique order, which, for the uninitiated, might be confused with disorder. This is why I argue that it is hard to categorize this city, to put your index finger on its pulse. When you feel like you have figured it out, it still manages to surprise you. When you say it is one thing, it transforms itself and shows a completely different aspect of its identity. Addis cannot be categorized as black or white; it is all the different shades of gray commingled. It is a city of fast-paced change, where traffic and rumors travel at breakneck speed. As car emission control is lacking (until recently, virtually nonexistent), the visibly bilious emissions coming from vehicles, particularly large IVECO trucks, suffocatingly envelop everything. The locals seem to be desensitized to the overbearing pollution, which, as is typical of most major Global South metropolises, clogs every pore in the human body and coats every surface with a dull dusty desert beige.

As pervasive as the pollution is the conspicuous presence of the diaspora in the city. Migration has seeped into every aspect of Ethiopian life, as none can escape the penetration of migration, particularly in a cosmopolitan city like Addis Ababa. Walking down the streets of the city, one is constantly reminded of the weight of the diaspora in the homeland. The urban fabric of Addis is intricately woven by local and transnational threads and the effects of migration are discernible in every aspect of Ethiopian sociocultural, political, and economic life. The observant social scientist can pick up clues as to the import of migration in the city's fabric, as it is literally woven into the urban landscape. Ethiopian identities have always been situated at the crossroads of multiple forces, through what is in fact a discursive construction. Transnationalism is therefore embedded in specific landscapes as the site of Addis points to the pervasive significance of returnees or the diaspora more generally. It is particularly visible in the hospitality industry, as shops, restaurants, hotels, and cafés are adorned with the names of faraway places, emulating the lifestyles of global cities. The businesses that pepper the city—Oslo Café, Amsterdam Restaurant, New York Bistro, La Parisienne Café, German Beer Garden—are constant reminders of foreign geographies. Moreover, these names testify to the presence of returnees and more generally the importance of the diaspora. Or perhaps the names are aspirational, the names of places that non-migrants dream of or harbor not-so-secret ambitions about. Yet the Jo-burg Cafés, the Kakuma Grocery Stores, the Beirut Bistros, and the Riyadh Restaurants are conspicuously missing from the Addis Ababa cityscape. Global South destinations do not appear to be as attractive or aspirational to potential migrants. For sure, no one dreams of the Kenyan refugee camps in Dabaab and Kakuma or of Bidi-bidi in Uganda, where many Ethiopians have languished for years if not decades.[3]

Addis Ababa has emerged as a complicit site for a whole range of social and cultural transformations operating on the local, regional, and global scale. Because of its urban primacy, questions of belonging are different in this cosmopolitan city. While space is contested on the basis of ethnic lines, the city also has a homogenizing effect; it serves as a sort of a melting pot as it simultaneously belongs to everyone and no one. Using the concept of city making (akin to nation making), Shimelis Bonsa Gulema concedes that there can be multiple interpretations of the city.[4] The "Addis Ababa *is* Ethiopia" understanding (which formulates the city as a complex microcosm of the nation) is countered by alternative interpretations that conceptualize "Addis Ababa as *not* Ethiopia" and "Addis Ababa as the *other* Ethiopia."[5] The city of Addis Ababa exhibits various manifestations of sharpening inequality, massive infrastructural upgrading, and cultural processes open to subjective interpretations. The city's, and by extension the country's, encounter with the "global" is negotiated and alternatively subverted. The vibrancy of the local and traditional cultures demonstrates the limits of the global culture encroachment. The local and the global are constantly negotiated and alternatively contested. This work is as much about the transformation of the city of Addis Ababa as its inhabitants, homespun and traveled alike.

CHAPTER 4

Saviorism and Returnee Belonging

> We have a responsibility to bring what we learned in the diaspora to the homeland. We [returnees] know what it takes to compete on a global market. We have an unparallel work ethic we were forced to learn [in the Global North]. We know how to market things. We know how to treat customers. This is all concrete knowledge that can benefit this country [Ethiopia].—Minilik (M, 35)

Sitting in the restaurant that Minilik recently opened in Addis, we discussed the impact that returnees (can) have on Ethiopia's economic and sociocultural landscape. As a business-minded individual, Minilik was excited about the economic potential of his homeland. Our conversation was periodically interrupted by employees coming to Minilik to solve one dilemma or another and phone calls from business associates or suppliers. He took these interruptions in stride, and I had been warned to expect them. Minilik exuded self-confidence, and his pronouncements, whether about business opportunities or the unique role of returnees, were assertive. He contended that returnees bring an unparalleled advantage that the local population lacks. Minilik emphasized the knowledge and skill sets that they likely bring to the homeland. He saw it as the responsibility of returnees, or more generally members of the diaspora, to teach local populations a supposedly superior Western business perspective. Minilik painted a rather stark us-versus-them picture of the relationship between returnees and non-migrants, emphasizing competition and animosity rather than cooperation and mutual benefit.

Contrasting Minilik's views with those of non-migrants renders an interesting two-sided understanding of returnee experiences in the homeland. I often heard from non-migrants that (some) returnees are "know-it-alls" who devalue local knowledge and by contrast admire anything Western. This chapter deals with these two opposing conceptions of the role of returnees within the homeland, from the perspectives of the returnees and local non-migrants. While the earlier chapters deal with returnee motivations (Chapter 2) and the joys and frustrations of return (Chapter 3) mostly from the perspectives of returnees themselves, this chapter highlights some of the problematic relationships returnees can develop with non-migrants. Chapter 3 amply demonstrates that returnees' privilege cannot be taken for granted in the context of the homeland; rather, that privilege is checked, contested, and negotiated at every step. This chapter takes the argument one step further by highlighting the potential for a deeply ingrained animosity between returnees and non-migrants.

A good place to start this discussion is with the different terminologies non-migrants have devised to refer to returnees within Ethiopia and other African contexts (summarized in Table 4.1). In West Africa, in countries such as Ghana, Liberia, and Nigeria, returnees are generally referred to as "been-tos." A "been-to" is a returnee who has been (or traveled) to a Western nation.[1] The term supposedly originated in returnees' self-pronouncement that they have "been to" such and such countries, mostly in the Global North. On the lips of non-migrants, it takes on a mocking tone aimed at conveying the presumably arrogant "know-it-all" attitude returnees often seemingly display toward non-migrants. In East Africa, different terminologies emanate from Eritrea, Somalia, and South Sudan. In Eritrea, returnees are colloquially referred to as "*beles*," a seasonal prickly pear, an edible des-

TABLE 4.1. AFRICAN TERMINOLOGIES FOR RETURNEES		
Term	Country / region	Meaning
Been-to	West Africa (Ghana, Nigeria, etc.)	Someone who has *been to* another country
Beles	Eritrea	Prickly pear
Nei ti cike ker	South Sudan	People who have seen the light
Returning qurbajoog	Somalia	Returning diaspora
Me'teche	Ethiopia	"I came from . . ."
Temelashotch	Ethiopia	Those who have returned
Watsupotch	Ethiopia	The what's-up folks

ert fruit that is part of the cactus family.² This term, applied interchangeably to diaspora vacationers and longer-term returnees, connotes that even though returnees can be beneficial to their homeland (as the *beles* fruit is indeed sweet), they can also be bothersome or irksome (as the tiny thorns render them painful to handle). The *beles* is contrasted with the tree *shibaha* to indicate those rooted in place, those who have never left. In Somalia, returnees are referred to as "returning *qurbajoog*," the latter word being the Somali equivalent of diaspora or those who have settled in foreign lands.³ "Returning *qurbajoog*" is an oxymoronic term reserved for returnees from the Global North, while those coming from the Middle East and Africa are described by the countries they returned from. The Somali terminology therefore indicates an ingrained hierarchy of migrant destinations. In South Sudan, returnees describe themselves with the metaphor *"nei ti cike ker"* (people who have seen the light).⁴ In other words, South Sudanese migrants presume some form of superiority over non-migrants by claiming that migration brings enlightenment.

In Ethiopia, the colloquial Amharic term for returnees is *"temelashotch,"* which is a mere descriptor and does not hold any positive or negative connotations. However, two additional terms are worth noting. One label accorded to returnees is *"me'teche,"* which loosely translates to "I came from . . ." This is equivalent to the "been-to" terminology from West Africa. Non-migrants explained to me that members of the diaspora have an annoying habit of always reminding those around them of their migration experience. While members of the diaspora employ *"me'teche"* to exploit their migration status, non-migrants use this term derisively. Similarly, returnees are sometimes referred to as the "watsupotch." The term is a local adaptation of the catchy American pop culture phrase "What's up" from the early 2000s. The use of such catchphrases marks a separate identity and brands the user. Ethiopian American returnees so often uttered this phrase that the local population started calling them "watsupotch," or the "what's up folks." As demonstrated with the derisive use of *"me'teche"* and "watsupotch," language is one way to understand or grapple with local understandings of migration in general and returnees in particular. The labels for returnees coined by non-migrants in the different geographies indicate the social context and reception returnees receive in their home nations. None of these labels are gendered but are applied indiscriminately to men and women. The different terminologies alternatively denote resentment, derision, or admiration.

Erasing and Drawing Boundaries

Most of the respondents for this study explained their understanding of their relative positions through a comparison between the situation in their host nation in the Global North, on one side, and the situation in the home nation of Ethiopia, on the other. While their migration experience helped them develop a transnational perspective, some of my respondents felt as if their lifestyle in Addis Ababa was not necessarily something new but rather a continuation of their lives in Europe or North America. Lydia (F, 30), a return migrant introduced in Chapter 3, argued:

> The life I am living here is not that different from my life in Germany. I know that most people in Ethiopia cannot afford to live like me, but there is no shame in that, is there? I mean, I see the inequality, but should I feel bad about it? Because I live better than most? And it is not like we're living such extravagant lives; it is just that we are living it in such a poor context.

Lydia demonstrated the internalized privilege of returnees. According to Pierre Bourdieu, class habits can be ingrained and taken for granted.[5] Bourdieu's theory on habitus and social capital provides a useful theoretical and methodological perspective to explore the everyday lives of returnees as lifestyle migrants. His work critically analyzes class practices and bridges the gap between structure and agency. Through a meso-level analysis of economic and cultural capital, Bourdieu explores how taste can develop and be deployed as a social weapon useful in demarcating socioeconomic hierarchy. The habitus, acquired through belonging to a particular social group, guides behavior and thinking. The complex mix of knowledge, behaviors, and attitudes appears natural or innate but is in fact learned. A focus on the habitus of privileged returnees allows us to simultaneously account for sociocultural and economic processes.

For some migrants, the promise of the West is not realized, and their return is filled with contradiction and precarity. They are in effect an extension of members of the diaspora who return for short stints and flash a lot of money, or big spenders who borrow a lot of money and become steeped in credit card debt. All for show. There is a performative aspect to their lives: They seemingly try to convince those around them (and perhaps themselves) that their lives in the West were good. In reality, they worked low-paying hourly jobs and were burdened with laden debt. They pretend at success in the hope of turning it into real success.

In the United States, privilege is associated with the invisibility of certain statuses, such as the male gender, white skin, heterosexual orientation, and so forth. In Ethiopia, a highly unequal society, privilege is eminently visible and often ostentatiously displayed. For the most part, class is displayed through dress, motor vehicles, and residences. At the same time, privilege cannot be disconnected from the global political economy.

Material inequalities and lifestyles are both causes and consequences of the hierarchical ordering of society at the local, national, and global levels. Some of the respondents believed that returnees and the diaspora in general were at least partly responsible for creating a visibly unequal society. Some attributed it to the ostentatious display of wealth gained through the migration experience. For example, Ashenafi (M, 34) explained:

> The diaspora is creating more inequality. In the U.S., you cannot tell someone's class by just looking at them. Everybody is wearing jeans, taking public transportation, or driving similar cars, but here [in Ethiopia] it is a whole show, and I do not understand why people are so showy, when others are barely surviving.

While the diaspora and returnees are generally expected to have unparalleled wealth, my respondents said that this is not really true. In fact, a few explained that the display of wealth was a show to secure good employment. Lenssa (F, 22) was one such individual.

> LENSSA: It seems like a lot of us are just pretending or faking it . . .
> HG: What do you mean "pretending"?
> LENSSA: Well, I am educated. I did get my master's degree from an OK school in the U.S., but I am not wealthy by any means. I need to work for a living.
> HG: But how is that pretending?
> LENSSA: I live a lifestyle that is beyond the means of most Habesha folks, but I am living off my savings, savings that I've worked hard over years to accumulate. Unless I secure a good job where I get paid either in dollars or euros, this [staying in Ethiopia] cannot be long term. So I feel like I am pretending. I drive the fancy car, wear the flashy clothes, spend money at the right places, while I am desperately looking for a job so I can continue doing this [living the privileged lifestyle]. It is about managing impressions, and perhaps the right person will open the right doors for me because they can see that I already belong to this group, but if I stop, people will forget me altogether, and I will be forced to move back to the U.S., back to my mediocre job.

Lenssa described her situation as "faking it until making it," saying that returnees have to appear to be doing much better than they actually are. She also explained that her lifestyle was a necessity for networking with an elite group of people. She felt a strong need to return and resettle in Ethiopia but did not quite iron out the details before her relocation. She jumped on the return bandwagon in the hope that her gamble would pay off. According to Bourdieu, cultural (e.g., educational qualifications) and social (i.e., social connections) capital can be converted into economic capital under certain conditions. Therefore, in the social field of returnees vying for position in the current economic boom, Lenssa could expect a rate of return on her investments through her network. Lenssa, just like other returnees, was mobilizing her social capital in search of a permanent position in Addis Ababa. The class dynamic in Ethiopia is highly visible yet elusive because of its fluid nature. Although there is a clear polarization of society between the haves and the have-nots, the urban and the rural, the migrants and the nonmigrants, the class system is marked by an extreme and rapid change of status. Therefore, within this background, return migrants find themselves navigating the complexities of being and appearing affluent.

Returnees are part of the system that creates high levels of inequality. The presence of returnees reifies existing social hierarchies and, left unexamined, perpetuates inequalities. They exercise their privilege, flex their muscles, and build up the nation. The home country is therefore a place of opportunity to improve their station and access career advantages. Because of their returnee status, they have access to better pay and better positions, even if they do not always have the necessary qualifications. Returnees (aspire to) occupy key positions in the home society by virtue of their migration experience (and sometimes despite their questionable expertise). They do this at the expense of local experts who lack the international migration experience. Returnees receive beneficial treatment from government officials and from employers (although employers decry the cost of hiring them compared to locals).

While returnees understand the level of inequality that exists within Ethiopian society and know that they, for the most part, occupy the higher echelons of the social hierarchy, they seem to take this privilege for granted. Yet returnees attempt to recreate the lives they lived in the United States or Europe in the poor context of Ethiopia. Abebe (M, 41) explained:

> I know most of the locals see us [returnees] as rich, but are we really? The lifestyle I live now is based on years—no, decades—of laboring as an immigrant in the U.S. The truly rich folks are the locals who build their Ground+10 [high-rise buildings] at twenty-seven, at thirty [years old]. I am not going to venture a guess as to where that money comes from, but we [returnees] are not rich compared to them.

While comparing returnees to the local rich, Abebe insinuated that their wealth was ill begotten while his own resulted from hard work. Tamerat (M, 45) put it more bluntly: "We're not rich. If you are looking for the truly rich, talk to the local *balehabt* [wealthy] who became overnight millionaires because of all the corruption that goes on." The returnees believe the local rich far surpass them in terms of wealth. They also believe the local rich, often nouveau riche, are vested in ostentatious displays of wealth. Moreover, the returnees compare themselves to those with more wealth and privilege.

In a 360-degree view of migration, returnees are constantly comparing and contrasting their experiences in the home and host nations. We can make two levels of comparison to contextualize and understand the relative privilege of returnees. First, we can compare the lifestyles of the returnees between Ethiopia and the Global North, as most of the returnees themselves are keen to do. Second, we can compare the lifestyles of the returnees with those of the local rich. How are the returnees different? There is a significant difference between *lame bora* (homegrown rich) and diaspora (migrants).[6] The current discussion focuses on the difference between life abroad and life as a returnee, but it is good to also compare returnees with the local non-migrant population.

The very act of migration at times confers on the returnee a status of symbolic upward mobility, even though the returnees do not necessarily have vast amounts of wealth. Their migration experience, coupled with their foreign citizenship or foreign residency permits, provides returnees with an unfair advantage. Returnees experience upward mobility through the act of migration, which enables them to claim a place in society previously unavailable to them. Migrants tend to move to higher occupational levels and also experience more upward mobility than non-migrants, which provides them (sometimes unwelcome) leverage in the local community. Returnees gain symbolic capital, which provides them an economic and sociocultural upper hand vis-à-vis the local population. The collective patterns of individual actions and choice in fact serve to justify and reify class, creating a specific codified subculture.

In general, returnees self-segregate on the basis of former places of living, organizations, and specific churches that cater to the diaspora and local rich (for example, by providing English-language services). They also segregate on the basis of age, country of migration, gated communities, and other characteristics. Aster (F, 29) admitted, "My friends are mostly diasporas. I don't really feel integrated into the rest of the society." In essence, Aster was pointing out the self-segregation that a lot of returnees practice. Returnees have significant informal networks and neighborhoods where they congregate. Members of the diaspora, potential returnees, also own property in this coveted residential area. Members of the diaspora have purchased an abundance of empty lots and houses in the hope of one day returning. These invisible lines between returnees and the rest are sometimes hard to penetrate.

The Privilege of (Unrestricted) Mobility

One of the returnees' key marks of privilege is their ability to move back and forth between the Global North and Global South. As Adamu (M, 43) put it: "Let's be clear: I know most in Addis do not necessarily live the way I do, do not have access to the things I do. I can also leave whenever I want because I have the coveted [American] blue passport." He highlighted that part of his privilege came from possessing an American passport, which allowed him freer movement between different countries and the ability to leave Ethiopia whenever he wanted. Similarly, Hagos (M, 34) explained: "Yes, I go back and forth between Ethiopia and Sweden. I still have my residency permit from over there."

Similarly, Alemneh (M, 47) highlighted that he could still return to the United States as he had maintained his U.S. citizenship:

> All in all, we're glad we decided to move. We still have our U.S. citizenship, so we can go back anytime we want, but the only thing that would send us back to the U.S. is if there is major political instability. If you can't live in peace, then what's the point? A lot of our friends from LA are curious, and they are exploring how they too can return. I can probably give a lecture series on return, the good, the bad, and the ugly.

Passport privilege is one of the biggest marks of difference between returnees and the local rich. The emphasis in this study is on voluntary returnees, not deportees or other coerced migrants. While the rich non-migrants also travel overseas, they are generally subject to the unwelcome scrutiny of Global South migrants with weak passports, who require visas to enter Global North countries. While their class shields them from some of the unpleasantness of the visa process, they are not as fully protected from it the way that returnees who come with their passports from the Global North.

In our unequal world, certain people have access to unrestricted movement between and across international borders, while others are denied this privilege. Mobility itself is the ultimate mark of privilege. Plenty of scholars have written about privileged passports and the benefits of documentation status.[7] The returnees in this study were cognizant of the lived realities of passport privilege as most possessed either citizenship or legal residency permits from the Global North countries in which they used to reside. In addition, they possessed the Yellow Card or Ethiopian Origin Identity Card,[8] which provided them with equal privileges as Ethiopian citizens, with some caveats. The Ethiopian government uses the Yellow Card system as a tool for mobilizing the diaspora to boost national economic growth. It is part of a broad development strategy seeking investments from members of the diaspora. While some nations actively encourage repatriation, the Ethiopian government has created an enabling environment for returnees but also actively seeks investments from members of the diaspora who have not returned or do not intend to return. Because the state designed the Yellow Card to attract investments, some non-migrants perceive card holders as having unfair advantages, unavailable or inaccessible to others. The privileges associated with the migration status of returnees and Yellow Card holders sometimes lead to resentment from non-migrants.

For instance, Lydia (F, 30), a returnee from Germany, reported being constantly pestered by a colleague who believed she had an unfair advantage in salaried employment:

> He always tells me, "You guys [meaning returnees or members of the diaspora] get the best jobs, the best assignments, you get paid in dollars, but for the same work that I do. The bosses would laugh if I asked for my salary in dollars!" I'm telling you, they [non-migrants] don't really like us . . . this guy from work I told you about also always wonders why I have come back because, as he tells it, "everybody in Ethiopia would leave if given the chance," so he cannot comprehend why I chose to come back and work here!

Lydia explained that her non-migrant colleague had argued with her about returnees with foreign passports not being made to pay extra taxes and getting the same rights and privileges as those who had maintained their Ethiopian citizenship. She said he resented the fact that she could request her salary in a foreign currency. Considering the rate of inflation, receiving a paycheck in dollars would make a significant difference for local workers. Lydia said, "He tells me that I should either give up my foreign passport or be treated like a foreigner." Her reporting of her interactions with this one colleague indicates that animosity is directed at returnees because the government accords them certain rights and privileges deemed unfair by certain individuals. Additionally, returnees have the ability to live in a Western nation, which is deemed to be an ideal position.

The West versus the Rest

Migration is highly racialized, and the salience of race for immigrants is undeniable. These ideas of racial hierarchies in migration have seeped into Ethiopian migrants' choice of destination countries. Migrants prefer destinations in the Global North, such as the United States and United Kingdom, and people look down on migrants who go to other African nations (notably South Africa) and the Arabian Peninsula (primarily Saudi Arabia). In what

Milena Belloni terms the "cosmologies of destinations," migrants rank the most desirable and least desirable destination nations.[9] The varied valorization of migrants based on destination nations can be seen as a by-product of a global racial system.

Ethiopian migrants rank destinations on the basis of their desirability, with Western nations (or more generally the Global North) as their top choice. By contrast, they see countries in the Global South (notably South Africa and Gulf States) as less desirable destinations. Migration aspirations are often associated with a hierarchical vision of the world and grouped in terms of desirable and undesirable geographies. Migrants' imaginaries of possible destinations take on subjective moral and symbolic meanings. These mental hierarchies are based on "images, rumors, perception, experiences of previous migrants."[10] Therefore, geographies are imbued with meaning and value judgments. These cosmologies of destination reflect imperialistic ways of thinking (and thinly veiled racial hierarchies) that have seeped into migrants' imaginaries. As a result, Ethiopian returnees can experience different homecomings by virtue of their different status as returnees from the Global North or the Global South. In other words, returning from a "high-status" country carries a social status. For the most part, members of the Ethiopian diaspora living in Western nations are assumed to have a higher socioeconomic standing than those residing in Middle Eastern nations.

This study focuses on individuals who voluntarily relocated from the Global North and who are thus generally better off economically than other returnees. Voluntary returnees, for the most part, have planned their journey and usually come armed with savings and a purpose. Migrants who return from the Middle East and those from Global North nations such as the United States also differ in their socioeconomic positions before migration. Only the relatively wealthy migrate in the first place, and the wealthiest of the group have a choice of destination nations. In other words, those who can, migrate, and those who have a choice migrate to the Global North. Therefore, a consideration of the experiences of returnees from Western nations comes with an understanding of their class position before migration. The combination of these three main factors—voluntary return, socioeconomic position before migration, and choice of destination countries—all work together to shape postreturn experiences.

Racial Pride?

When I told some of my African American and Jamaican friends that I was moving back to Ethiopia, they were so supportive of the idea. "Back to the motherland" and all of that. They kept telling me, "We all should go to Africa," and I believe there was a part of me that believed in that romantic idea, I guess. There really was no question on whether I would belong. But after living here [in Ethiopia] . . . I did not realize how different I actually am. Local and diaspora sensibilities are different. It can be a bit unnerving. I was not really prepared for the culture shock. The way we view our homeland from the diaspora is not the same as people who have never left. It is so different.—Henock (M, 33)

Henock was a young returnee who identified strongly with Rastafarian music and culture while living in the Washington, DC, metropolitan area during his teenage years and early twenties. Growing up as a young Black man, he often clashed with his parents on account of his views on race and what he saw as his parents' lack of understanding of U.S. race relations. Because of the influence of his Jamaican and African American friends, he even somewhat resented his parents for taking him out of the "motherland" to bring him up in the West. Henock could not wait to go back to live in Ethiopia, although he had left his homeland at a very young age and most of his family lived in the United States at the time. In college, he double majored in computer science and Africana studies with the aim of building a useful skill that he could bring back to his home country and gaining a better understanding of his racial identity. After receiving his degree, Henock worked for a few years in the United States both to gain some useful work experience and to amass some savings that he could use as a starter fund for his relocation. He also prepared himself for relocation by taking yearly trips to familiarize himself with the landscape of the homeland and scout out any business and work opportunities. After much planning and preparation, Henock relocated to Ethiopia in 2016 and began running his own small independent technology firm in Addis Ababa. A few of his ventures did not succeed, but he held on to the hope that he would have a breakthrough and make a big splash on the Addis technology scene. He also adamantly believed in educating the next generation of technology entrepreneurs and spent a lot of his free time teaching in different schools and nonprofit organizations. He strongly believed that his presence and investments mattered to his homeland. With neat locks down to his shoulders and a ready smile, Henock blended into the cosmopolitan landscape of Addis Ababa. He saw Ethiopia as "the Black motherland" with her doors open to all Black people regardless of their origin. Henock employed the language of Rastafarians, with whom he identified culturally, if not necessarily religiously.

Idealistic returnees such as Henock are interested in Ethiopia's, and by extension Africa's, rise as an economic power. While they still lived in the Global North, they were conscious of the negative perceptions of Ethiopia and the racialization of the African continent and by default all Black people globally. They are emotionally exhausted by the constant negative depictions of their country, their continent, and their people. They emphasize that promoting a unified Ethiopian identity and more global Black consciousness should be a high priority. They support national endeavors such as the Grand Ethiopian Renaissance Dam (GERD), slated to be the largest hydroelectric dam on the African continent.[11] The emphasis frames a vision of an Ethiopian Renaissance, and by extension an African Renaissance, within a postcolonial discourse, and they see themselves as an integral part of translating that vision into reality.

For instance, Tamerat (M, 45) argued, "It is time that we stop talking only about the past, about Axum and Lalibela, but start working towards a future we can all be proud of . . . to show the world that we are not just an ancient civilization but a modern one as well." Tamerat did not consider it sufficient to recall Ethiopia's ancient glory. He saw more importance in building the economy of the country presently. He said that we need to learn from countries such as India and China to build up education and manufacturing and become a leader within the African continent and beyond. He insisted that we could best do this by overcoming ethnic differences and unifying toward a common goal. He argued, "We are the center of African politics, and it says a lot that we are still stuck in our local tribalism. If we can't overcome this, what hope is there for the rest of Africa?" He referred to the fact that Addis Ababa is the headquarters of the African Union (formerly the Organization of African Unity, or OAU) and has historically been a leader for postcolonial African politics in many ways.

Redeit (F, 28) argued along similar lines that Ethiopians need to transcend ethnic division to build a better future for all. She also posited Ethiopia as an African leader:

> Racial pride to me means reminding the world that we were never colonized. We never bowed down to the white man. United, we fought against the Italian invasion and beat them not once but twice.[12] Why can't we come together again? Why can't we show the world that our strength is our unity? Why can't we transcend ethnic differences to build up our country? To build up Africa?

The returnees are highly cognizant of how Ethiopia is viewed from the outside. When they argue for bettering Ethiopia's image, they are positing a win for Ethiopia as a win for all Africa and by extension for all Black people worldwide. Ezana (M, 35) argued along similar lines:

> I abhor how Americans view my country [Ethiopia] and my people [Ethiopians]. It is always conflict and AIDS, always recalling the

famine from like forty years ago. The assumption is that we are poor, we are uneducated, we are less than. By association, all Africans, all Black people are lacking somewhat, unacceptable. How long are we going to tolerate these stereotypes? When are we going to change the narrative?

Ezana desired to return to his homeland in part to contribute to the country's growth. He felt unsatisfied living in the diaspora, "contributing to another man's country and not even being appreciated for it." He viewed his labor in the diaspora as less meaningful than the work he could do and the amount he could contribute to Ethiopia.

After a long discussion with Sammy (M, 29) about his experiences surrounding race relations in the United States, the conversation switched to ethnicity. I asked him what he thought about the existing ethnic situation in Ethiopia. He became visibly agitated and burst out:

> I don't understand what everybody is up in arms about, Oromo this and Amhara that.... Don't they know that the rest of the world does not care about their tribal childishness? The rest of the world sees us as Black and poor, not Amhara and Oromo. It would befit us to get rid of our small differences and work together to change how Africa is viewed by the rest of the world. We're a poor nation, and we need to come together to build a better society and not become even more fragmented. It just does not make sense!

According to Sammy, Ethiopians should concern themselves with the country's economic and global standing rather than becoming "distracted" by ethnic rivalries. Minilik (M, 35) argued along similar lines: "Outsiders don't see you as Amhara or Oromo; it is your skin color that matters, or your bank account." Similarly, Zechariah (M, 32) felt that Ethiopians have "bigger fish to fry," meaning that Ethiopia's global standing is more important in his view. He wished to "rebrand" Ethiopia, to present the country, and by extension the continent of Africa, in a positive light to the rest of the world. He explained:

> I never understood how the rest of the world saw Africa and Africans in such a negative light. This was home for me. I grew up between Ethiopia and Kenya and only went to the U.S. when I was ready for college, and then I went to Oklahoma! What a change that was ... I met so much negativity associated with my continent, and all people knew about Ethiopia was the famine in the 1980s! That was so long ago.... I knew I had to change this image.

After the devastating famine of 1984, Ethiopia tried to rebrand itself by sending cultural ambassadors all around the world to showcase the different cultural songs and dances of Ethiopia. One of the biggest cultural exports and global propagandas of the Derg regime (1974–1991) was the development and tour of the 1987 *Hizb le Hizb*, or People to People, a multiethnic music and dance production presented by the National Theater under the direction of Mulatu Astatke.[13] Zechariah employed the same idea of rebranding the country using print media in his work for a nationally recognized and globally distributed magazine. At times, returnees' vision of the homeland is at odds with the local conception. This can lead to significant animosity between returnees and non-migrants.

Saviorism

I don't think I really need to tell you this, but the locals just don't want to work. They expect to get something, everything, from nothing. They think we got our money from trees just because we lived abroad. They're so lazy. They just want to sit around and talk, talk, talk, all day, every day. I am getting fed up with it.—Adamu (M, 43)

A divorced father of two, Adamu lived in the United States for over eighteen years before relocating to his homeland. In the United States, he worked primarily as a taxi and truck driver. After he accumulated some savings, he returned to Ethiopia, a country he had left relatively young, to start a small construction and real estate business. Although he had no background in either field, he purchased some large construction equipment and rented it out to build his capital. He also made local partnerships to get his business off the ground. However, he felt frustrated by what he considered a lack of work ethic among the local non-migrant population. He also felt that some nonlocals, including close family members, had used him as a "cash cow" as they assumed that he had unlimited wealth. He said that he felt some animosity toward local non-migrants. Adamu added, "Some of the [local] workers are just infuriating. *Eleh asetcherash natchew*. [They make you lose your patience.]"

Adamu became increasingly frustrated by his business interactions, and he was not the only one. Aster (F, 29) stated, "They definitely have a different way of doing things here [in Ethiopia]. The pace of business is so slow, it's a wonder anything gets done at all." After returning from the Netherlands, where she lived the majority of her life, Aster worked in the nonprofit sector. Although she loved the mission of the organization that employed her, she was sometimes dismayed by what she considered the inefficiencies and blasé attitudes of some of her coworkers. Aster, as a young woman returnee, experienced some friction due to the organizational culture. She felt limited by the expected deference to older men, as her coworkers often interpreted her open disagreement and suggestions of different approaches as disrespectful. Even aside from the age and gender dynamics, she found the work culture in Ethiopia to be highly ineffective and unnecessarily bureaucratic.

Abigail (F, 32), who returned from France to open a restaurant in a posh neighborhood in Addis, echoed Aster's expressions, explaining, "I just wish they [her restaurant staff] would listen to me. They just want to do everything the way they're always done it, same as everybody else. *Sew ayseletenem ende?* Don't people change and modernize?" Abigail used the interesting language of "modernization" to portray the locals as backward and returnees as advanced.

While some of the earlier respondents only implied that their professional approach to work was superior to that of the locals, Noah (M, 33) took it to a whole other level. He stated, "Let's be real: we [returnees] have the upper hand. We have a foreign experience locals lack. We speak the language. We have been exposed to a different, a better way of doing things. We can navigate an international business space. They [non-migrants] lack these skills. *Lemen yewashal*? [Why lie?] Why pretend otherwise?" Noah clearly stated that returnees are better skilled and more proficient than any local businessperson. He went as far as saying, "If only the government would let some of its office be run by returnees or anyone with some foreign experience. We would actually be able to accomplish something. *Ye ezih ager sew, wey ayesera, wey ayasera.* [People in this country don't work or let others work.]" Noah extended his analysis from his own personal business interaction to argue that returnees would be more adept at running the country than local non-migrants.

Returnees mostly have a "saviorism" mindset. Because of their life and work experiences in Western countries, they see themselves as the hope of the nation. Upon returning, they bring back their ideas, attitudes, and behaviors, with an emphasis on the superiority of Western ways. While the returnees are of Ethiopian origin, their prolonged contact with Western civilization and acquisition of "modern" ways in the diaspora have transformed them. The returnees' cultural affinity with the West and their ability to straddle both worlds constitute some of their biggest assets, and returnees play them up to the best of their ability. The intervention of the returnees, however well meaning, is self-serving and often benefits their own fortunes rather than (solely) the local population.

Ideas of saviorism are strong among returnees. Returnees perpetuate a fetish for all things Western, while at the same time lamenting the pitfalls of local understandings. Returnees (aspire to) occupy key positions in the home society by virtue of their migration experience (and sometimes despite their questionable expertise). They do most of this at the expense of local experts who lack the international migration experience. Returnees overvalue the benefits of Western attitudes, particularly around work ethic, and devalue certain aspects of the home culture, particularly painting locals as "lazy." Returnees see themselves as having a superior work ethic (which sometimes is interpreted as moral superiority). For instance, Abigail (F, 32) stated, "Our people don't really like to work. We have to show them the way." Ezana (M, 35) echoed this statement, contending, "We developed a work ethic in the West that is just not present in Africa. It is our responsibility to build a better work culture." Hagos (M, 34) took it one step further, arguing, "Those of us who have lived in Europe, in the U.S., we know better. Ethiopia is so backwards in so many ways. There is so much we can change. We can infuse much-needed technology from the food industry to whatever.... If only they would let us work and show them a better way." While these respondents might mean well, their statements denigrate the local knowledge, work ethic, and culture while playing up the benefits of having lived in a Western nation. As a result, the relationship that returnees establish with the local population can be depicted as well meaning and benevolent but condescending. The benevolent condescension is premised on the foreign experiences of returnees. There is a damaging dichotomy between the returnees and non-migrants. Some of the returnees employ the language of neocolonialism, indicating that they need to "lead" the development of the country.[14] This seductive and harmful language filled with condescension creates a rift between the returnees and non-migrants. Returnees propagate a dangerous and misguided myth of their superiority akin to the language employed by colonizers and Western development bureaucrats (but it is even more hurtful because it is coming from one of their own). In effect, returnees enact a sort of symbolic whiteness by emphasizing their foreign experiences. Returnees inhabit a liminal space, outwardly Black but inwardly indoctrinated into Western ways.[15] Returnees, with their social identities and location premised on the foreign experience, have internalized certain norms and ways of thinking.

The dichotomy between superior and inferior, savior and saved (or in need of saving), replicates colonial hierarchies in different parts of Africa and the world. Returnees espouse colonial civilizing-mission ideologies. We can draw parallels between this paternalistic "saviorism" with the "white man's burden."[16] Black returnees to the African continent have at times been said to carry the "Black Man's burden."[17] The humanitarian endeavor to "save" Ethiopia has uncomfortable parallels with the civilizing mission as returnees adopt a language akin to European colonialism. The idea of "lifting," "modernizing," and "developing" Ethiopia is deeply imbued with ideologies of saving the Black race, the African continent, or at the very least the Ethiopian nation. The problem with this "saviorism" is that it assumes that the local population cannot "save" itself. It also raises the question: What does Africa need saving *from*? The discourse of saving Ethiopia, or more generally saving Africa, paints local, non-migrant Africans as inferior and, by extension, returnees as superior. Armed with the "superior" knowledge of the West, returnees, mostly unaware that they are mimicking white savior terminology and behavior, see it as their "responsibility" to save the continent. The returnees are anxious about how the country is perceived globally, and they also comment on the state of local affairs.

While returnees' "savior narrative" may not be overt or insidious, and it may be a reaction to racial oppression and disenfranchisement in the West. Returnees still maintain their desire to "lift up the race" as their destiny. They equate "saving" the Ethiopian nation with "saving" the Black race. While they are mostly unaware of the racialized language they employ, returnees (inadvertently) perpetuate the myths of a white racial superiority. Some of their actions and attitudes can be perceived as the detrimental extension of the white savior complex. They perpetuate the mindset that external forces will come to save the day and that this foreign intervention is not only necessary but desirable. The (white) savior complex is a kindhearted but utterly racist set of beliefs, actions, and attitudes insisting that places like Africa are doomed without the seemingly benevolent, but in reality destructive, intervention of white people (regardless of their own level of expertise).[18] The allure of saviorism has saturated our contemporary logic. The redeemers are the migrants, and more specifically the returnees, and those in need of redemption are the non-migrants. While the history of foreign intervention in Ethiopia is complicated, the attitudes of returnees are just as pliable and at times contradictory.

We can draw parallels between the saviorism of contemporary Ethiopian returnees and of Black American settlers in Liberia at the founding of the modern country. The Americo-Liberians socialized in the United States during the time of slavery regarded Western culture as superior to that of the African continent. This is despite their relocation to Africa to escape the prevalent oppressive enslavement of Black people in the United States at the time.[19] Returnees are similar to the Black settlers in Liberia: although they share racial similarities with the local population, there is still a significant divide between them and non-migrants. The returnees are also prejudiced against some local practices. In the case of Liberia, the Black American settlers regarded themselves as superior because of their exposure to American culture and Christian religion, among other things.[20] They attempted to recreate American architecture, economic structures, and legal norms and even preferred the American style of dress despite the unrelenting heat of West Africa. Driven by their strongly held belief that their ways were superior, they took it upon themselves to "civilize" and "Christianize" the local Africans in ways that mimicked European colonization. The cultural differences and the condescension of the Black American settlers therefore became a source of friction between the newcomers (returnees) and locals (non-migrants). While the Black American settlers sought to maintain positions of power and influence in their new society, the Indigenous Liberians accused the Black American settlers of having a superiority complex and constantly reminded them that they were formerly enslaved.[21] Similarly, the "saviorism" of Ethiopian returnees does not go uncontested. Non-migrants, in turn, challenge, denigrate, and look down on returnees. One of my respondents, Robel (M, 33), informed me that a coworker once berated him, saying, "*Ye nech asheker neberk* [you were the white man's servant], and now you come to boss us around?" This harsh criticism was directed at Robel in particular and returnees more generally.

Nonetheless, returnees' conception that exposure to Western ideals gives them better qualifications enhances the soft power of the countries of migration: Global North countries.[22] This soft power is premised on the real or imagined successes of the diaspora. According to some, the diaspora and returnees are the imagined salvation of the homeland. Returnees emulate the cultures of the host nations and shape a desire for exit and other preferences in the home country. They promote Western values in workplaces, private relations, and society at large, through interpersonal relationships and their media presence (popular depictions).

Within the context of return migration, returnees inadvertently become the vessels or tools of the diffusion of Western ideals.[23] The reality of imperialism in our contemporary world is that rich, developed nations dominate poor, underdeveloped countries in political, economic, and social arenas. Returnees effectively convey norms and values through their migration experiences. They exert undue influence solely by virtue of their migration. The extent of returnees' influence depends on many factors, including age, education level, experience, and wealth. Their influence is not always negative, but at times they convey a problematic notion of the West as racially superior. Returnees, socialized into the norms and ideals of the West in a global white supremacy, inadvertently become tools of Western soft power.

On Returnee Belonging

Part of returnees' well-meaning saviorism is triggered by the racialization they experienced while living in the Global North. They were constantly reminded of their supposed inferiority and their homeland's socioeconomic poverty. Consequently, they rush to rewrite the African story as a phoenix rising from the ashes. However, their eagerness to see more socioeconomic and political development inadvertently transforms them into unwanted, obnoxious Black saviors. They fail to realize that they have adopted the same negative lens they decried while living in the Global North. However well-meaning their intentions, they lord their supposed superiority over local non-migrants.

Consequently, local populations do not always accept returnees. Similar to the love/hate relationship between the homeland and diaspora, the presence of returnees is simultaneously praised and denigrated. While some appreciate returnees and value their education, know-how and investments, others resent their presence and attitudes. Non-migrants feel some resentment as they see the diaspora as having unfair advantages and bringing in too much competition. Some non-migrants also blame the presence of returnees for driving up the cost of living in the homeland. In addition, they believe the diaspora's existence increases non-migrants' desire to migrate. Although all of this is outside the control of individual returnees, they must contend with these perspectives as part of their daily lives. While some returnees expect a welcoming society upon their return, they do not always find one. Some even expect the home society to be grateful for their return, and more specifically for the savings and skills they bring back to the homeland. They are disappointed when their expectations do not materialize. On the other hand, returnees often resent the expectation that they will be a golden goose or cash cow.

When I solicited non-migrants' perspectives on migration and their own desire (not) to migrate, I was also interested in how they perceived the visibly growing presence of returnees. The following questions animated my interactions with non-migrants: Does the presence of returnees have a socially empowering role? To what extent does it contribute to the perpetuation of social inequality? Although non-migrants and returnees seem to share a sense of solidarity, there is also hidden, thinly veiled animosity between the two groups.

Non-migrants often accuse returnees and the diaspora more generally of driving up the cost of living. The unaffordability of basic life necessities consequently increases people's desire to migrate, creating a circular loop that is hard to escape. Non-migrants also expect returnees to be flush with cash, and accordingly, friends and family sometimes treat them like a cash cow or golden goose that will indiscriminately give money. When this unrealistic expectation is not met, non-migrants can develop a level of resentment and even accuse returnees of being stingy with the wealth accumulated from abroad. The predicament of return and social inequality is thus important to consider.

At the same time, returnees may also have an unrealistic expectation—that of gratitude or welcome for returning. However, when this does not materialize, again, resentment and animosity can develop between non-migrants and returnees. Therefore, Ethiopian migrants and non-migrants hold opposing views on migration; on one side, there is the argument that "you have to leave in order to be respected," and on the other, the sentiment that "once you leave, you're lost" prevails. In the relationship between non-migrants and returnees, a lot of emotions circulate, including anger, envy, disdain, pity, and ambivalence.

Non-migrants feel as though returnees look down on them. As one non-migrant, Abel (M, 23), explained to me, "Just because you came from another country, it does not make you better than us!" Dereje (M, 53) emphasized that returnees are self-interested individuals: "They're not all like the guy from Makedonia" (a reference to Benyam Belete, a returnee who established and operates the largest home for the elderly and mentally ill, providing basic needs such as food, shelter, clothing, medical services, and so forth). Other researchers have noted that returnees sometimes look down on (disparage) non-migrants as "returnees tend to embrace the dominant imagery that portrays the country of origin or return as an underdeveloped space and themselves as 'more developed and advanced' by virtue of having resided in a developed Europe."[24]

When I asked non-migrants whether returnees belong back in the home country, I received a range of answers. We can see the responses on a spectrum rather than in neat categories. In general, I found a correlation between non-migrants' perception of the desirability of migration and their answers to the question of whether returnees belong and integrate well in the home country. This correlation can be gleaned from the responses of the three groups introduced in Chapter 1: the indignant patriots, the hopefuls, and the ambivalents. On one end of the spectrum, the indignant patriots supported the return and reintegration process. They encouraged return and stated that the home nation would embrace returnees. Negussu (M, 64) even quoted from the biblical story of the long-lost child returning to the father after squandering his wealth in faraway lands. Return, in his view, was akin to redemption. The indignant patriots further posited returnees as potentially positive social actors who would benefit the homeland through the knowledge, skills, and savings accumulated during their migration years. Return was thus mostly positive from the point of view of the indignant patriots.

The hopefuls, at the other end of the spectrum, were against return migration for two main reasons. First, they could not understand why anyone would want to return to the land they were trying to leave. Second, they viewed returnees as competition for limited jobs and resources. They believed that the returnees as a group had an unfair advantage on the job market or in business due to their foreign experience. The foreign experience translated into language skills, educational credentials, and savings that non-migrants generally do not possess. In the business field, returnees are perceived as having access to much-needed foreign exchange and preferential lending terms from local banks. The perceived unfair advantages premised on the migration experience therefore rendered returnees unwelcome in the homeland from the viewpoint of the hopefuls.

Finally, the ambivalents offered a tempered response. While some questioned the motives of the returnees, the ambivalents generally believed that returnees had the right to relocate back to their home country if they so desired. Yet the ambivalents recognized the transformative effects of migration and sensed that returnees are no longer the same people who left. Moreover, the city of Addis and the country of Ethiopia have also experienced significant changes over the years. The ambivalents recognized that it might be hard for some returnees to negotiate these transformations. However, the ambivalents believed that if returnees could overcome these challenges, they could potentially make a positive contribution to the home society.

Regardless of non-migrants' individual stance on migration (positive, negative, or somewhere in between), respondents indicated that the diaspora and particularly the presence of returnees have transformed the social fabric of Addis Ababa. This, however, does not imply that returnees' belonging in the home country goes unchallenged. This chapter deals with returnees' views of non-migrants and vice versa. This chapter also sets the stage for the process by which returnees become repeat migrants. Returnees are at times placed on a continuum from pilferers trying to take undue advantage of the local non-migrant population to saviors who will be the country's saving grace. While these are the two extremes, most returnees exist along this spectrum in the minds of non-migrants.

Returnees exhibit a duality as they are interested in both erasing and drawing boundaries between themselves and non-migrants. Return can be seen as a way of subverting the global system as some returnees feel stigmatized because of their race in the host nation. In the home country, the external ascription of a "returnee" proves to be powerful. Even when returnees do not divulge their migration status, non-migrants label them as "diaspora," mainly because their speech or attire.

Despite their different backgrounds, returnees engage in a form of saviorism in their homeland based on their experiences in the Global North, whether this is warranted or not. Their migration status provides some form of unquantifiable social capital to returnees. Although there is an economic component, their social capital partly derives from their association with Western culture and thus their perceived proximity to whiteness.[25] They have in essence absorbed the norms and values of the West, particularly in terms of a capitalist work ethic.[26] The worship of the West fades with time for some, while others seem to be perpetually stuck in their adoration of Western ways and ideals. There is a seeming contradiction and hypocrisy to the returnees' views of living in Ethiopia: while they enjoy a more relaxed lifestyle in their home country, at the same time, they lament the lack of a strong work ethic. Regardless of which way the pendulum swings, returnees are still engaging in a (Black) civilizing mission. Saviorism is a tenacious idea that is hard to let go, particularly as those engaged in it do not recognize the ills associated with the practice.

Critiques of saviorism in Africa have traditionally (and rightly) focused on white humanitarian interventions, where the African people serve as a backdrop for the "good-hearted" white savior. Part of the issue is the power imbalance between the "helpers" and the ones who (supposedly) need a helping hand. While humanitarianism has self-exonerating undertones and seeks to conceal the hierarchical relationship, a critique of saviorism highlights the power imbalance. Ethiopian returnees do feel a duty to their fellow, less fortunate country folks. They may not engage in direct philanthropy, although some do. Yet, although returnees are sensitive to the pain of others, they are not true agents of change because they often do not challenge the status quo. Their interventions do not truly empower those on the receiving end. Rather than saviorism, we should discuss the concept and practice of solidarity. Solidarity can be a more timely and politically nuanced version of philanthropy. It generally involves an empowering dynamic that goes beyond perpetuating a particular status quo.

I systematically asked returnees what would make them remigrate back to the host nation or to a third nation. Although some respondents mentioned family reasons (e.g., children's education), health concerns (e.g., the availability of proper medical care in old age), and economic concerns (e.g., significantly better job opportunities), almost all respondents unequivocally stated that if the peace and security within Ethiopia deteriorated, then they would have no choice but to reemigrate. In other words, the political stability of the nation was of the utmost importance to returnees. Therefore, if the Ethiopian government would like to continue reaping the benefits of return migration, it would have to unequivocally bolster the peace and security of the nation. It goes without saying that this would benefit not just returnees but everybody residing in the country and the East African region overall.

INTERLUDE 4

Little Ethiopia in America

When I draw a mental map of the Ethiopian diaspora, Washington, DC, represents a central node. The metropolitan DC area (the DC-Maryland-Virginia triangle, or DMV, as the locals call it) is home to the largest Ethiopian immigrant population in North America, perhaps in the world. The DMV area has been home to a substantial Ethiopian immigrant population since at least the 1970s, a fact that has certainly attracted the attention of scholars.[1] Many scholars have written about the benefits and challenges of ethnic enclaves, as these spaces provide a sense of comfort, engulfing the immigrant in the familiar while insulating them from the larger community.[2] Ethiopian immigrant entrepreneurs are thriving and making a place for themselves both literally and figuratively. It is no wonder that the cityscape reflects this presence. I have a couple of favorite restaurants in the DMV area, places I have frequented over the years: Addis Ababa Restaurant, Lalibela Restaurant, Harar Coffee and Roastery, Nile Ethiopian Restaurant, Ethiopic Restaurant, Das Ethiopian, Abyssinia Ethiopian Restaurant, Habesha Market and Carry-Out, Ethio Café. When I step into these spaces, the aroma of the cuisine greets me, enveloping me like a comforting warm blanket on a cold day. The distinct East African phenotypes that pepper these restaurants bring an added sense of comfort, familiarity, and community tinged with a little bit of nostalgia. It is always interesting to me that despite the stereotypical image as a perpetually famine-stricken country, one of the most ubiquitous Ethiopian cultural exports is its cuisine.

Whenever I miss Addis but cannot hop on a transatlantic flight, I embark on the five-hour drive to DC instead and find refuge in the Shaw or downtown Silver Spring neighborhoods. It is my unparalleled cure for homesickness. I know where to find the best *gomen be sega*, a steamy collard green stew; the most delicious *tibs*, spiced and sautéed meat; and the most generous portions of my favorite comfort food, *firfir*, a mélange of sauce in injera, all within a short distance from one another. I often make the obligatory stop at the acclaimed Ethiopian filmmaker Haile Gerima's café and bookstore Sankofa, where I am sure to find not only the best coffee but also conversation. This unapologetically Black space has been a center for the community since the late 1990s.

Driving down the streets in the DMV, one can see Ethiopian immigrants inscribing themselves into the landscape, in *fidel* a constant challenge to anyone who has ever dared to argue that Africans are unlettered. The Ge'ez Ethiopic lettering and the green, yellow, and red of the Ethiopian flag are ubiquitous in certain neighborhoods. Just as Ethiopian returnees have inscribed themselves into Addis Ababa's landscape with business names reminiscent of their host countries and cultures, Ethiopian migrants have imprinted themselves into the landscape of their host country with business names reminiscent of their home country. In fact, Little Ethiopia engages all the different senses: sight (signs in *fidel* script, including on public trash and recycling receptacles), sound (Ethiopian music blasting through loudspeakers), smell (the aroma of Ethiopian cuisine wafting through the open doors), touch and taste (the use of a warm injera to scoop some sauce and the unique taste of the seasoning).

Ethiopian immigrants in the United States (like other immigrant groups in other parts of the world) maintain a strong sense of the homeland and have consequently reproduced their community across borders. They have recreated their homeland in this new place of residence, clustering with others of similar backgrounds. They opened their own (Evangelical and Orthodox) churches, cultural centers, and businesses, particularly restaurants and grocery stores.[3] The book *Yegna Sew be America* (An Ethiopian in the United States) by Nebiy Mekonnen,[4] first written as a series in the newspaper *Adis Admas* and then collected into a book, is the perfect ethnography of the Ethiopian community in the Washington, DC, area.

The Ethiopian immigrant takeover of certain neighborhoods in the DMV area came in waves. In the last decades of the twentieth century, Ethiopian businesses proliferated in the Adams Morgan neighborhood, more specifically around Eighteenth Street between Columbia and Florida Avenue. In the 1980s, Ethiopian ethnic entrepreneurs opened their restaurants, nightclubs, and grocery stores, forming the beginning of an ethnic enclave, which would have made it the initial Little Ethiopia. The vibrancy the Ethiopian community created in once dilapidated neighborhoods was the first sign of gentrification, a topic Dinaw Mengistu explores in his debut novel *Children of the Revolution*[5]. Unfortunately, most of these businesses became a victim of their own success; their vibrancy attracted others to the once "undesirable" areas of Adams Morgan and triggered white migration, leading to rising rents and soaring real estate values. The area is now filled with luxury condos, yuppies, wine bars, trendy brunch places, and smoothie joints. Increasing rents led to ethnic businesses closing, leases not being renewed, and, on a few occasions, even people being evicted.

As the rising rents pushed them out of the quickly gentrified Adams Morgan neighborhood, the ethnic Ethiopian businesses shifted east by the 1990s, moving into yet another poor neighborhood with low rent and low property values and starting the process once again. A new cluster formed on Ninth Street between U and T Streets in the Shaw neighborhood, where you could find anything from the ubiquitous restaurants and cafés to hair salons and music stores. Having learned from their mistakes in Adams Morgan, the Ethiopian businesses started buying up property in the area instead of renting, even when it was considered to be a risky investment. Although they did not see themselves as such, the ethnic Ethiopian businesses were yet again the first gentrifiers of another neighborhood in Washington, DC: Shaw. The Ethiopian yellow pages grew to hundreds of pages over the decades, listing thousands of Ethiopian-owned businesses, including real estate, computer training schools, tax centers, and other mainstream businesses. According to the Ethiopian Community Development Council and the Ethio-American Chamber of Commerce, there are over 1,200 Ethiopian-owned businesses in the region as of 2020.

In the early 2000s, the DMV Ethiopian community, like their counterpart in Los Angeles, sought official recognition.[6] Community leaders hoped that the official recognition would serve as an acknowledgment of their socioeconomic contributions and inspire more political activism within the community. The city government officially designated a region in Los Angeles Little Ethiopia in 2002, after the successful lobbying of the local Ethiopian community. Little Ethiopia in Los Angeles maps onto the commercial strip and business corridor on Fairfax Avenue, a one-block stretch in Midtown between Olympic and Pico Boulevards. The designation was a significant accomplishment, particularly considering the much lower number of Ethiopians in Los Angeles compared to the DMV area.

Ethnic neighborhood labels were not always pursued by immigrant groups. Rather, places were given these names vernacularly by outsiders, and they were usually seen as pejorative labels denoting poverty, squalor, and otherness. Only in more recent years have immigrant groups embraced such labels, even going as far as to lobby city officials for the recognition: Little India, Koreatown, Thai Town, Little Saigon, Historic Filipino Town, or Hi-Fi. The Little Ethiopia designation indicates that the Ethiopian community's presence is not transient. In other words, it conveys an unequivocal message: "We're here, and we're here to stay." Inspired by their compatriots in Los Angeles, the Washington, DC, Ethiopian community submitted their proposal to city officials in 2004. However, getting public recognition of a Little Ethiopia in the Shaw neighborhood has been thorny to say the least.[7]

Attempts at renaming the Shaw neighborhood Little Ethiopia were met with significant resistance from African American community members who have a historical claim to the area.[8] Shaw was once a historical epicenter for African American culture, an area for Black Broadway, jazz clubs, and restaurants, particularly in the first half of the twentieth century. Performers such as Duke Ellington graced the stages of the local establishments, such as Howard and Lincoln Theatres. Langston Hughes blossomed as an artist there. The year 1968 marks the decline of the neighborhood, after the assassination of Martin Luther King Jr. and the ensuing race riots. The area fell into disrepair, burned and looted, during the 1968 race riots and did not recover for a couple of decades. As newcomers, Ethiopian immigrants took no notice of the history of the place and did not bother forging relationships with long-term African American residents, who understandably felt slighted. The Ethiopian community's attempts to be recognized for revitalizing the neighborhood through their ethnic businesses were therefore viewed as inappropriate if not outright offensive. The African American community faulted the Ethiopian community for not taking into consideration the importance of this neighborhood to African American history.

The contestation over the name of the neighborhood leads to a number of critical questions, notably Who has a rightful claim to a neighborhood? In contested spaces such as Shaw neighborhood, this is not always an easy question to answer. This case demonstrates that ethnic labeling does not arise simply from an area's demographic composition but rather from political processes. It can unify as well as fragment an area and neighborly relationships. The tension that emerged between the Ethiopian community and local African American residents is a case in point. The Ethiopian community's attempt at recognition exacerbated the ethnic tensions between these two Black groups with different migration histories. While some Ethiopian businesses stressed the shared African heritage with African Americans, some long-term African American residents were outraged by the Ethiopian immigrant takeover. Perhaps counterintuitively, the relationship between new Black immigrants and African Americans is not easy or straightforward.

The conversation raised the question of why Black immigrant entrepreneurs were succeeding while local Black businesses floundered, creating even more animosity between the two groups.

Sixteen years later, in 2020, the DC Council approved a ceremonial resolution to rename the Ninth and U Street business corridor Little Ethiopia.[9] This took place in the middle of the Black Lives Matter movement, highlighting the strengthening relationship between African Americans and Ethiopian Americans. There is a recognition from both sides that the accomplishments and contributions of the Ethiopian community should not come at the expense of the erasure of African American history in the District. The resolution affirms the "partnerships with the African American community in the fight for social justice and civil rights," recalling the initial settlements of Ethiopian immigrants in the Adams Morgan area before the relocation to the "historical African American Shaw neighborhood." It reads like a smorgasbord of Ethiopian history, referencing Lucy, the Axumite Empire, Queen of Sheba, Emperor Menelik, the Battle of Adwa, the establishment of the Abyssinian Baptist Church in Harlem, Duke Ellington's travel to Ethiopia, Ethiopia's contribution to the Pan-African movement, and its effects on the civil rights movement in the United States. Even if it is a ceremonial resolution, it strikes a reconciliatory tone. It further calls attention to the sister city agreement between Addis Ababa and Washington, DC, and the renaming of Gazebo roundabout in Addis as Washington DC Square. This adds weight to the reciprocal relationship between the two cities, both political centers for their countries and regions, although the power asymmetry is undeniable. By showing respect and honoring the histories of African Americans, the Ethiopian community has perhaps finally taken a cue from land acknowledgments for Native Americans (Indigenous peoples), a practice that has caught on recently in the United States.

Although Washington, DC, proper was historically the epicenter of the Ethiopian diaspora in North America, the diaspora is now more spread out and less centralized. The multiple Ethiopian community nuclei include downtown Silver Spring (extending into Takoma Park) in Maryland and Alexandria in Virginia (around the Skyline area of Fairfax County), all within an hour's drive of one another, not accounting for the unpredictability of traffic patterns. This outspread is due both to Ethiopians who have left the District because of gentrification and to the growth and maturation of the community. Little Ethiopia is not the only immigrant enclave to have left DC proper in recent years. Regardless, as (Black) African immigrants, the Ethiopian diaspora is a significant socioeconomic and political force in the DMV area. As the mecca for the Ethiopian diaspora, the Washington, DC, area also attracts repeat migrants.

CHAPTER 5

Repeat Migration

Ever Greener Grass or Next Logical Phase?

I packed my bags the first time I left Ethiopia, saying, "This is it!" After a decade, I packed my bags once again, saying, "This is it." Now I am back [in the United States], but I can't say "This is it" anymore.—Nahom (M, 42)

Nahom and I were sitting in Kaldis Social House (KSH) in downtown Silver Spring, Maryland, a coffeehouse that felt like a spacious living room rather than a transactional space. With its large glass windows, muted lighting, concrete floors, oversized leather chairs, and wooden tables, and with the hearth of the place as the open coffee bar, it gave a sense of community and camaraderie. Patrons were quietly reading or working on their laptops. There was a quiet hum to the place. Snippets of conversation wafted my way. Amharic, one of the most widely spoken languages of Ethiopia, and English blended seamlessly, the line between foreign and familiar unclear. KSH, which opened its doors in 2014, had successfully broken into the seemingly saturated coffee shop craze and showed no signs of abating. A convenient space for gathering and socializing, KSH had grown significantly in the post–COVID-19 years. Doubling in size and offering a variety of services, including a rooftop bar. Its popularity among the young, the stylish, and those with disposable income was obvious. Owned by a first-generation Ethiopian immigrant, KSH showcased Ethiopian coffee culture, the oldest in the world, as most Ethiopians are proud to remind anyone who would listen. The coffee bean originated in southwestern Ethiopia, and more specifically the Mankira Forest in the region of Kaffa. According to a popular Ethiopian legend, Kaldi is the name of the goatherd who supposedly discovered the coffee bean.[1] Kaldi (and to a lesser extent Mankira) have consequently become popular names for coffee shops and coffee products. Most Ethiopians would recognize this name, particularly as it is also the name of the largest coffee chain in Ethiopia. While in Addis, I often met with my respondents at different Kaldis locations as they were popular hangout spots. Here I was on the other side of the world, in the Washington, DC, area, still interviewing Ethiopian migrants in a Kaldis coffee shop while sipping my macchiato. I wonder, since the Ethiopian Kaldis is seen as an imitation of the American (now global) Starbucks chain, does this mean that the Silver Spring KSH is an imitation of an imitation? (To top it all, the owner used to work at Starbucks before opening his own coffee shop, bringing the interconnections full circle.) Spaces like KSH also make me ponder the interconnectedness of migrant geographies.

As we were sitting in KSH, Nahom (M, 42), a repeat migrant, explained his different migration journeys over the years: "I don't know if I have 'the grass is greener syndrome,' but I have done the tour Addis, DC, Addis, and now I'm back in DC again." The first time he left Ethiopia, Nahom expected his migration to be permanent. However, after living in the United States for a decade, he decided to return and resettle back in his home country because of a combination of family reasons and economic opportunities. While he was in Addis, he felt that his migration journey had come full circle, Addis–DC–Addis, and reached a sort of natural conclusion. Unfortunately, his plans did not pan out the way he anticipated, and he opted to migrate once more to the United States, adding yet another leg to his migration journey: Addis–DC–Addis–DC. At every step, Nahom expected his move to be permanent. In his own words, each time he said, "This is it." After returning to the United States as a repeat migrant, he became more cautious. He stated, "Perhaps it is a sense of restlessness, but I felt dissatisfied once the initial euphoria of return dissipated. The rosy colored lens through which I saw my homeland for all the years I lived abroad and maintained during my short trips home could not be sustained in the long term. When you're visiting for a few weeks versus when you are really living, those two cannot be compared." Nahom was no longer willing to authoritatively declare, "This is it." Nahom highlighted the impermanence of his current migration status after the third major relocation in his life. As a repeat or circular migrant, he sometimes had qualms about being perceived as indecisive, unable to make up his mind about where to live. He even represented his repeated migrations as a "grass is greener *syndrome*" (emphasis mine), almost equating it to a diagnosable medical or psychological condition. The restlessness and disquiet were echoed by other repeat migrants. They described a sense of unease or emotional perturbance when their initial plans did not materialize as they had hoped. This adversity engendered distress, anxiety, a sense of malaise, and even angst. This state of unrest set in motion a repeat migration. We can posit all of the above as migra-emotions specific to a particular type of repeat migrant.

After initial migration and return, the next step in the cycle is repeat migration. Bringing the conversation full circle, this chapter shifts the attention to Ethiopian repeat migrants currently residing in the United States. Repeat migrants are the last group in this 360-degree view of migration, which started with a discussion of non-migrants. Not all Ethiopian return migrants stay in the home country long term, and for some, the next step of the journey is repeat migration. I argue that return and repeat migration represent two sides of the same coin indicating an increasingly mobile population.

Repeat Migrants: Next Logical Phase?

Migration streams engender counterstreams as we have amply seen through this research. We therefore cannot posit return migration as the end of the migration cycle. Even though returnees may envision a permanent return to their homeland, this does not preclude another migration back to the host nation or to a third nation. Return migration can thus subsequently fuel reemigration or repeat migration, especially since recent advances in telecommunications and transportation render connectedness much easier.[2] Repeat migration has been called many different things: circular, recurrent, secondary, back-and-forth, multiple, rotating, circuit, shuttling, revolving-door, yo-yo, va-et-vient, and pendular migration.[3] Although there are slight differences between these different labels (some with negative connotations), the umbrella category of repeat migration is large enough to encompass any migrant who moves between an origin country and one or more destination countries repeatedly for stays of varying durations. While repeat migration can be either planned or unplanned, it involves systematic movements of migrants between home and host nations. It implies substantial periods of residence, ranging from a few months to a few years, in both locations. Moreover, repeat migration does not have to be (primarily) motivated by work.

Repeat migrants do not necessarily lose their connection to the host nation while living as returnees in the home nation. Repeat migrants maintain contact with the host nation just as returnees kept their connection to the home nation during their migration years. Repeat migrants are likely to have established a network of friends and contacts that might tempt or enable a reemigration. Moreover, repeat migrants do not necessarily lose or give up their residential permits in their host nations. Some migrants may choose to maintain dual citizenship to secure their continued cross-border mobility. Therefore, migrants continuously perpetuate a transnational stance, maintaining a foot in both home and host societies.

Repeat or circular migration has been optimistically characterized as a triple win, benefiting the host country, the home country, and the migrants themselves.[4] Circularity has additionally been praised for increasing flows of financial, human, and social capital between different geographies, particularly as it relates to socioeconomic development and technology exchanges. However, the representation of an all-around positive-sum game and the optimistic "win-win-win" discourse need to be tempered with discussions of the many downsides involved in repeat migration. Repeat migration can have both positive and negative outcomes. Like other types of migration, repeat migration has costs and benefits for the migrant and the home and host societies. Just as returnees have been posited as failed migrants, repeat migrants are at times depicted as failed or disillusioned return migrants.[5] Outside of this cost-benefit analysis, repeat migration is significantly changing the face of migration permanence.

For this study, repeat migration describes the process wherein individuals return to their country of birth and then emigrate back to their original host or to a third country. Some of the return migrants I first interviewed in 2011 or 2014 later migrated back to the host nation; therefore, the stage of their life in transit has changed over the span of this study. It was comparatively harder to identify and solicit interviews with repeat migrants compared to non-migrants or returnees, as repeat migrants do not congregate in one particular location. In general, two types of repeat migrants—the young professionals and the retirees—were willing to share their migration experiences with me without much problem. However, the third and fourth types of repeat migrants—the disillusioned and the inadvertents—tended to be more resistant to opening up about their migration experiences. Even after I secured reliable referrals, I found it hard to convince repeat migrants to actually sit down for an interview with me. Most individuals did not flat out refuse to be interviewed, a feature of Ethiopian culture. More often, they agreed to the interview but found excuses to delay until I gave up.

This chapter explores the migration histories, motivations, and experiences of Ethiopian repeat migrants currently residing in the United States. Ethiopian repeat migration should be understood as part of a circular system of social and economic relationships. An examination of the dynamics of repeat migration reveals that it is the next logical step of the return migration process. Just as initial migration is not permanent, return migration also exhibits impermanence. The migrants follow a pattern: migrate, return, repeat.

Taxonomy of Repeat Migrants

I identified four trends among the repeat migrants I studied—young professionals, retirees, the disillusioned, and inadvertents—which I describe in detail in this section. The plurality of these migrants' considerations provides a nuanced understanding of the different motivations, experiences, and lifestyles of Ethiopian repeat migrants. It further enables us to interrogate belonging, privilege, and inequality in a circular system of social and economic relationships between the Global North and the Global South. I interviewed sixteen repeat migrants, including four young professionals, four retirees, four inadvertent migrants, and four disillusioned migrants.[6] A few caveats are necessary before I continue. First, I want to clarify that these different trends among the repeat migrants I studied do not represent the totality of perspectives or emotions experienced by all repeat migrants. In other contexts, other researchers might uncover other types of repeat migrants. Nonetheless, these categories enable us to capture and describe some of the prevailing sets of reasons for repeat migration and speak to the diversity and complexity of the emotional landscape of the migrant who chooses to migrate again after return. When we examine the emotional landscape of individual repeat migrants, similarities emerge that speak to the experiences driving the group, features that affect the counterstream. Second, although this sample gives the impression that young professionals and retirees make up the largest group of repeat migrants, the distribution reflects those who were willing to talk to me. For reasons that will become obvious later, individuals in the disillusioned category in particular (even more so than the inadvertents) were hard to draw out. They were less open to talking about their experiences. In one case, it took me a full two years to build a relationship and establish sufficient trust for the individual to sit down for an interview. I suspect that there are more individuals who fit the set of concerns articulated among these disillusioned respondents.

The Young Professionals

Young professionals are most often written about in the existing literature under the auspices of brain circulation.[7] They are an elite group of highly skilled professionals, globally upwardly mobile, who can easily relocate between different geographies thanks to their high levels of education and coveted multicultural skill sets. This shared story should be the least surprising among repeat migrants, perhaps with the exception of their skin color as most often, highly educated, globally mobile professionals are conceived as white. Generally, they are in the early or middle stages of their careers. They used the return migration process to gain international experience and move their careers forward while at the same time reconnecting with family and their homeland. Most young professional repeat migrants first moved to Ethiopia to live as returnees with the intention of not staying for more than a couple of years. This perspective of return as a temporary move makes the repeat migration process easier for the young professionals than for others who engaged in return migration with the intent of a more permanent settlement.

Consider the case of the repeat migrant Saron (F, 29), who viewed her migration through the prism of her work:

> My family moved to the U.S. [from Ethiopia] when I was just a child. I was only five [years old]. I did not have much recollection of Addis at the time. Growing up in the U.S. and hearing my parents' stories of Ethiopia, I always desired to live in Addis, at least for a short time, to try it out, a year or so.... The few family trips we took over school summer break always left me wanting more. After college seemed like the perfect time to finally do what I always wanted. Of course, I had to justify it to my parents by making it work related. It is not like we're wealthy enough to be able to afford a gap year. I got the perfect opportunity when I secured this paid internship, which was initially only for six months. I loved it so much in Addis that I was able to extend it for another almost two years. It has helped me build my language skills and get really relevant work experience. I came back to the U.S. after a little over two years total in Addis. Once I finish my MA, together with my international work experience, I will be very marketable on the job market.

Saron described her two and a half years of working and living as a returnee in Ethiopia as "sort of killing two birds with one stone." She stated, "I know how much my parents sacrificed for me to be able to get to where I am. I am very aware of that. I am grateful for it. . . . I don't know how else to express it honestly. I wanted something more exciting in my life. I wanted adventure. My two years in Addis is only the beginning of that adventure." While Saron was cognizant of some of the economic benefits that accompany living in the Global North, which her parents' sacrifices allowed her to access, she desired to return to her ancestral homeland. During her stay in Addis, she gained a much-coveted international work experience in her field of sales and marketing while fulfilling a childhood dream of living in Ethiopia. As a career-minded young migrant, Saron secured an initial internship that enabled her to build her work experience internationally before pursuing her second degree. She later came back to the United States to finish her graduate studies and embark on the next stage of her career.

Similarly, Rihan (F, 42), who worked in international aid and development, stated, "You have to do things the smart way. I couldn't place my career on hold and just return, so I had to figure out a way to be able to do both: take my career to the next level and return. I needed it desperately at the time [living in Addis]. I had felt disconnected from my culture, my people. I was so desperate to live in Ethiopia, at least for a little while. It was such an eye-opening and healing process for me. I wouldn't be who I am today without the years I spent back home [in Ethiopia]." Rihan had a strong desire to live in Addis Ababa to both be among kin and gain international experience in her field of work. She managed to tap into her social and professional network to secure a lucrative two-year contract with an international development agency, which enabled her to return to Ethiopia. As she was not willing to put her career on the back burner while pursuing her other interests, she found a strategic and creative way of doing both. She admitted that it would have been challenging, particularly as a woman, to just uproot herself without a stable job waiting for her on the other side. Moreover, her Ethiopian background and Amharic language skills came in handy for her position. Even though her initial contract was for two years, she was able to extend it for another three years. During this time, she reconnected with her family and homeland while also advancing her career goals. Her return to Ethiopia thus both benefited her career (providing international work experience) and assuaged her long-held desire to live in her home country with her extended family. After working as an international aid development worker for a total of five years, Rihan then took a different, higher-paying position back in the United States. At the time of the interview, Rihan was working at the United Nations headquarters in New York City and contemplating a move to Geneva, Switzerland.

Hiyaw (M, 33) was another career-minded young person who used his return migration for a double purpose: professional and personal reasons. He was born in the late 1980s, and his family first migrated to the United States as refugees when he was a child. As a political scientist, he was interested in researching his home country's political administration while contributing to the establishment of a more democratic system of government. He also wanted to reconnect with a homeland his family had been forced to flee because of political instability. He secured a high-profile grant that enabled him to work with a local think tank for two years, doing political analysis while writing his doctoral dissertation. After he completed his Ph.D., he secured a postdoctoral position that brought him back to the United States. At the time of the last interview, Hiyaw was nearing the end of his postdoc and applying for academic and research positions, mostly in the Global North. However, he did not preclude another return migration to Ethiopia "under the right circumstances," where both his personal and professional interests aligned. Hiyaw, as a highly skilled individual, could enjoy the benefits of mobility in an interconnected global economy.

As we see from these narratives, the young professionals are career-minded individuals who have found creative ways to return to their home country for short periods of time, ranging from two to eight years. They have fulfilled their personal desire to live among kin in the homeland while advancing their careers to the next level. As Zema (F, 39), they were able to fulfill two goals with one move. The young professionals never intended to stay long term in the home country, and their repeat migration processes generally went smoothly. At the same time, they do not necessarily close the door on future return migrations under the right circumstances.

The Retirees

Retirees are interesting to consider among repeat migrants, as most of the literature focuses on retirees as returnees.[8] Retirees may engage in return migration with the idealistic plan to live out the remainder of their lives in their home country. They return after accumulating savings or at the end of their careers. Respondents enjoyed the relaxed and sociable lifestyle reconnecting with family and friends in the home country. As discussed in Chapter 2 they also returned with the expectation that their retirement funds would better stretch to meet their needs in Ethiopia than in the migration host country. They benefited from cheap hired domestic labor and the other privileges of living an upper-middle-class lifestyle as returnees. Despite all these perceived advantages, some retiree returnees become repeat migrants for a number of reasons. More specifically, two things can compel retirees to return to the host country once again: health and family.

Gash Mengesha (M, 68), first discussed in one of the three vignettes in the Introduction, conceded that health was the main reason he and his wife resettled in the United States. *Gash* Mengesha developed heart disease that required a series of surgeries and close monitoring by a specialized team of medical professionals. "What can you do when your body fails you?" *Gash* Mengesha asked rhetorically as a way of explaining what compelled him to engage in repeat migration. "This was not the plan. You know that expression 'You make plans and God laughs'? Well, that's my life!" He expressed disappointment in his inability to continue living his dream as a returnee permanently resettled in his homeland. Practicality required that he let go of a dream he had long harbored. When *Gash* Mengesha and his wife left the United States to live as returnees in Ethiopia, they held on to their green cards, not needing or desiring to change their citizenship. To maintain their residency status, they traveled back and forth every six months, never intending to fully resettle in the United States. The back-and-forth movement led to a more permanent resettlement in the United States for health reasons. In a way, they maintained a foot in two continents, a fact that helped them transition into a smooth resettlement as repeat migrants.

Another retiree in the same boat, *Gash* Agonafer (M, 84), worked for the U.S. government as a postal worker for over two decades and collected generous retirement benefits. While he still wished to spend the majority of his retirement back in his home country of Ethiopia, his health concerns and his need for long-term treatment disrupted this dream, and he ended up as a repeat migrant resettling once more in the United States. *Gash* Agonafer stated:

> My health is not what it used to be, and the health-care system in Ethiopia has a long way to go. Even though I had insurance in the U.S., processing claims from medical institutions in Ethiopia was almost impossible. . . . I was coming back and forth to the U.S. regularly, but even that was not enough. I need some more longer-term treatments that meant I had to move back . . . even though that was not the plan at first.

Gash Agonafer explained that his ailing health and the lack of quality care in Ethiopia prompted him to engage in repeat migration. He initially went back and forth between treatments but became increasingly unable to sustain the repeated long transatlantic flights. He reluctantly decided to make the United States his permanent home because of his increasingly precarious health.

As retirees age, they encounter health concerns they might not have previously considered, and these factor into the meanings they apply to potential countries of residence. They often lament that the quality of care in Ethiopia is not up to the standard they have become used to in the host nation. Even basic medications for common health ailments such as diabetes and blood pressure may not be readily available or covered by their insurance outside of the host country. Therefore, aging retirees may engage in repeat migration, either spending a few months of the year in the host country for their checkups or fully packing up and relocating. Although retirees are not the only ones who have complained about the state and quality of the health-care system in Ethiopia, the compounding health issues they experience as they age renders them particularly sensitive to the issue.

In addition to the health reasons previously discussed, offspring settled in the host nation may make it difficult for retirees to fully settle as returnees in their homeland. Retirees may feel disconnected from their progeny during their return migration. They therefore engage in circular migration, where they spend a few months of the year reconnecting with their children and (for some, more importantly) their grandchildren. Because of the location of their progeny, retired returnees feel a pull back to the initial country of migration. Meselu (F, 65) explained, "It is like an invisible spring was always pulling me back to the U.S. I did not want to miss out on my grandkids' childhood, feeling disconnected from them being oceans apart." Meselu, a retired retail worker, lived with her husband and her four kids in the United States for fifteen years before relocating to Ethiopia. She described the tug of familial connection as an "invisible spring" that was constantly pulling her back to the United States, where her grandchildren resided.

Eteye Elelta (F, 72) also relocated back to the United States for family reasons. *Eteye* Elelta described how her experience as a returnee soured upon the death of her husband, who unfortunately passed away from a stroke shortly after they relocated to Ethiopia. After her husband's passing, she could not see herself living in Addis by herself. She said, "I would rather live here [in the United States] with my children than be by myself back home [in Ethiopia]. I hated being there after I lost him. It was more his dream to return [to Ethiopia] in the first place. . . . I never wanted to be far from my children and grandchildren. What is home but where your family is?" Even if she had a few siblings and extended family in Addis, *Eteye* Elelta was profoundly affected by the death of her husband of close to forty years. She also strongly believed that her husband might have survived his stroke if they had been living in the United States and he had received proper and timely medical intervention. She considered her children her solace and provided a poignant definition of home and belonging as the place where her family was located. As her children had settled in the United States, she felt it was also her home.

Retirees can therefore become repeat migrants for health or family reasons, or sometimes a combination of those two factors. As retirees are not the most common type of repeat migrant featured in the research literature, their experiences shed light on a particular type of migratory movement seldom addressed. Retiree respondents often enjoyed living as returnees in the homeland, experiencing both sociocultural and economic benefits, and most ended up as repeat migrants reluctantly and would have preferred to stay in the homeland if their progeny lived close by and the requisite medical care was available. Retiree repeat migrants in this study were motivated by pragmatism. Acquiescence is often categorized not as an emotion but as a behavior. Nonetheless, the tacit acceptance of a disagreeable, unwelcome situation is a pragmatic emotional response.

The Disillusioned

Nahom (M, 42), introduced at the beginning of this chapter, returned to Ethiopia in 2003 after residing in the United States for over thirteen years.

He initially migrated to the United States with his family at the age of seventeen, and he finished his last year of high school and took some college courses there. Even though he resided in the United States for over a decade, he reported never feeling quite at home during his stay. He described himself as a restless soul, uprooted from his home and comfort zone. It did not particularly surprise his family when he decided to return to Ethiopia at the age of thirty-one. Nahom admitted that his parents nursed a not-so-secret desire that he would find himself a wife and settle upon his return:

> I returned [to Ethiopia] like the prodigal son to be embraced with open arms by my homeland.[9] . . . That was supposed to be the end of the story, the fairy-tale happily ever after, the ending most migrants dream of . . . but nope! That was not it for me. I could not stay [in Addis], so I have uprooted myself once more, and find myself in the U.S. yet again . . . for good *beye heje, wey gud beye temelesku*. . . . Back home is where I should have belonged without question. . . . I have so much mixed feelings about my return, and now that I am back in the U.S., people eye me with suspicion or pity or whatever, like I am some wounded animal that they have to be careful around.

Nahom had a poetic way of expressing himself. First, he equated himself with the biblical character of the prodigal son but explained that return was not the "happily ever after" he expected. Second, he used a common expression that was often quoted to me in Addis Ababa to sum up the experiences of return migration as failure. The expression "for good *beye heje, gud beye temelesku*" is a play on the English word "good" and the Amharic word "*gud*" in the Ethiopian tradition of wax and gold.[10] Although the words "good" and "*gud*" are homophones, pronounced exactly the same in the two languages, they have vastly different meanings. In Amharic, "*gud*" roughly translates as "woe," "calamity," or "unexpected occurrence." In a direct translation, the expression states, "I went saying it is for good, but I came back saying woe (unto me)." In a contextual translation, the meaning can be rendered as follows: "I returned to my homeland envisioning a permanent resettlement, but the realities of return made me flee." This expression highlights the fact that returnees envisaged their return to be a one-way street, a final move, but the reality of return did not meet their expectations. Therefore, they reemigrated once again, either to the country of their previous residence (most likely) or to a third, new nation (very rarely).

When I first met Nahom in 2016 in Addis Ababa, he was already contemplating a repeat migration to the United States, wondering what his friends and family would say. I met up with Nahom again in 2019 in Washington, DC, where he had been back for over a year. At the point of the last interview, Nahom was forty-two years old and still single, foiling his parents' plan to get him married off in the home country. He expressed his high level of dissatisfaction with his entire migration experience, stating, "I feel like I am zigzagging between continents. I feel disconnected, like I am floating around in some impermanent state. I am tired of starting from scratch every time. I am not sure I've made the best decision by leaving in the first place, but you don't know until you try, right?" The combined dissatisfaction with work, the everyday annoyances of living in a developing nation, and the disconnect Nahom felt with his kin in the home country led him to embark once more for the supposed greener pastures of the United States.

Like Nahom, Ayana (F, 45) experienced the challenges of living as a returnee in the homeland. Ayana's business in the hospitality industry was off to a good start as there was a strong demand for her skill sets. She was thus very certain that her return would be permanent, and she accordingly informed all her friends and family that she was back in Ethiopia for good. However, after being back in Addis Ababa for a few years, Ayana started having doubts and fantasizing about repeat migration. Every negative interaction she had while living as a returnee solidified her desire to leave her homeland once more. She stated:

> My language skills were nowhere as good as I thought it was, plus not knowing how to read and write in Amharic put me at a severe disadvantage. Signing anything at government offices was a challenge. I needed to bring an interpreter with me at every step. Imagine that, having an interpreter for your own language! . . . Once they [government officials] saw that I was a diaspora, I became a mark.

She described how some of the officials targeted her demanding bribes to do their work. Initially unwilling to abide by this informal system, she quickly adapted but found the financial and emotional cost of doing business to be unsustainable. She asserted, "They say no matter how far a mule travels, he will never come back a horse. I guess that's what I was trying to do, to be someone I was not. I learned the lesson the hard way." After living in Addis for close to eight years, she felt increasingly frustrated by aspects of her life upon return. For instance, she mentioned small annoyances such as the unreliability of the basic necessities of tap water and electric power. She lamented the lack of professionalism compared to her experiences in the United States. More importantly, Ayana reported feeling disconnected from her extended family and her close relations. She acknowledged that her decade-long sojourn in the United States had changed her, and she could not fully bridge the gap upon her return. The home society had transformed during her absence, and she felt disappointed in her inability to truly "go back home" as the home she knew as a child no longer existed. This is a common expectation and source of disappointment among migrants who expect things at home to remain static.

The disillusioned repeat migrants I spoke to were mainly motivated by their utter disappointment in the return migration experience. They left the host country with high expectations of all that they would accomplish in their homeland, but the reality fell short of their expectations. The disappointments can stem either from structural or systemic challenges (such as financial, political, or bureaucratic concerns) or from interpersonal challenges (such as gendered and sociocultural considerations). In a way, the disillusioned struggle with the thought that they are "failed" return migrants. The existing literature deals with the perceptions of return migration as failure (failure of integration, failure of accumulating savings, etc.),[11] but there are no works that deal with repeat migration as a failed return migration experience. It is consequently important to analyze disillusioned repeat migrants.

Hunde (M, 43) was another repeat migrant who struggled with disillusionment. Born in Addis Ababa, he first migrated to the United States at the age of nineteen to attend college on the East Coast. After graduating with a bachelor's degree from his university, he worked for a few years, got married, and moved to Texas. He and his wife of Ethiopian descent decided to return and resettle back in their home country. Their extended families enticed them to return with promises to set them up in lucrative business ventures. Hunde would work a salaried job while his wife set up the business. Unfortunately, none of their plans on the business front materialized. They did not have the funds or the business connections needed to facilitate their venture. They found life in Addis to be too expensive as Hunde's salary was not sufficient to cover their expenses. Moreover, they found that the culture they left behind was not the same upon their return. Hunde explained, "None of our old friends were there, none of our neighbors, no one we grew up with. Everything has changed so much! I don't recognize it. It was so cutthroat, everything is money-money-money, no respect for others." He listed all the things he lost during his absence. Hunde expected to almost pick up where he left off seventeen years before, not realizing that such a big gap would take time and effort to overcome.

Hunde said, "If you think I had it hard, it was even harder for Lelisse [his wife]. It is so much harder for women. When she would go to government offices on official business, they would proposition her to get anything done!" Hunde went on to explain that his wife, as a woman, was vulnerable to catcalls, lewd remarks, and even physical molestation in public spaces. All of this compounded her distress. Hunde added, "[Lelisse] came to the U.S. incredibly young; at least I was a teenager. . . . She had forgotten more of the culture than I had; she had become too Americanized. Simple concepts like personal space, which is completely nonexistent back home, would irritate her. She got tired of it rather very, very quickly." These gendered challenges that affect women in particular are discussed in Chapter 3. In addition to the prevailing gender norms in Ethiopia, non-migrants use these gendered aggressions to check the privilege of returnees and purposefully frustrate their plans.

Lelisse's business venture was also a colossal failure filled with false promises, "shady" people, and disappointment. Hunde explained some of the challenges of doing business in Addis as returnees who had not tapped into the social networks that would have allowed them to succeed: "You gotta know the right people. You can't google anything. It's more about who you know, but people are closed off; they don't want to share their business connections." After less than a year's stay in Addis, the couple started looking for ways to reemigrate to the United States. Hunde took his GRE (an American standardized graduate school entry test), enrolled in a master's program, and moved back to the United States with his wife after a little more than a year of living as a returnee in Addis. Lelisse also found a job, and the couple settled back into the life they had left behind in Texas. Their readjustment to life in the United States as repeat migrants was much easier than their adjustment to life as returnees in Ethiopia.

I interviewed Hunde four years after he and Lelisse resettled back in the United States. It took me two years of building a relationship with Hunde before he would finally sit down for an interview with me. Hunde's wife, Lelisse, however, still refused to discuss her experiences as a returnee. When I asked Hunde if he would ever consider resettling back in Ethiopia, he gave me a candid answer: "Initially, I said never, never again, over my dead body, not even then . . . but now, I would not completely discount it. I would be open to returning. I would do a better job at preplanning it, but I don't think it is a horrible or dreadful idea." Hunde's assessment of his return had softened over the years. In hindsight, he also admitted that he and his wife had not fully thought out their return before actually making the move. He saw the error of his ways and would not completely close the door on embarking on another, perhaps better-planned return to his home country at an unspecified future date.

While I was conducting fieldwork in Addis Ababa with returnees, numerous people recounted stories of repeat migration motivated by a failed return experience. The hearsay narratives I collected mostly followed the same patterns: An individual or family relocated to Ethiopia expecting their return migration to be permanent. However, the returnees encountered financial and social challenges that they could not overcome and therefore packed their bags once more to emigrate. The repeat migrants generally moved back to their former host country, although most often to a new city, far away from their former social circles. Having heard this story repeatedly, and eager to connect with these "failed" return migrants upon my own return to the United States, I collected a series of referrals. However, as described in detail earlier, despite my repeated solicitation to secure interviews, a significant number of repeat migrants were not open to my overtures. Indeed, the disillusioned proved to be inaccessible repeat migrants as very few were willing to openly discuss their misadventures in return migration.

Salem (F, 45) was one of the few repeat migrants who was eager to talk to me. She was adamant that return is not "a bed of roses" and that people need to know that. She remigrated back to the United States after spending a couple of very frustrating years in Ethiopia as a returnee. A mutual acquaintance connected us after hearing my frustrations with identifying and securing interviews with repeat migrants. Salem and I met in a quiet café in a posh suburb in Virginia. Salem came from a wealthy family in Ethiopia and had access to some of the best education in the country. After moving to California in the 1990s, she spent a few years working in real estate and interior design, building a lucrative career. When she first moved to the United States, she was plugged into a supportive community and experienced a smooth transition. Although she had visited Ethiopia a few times before relocating, she did not fully plan out her return. Some of her troubles stemmed from this insufficient planning. She initially returned to Ethiopia to sort out inheritance and land ownership issues after a parent's passing. She had not planned to stay long term, but over time, her desire to build on a business opportunity helped her overcome her reluctance. On the relationship front, she was going through a divorce, which helped solidify her decision to stay in Ethiopia on a more permanent basis. Additionally, she was laid off from work as a result of the U.S. housing market crisis in 2011. Because of all these compounding factors, Salem sold her house in California to build one in Addis. While she was describing all these challenging moments from her past, Salem maintained her composure even though it was obvious that she was recounting painful moments to a complete stranger. Our conversation shifted quickly from the motivations for her return to her experiences while living in Addis. Salem highlighted three areas of her discontent while living as a returnee in Ethiopia: finances, bureaucracy, and gender. She had sold her home after her divorce in California to finance her new house construction and business ventures in Addis. She felt incredibly financially stretched as things took longer than planned and required more resources than she had at her disposal. In addition, she found the Ethiopian legal system to be chaotic and hard to navigate. These challenges were compounded by gendered expectations. As a youngish, single woman from the diaspora, Salem was seen as an easy target on many fronts. She reported that locals tried to take advantage of her financially, expecting her to be wealthy. She felt that as an unattached woman she did not get any respect, particularly in government offices. As she was describing all of these challenges, Salem became increasingly animated. She stated:

> Do you know how often I got propositioned? All the lewd men I encountered? They wanted one of two things from me: sex and money. When they realized they were getting neither from me, they lost interest. They even went out of their way to make sure that my plans failed. So vengeful. So incredibly vengeful.

Salem had some choice words for all the men who purposefully stood in her way. Her anger was defensible and her exasperation unsurprising. She summed up her experience: "I was constantly reminded that I did not belong [while in Addis]. It did not feel like home. I expected it to be easy, I kept telling everyone 'I am going back home,' but it was no longer home." This explanation prompted my obvious next question: "Where is home for you now?" She gave me a philosophical answer: "Home is where I can live in peace." Unfortunately for her, that was no longer in Ethiopia.

All of these challenges compounded Salem's disappointment in her return, and she remigrated back to the United States after living five years as a returnee. She told me, "I am angry, mad, sad, disappointed, and everything in between. I went back to Ethiopia with such high hopes, but everything is a mess. My life is a mess. I still cannot believe everything that happened, happened. If you talk to me in five, ten years, I may have words of wisdom, but what I have right now is all this anger and regret bubbling up in me. I still have not processed it properly." Salem's composure clearly showed how deeply the disappointment and other emotions affected her, even years after she remigrated back to the United States. To compound matters, her second resettlement in the United States proved to be much harder than her initial one almost two decades prior. She could not go back to the life she had worked hard to establish. First, instead of relocating back to the West Coast, Salem opted for the East Coast, where she did not have an established network. This was partly due to her desire to avoid her old social circles. Second, because Salem had not fully resolved all her pending financial obligations in the United States before leaving for Ethiopia, her credit was negatively affected. She explained, "I had left one too many things hanging. I had one leg here [in the United States] and one leg there [in Ethiopia] for a while. It drained me financially. I was so stretched. I did not sort out all that I needed to before I left [the United States], which in the long run came back to haunt me." As Salem explained, neither return nor repeat migration was an easy process for her.

As we can see from these four different cases, repeat migration can be motivated by some form of disappointment. Challenges to belonging can result in displacement, which is an all too familiar condition for migrants. Displacement is not just a physical measure, change of location, or geographic shift; it can include experiences of marginalization and alienation. As with belonging, there is an emotive side to displacement. Displacement can take the form of general unease, insecurity, homesickness, anxiety, and a range of other negative emotions that cause individuals to feel alienated in their social worlds. While it is not surprising when migrants feel displaced and alienated in destination countries, it is more unexpected when they feel that way in the home country after a planned voluntary return. The disillusioned repeat migrants all reported feeling foreign, disconnected, and taken advantage of in the home country because of their status as returnees. Their expectations and the realities of their return experience did not align properly, and this misalignment was the main source of their disappointment. They saw their return experience as a failure. Our interactions made it clear that discussing their misadventures in return was painful.

The Inadvertents

Nardos (F, 23) explained that she did not have much choice in her return migration experience. Her parents sent her back to Ethiopia for disciplinary reasons as they considered her a "problem child." They believed that finishing high school back in the homeland, away from some of the corrupting influences in the United States, would be the best solution for her. Unlike her older siblings, Nardos was getting very low grades and "hanging out with the wrong crowd," according to her parents. They therefore sent her to Ethiopia as a form of disciplinary intervention.[12] Consider this exchange I had with Nardos:

> NARDOS: It is called *tsebay maremya* [loosely translated as "attitude adjuster"]. It sounds so innocent, doesn't it? If you didn't know, *tsebay maremya* is also what they call prisons back home. Yep! My parents sent me to Ethiopia as *tsebay maremya*.
> HG: Were you misbehaving in any way?
> NARDOS: I sure did not think so at the time. I was so angry at my parents. How dare they? I mean, I was an American citizen, and they are freaking sent me to a third world country!
> HG: Do you regret the time spent in Ethiopia?
> NARDOS: Perhaps not as much in hindsight . . . but I don't see myself living there anymore.

Nardos described her high school years in Ethiopia as transformative. She was able to calm down from her teenage "overacting" (her own word) and grow into the person she eventually became. Although she was eager to return to the United States, Nardos had, over time, developed something of an appreciation for her parents' choice. When Nardos finished high school and turned eighteen, she returned to the United States. She convinced her parents that she would be better off attending college in the United States, but she dropped out after taking some courses. Nardos did not therefore have much choice in her initial return migration, but she strongly desired her repeat migration and preferred to live in the United States, where she had more freedom and thus a higher comfort level than she had experienced in Ethiopia.

In what she described as a complicated and frustrating affair, Nafkote (F, 37) relocated her family back and forth between Ethiopia and the United States as she waited for her husband's immigration paperwork to be regularized. After Nafkote became a naturalized U.S. citizen, she traveled back to Ethiopia to marry her high school sweetheart, with the intention of living in the United States once the paperwork was sorted out. U.S. Citizen and Immigration Services, however, questioned the truthfulness of the marriage for whatever reason and denied her husband entry. Nafkote moved back to Ethiopia to have her first child and live with her husband as they waited for the paperwork and mounted a legal battle with the U.S. Citizenship and Immigration Services. While in Ethiopia, Nafkote started a small café, which required her to drain all her savings, while her husband worked at a nongovernmental organization. This ordeal with immigration paperwork took up the better part of ten years, during which time Nafkote and her husband became parents to two children (aged five and seven at the time of the last interview). Nafkote stated:

> I think my story is a bit unusual. U.S. Immigration has condemned my family to live in limbo all of these years. If I had not moved back [to Ethiopia], my children would have grown up without their father. They might not even have been born! I thought being a U.S. citizen would have protected me from some of these things that I went through, but no, I ended up living an unsettled life. I am still living in uncertainty. We never had the chance to do the normal things young families do, like invest in a house, build a career, give stability to our children . . . I feel like these were stolen years from my life.

Nafkote remembered her "limbo" years with regret. She resented her inability to freely choose where to live and raise her children. The fact that she did not have a good time in Ethiopia also compounded her dissatisfaction.

Nafkote was particularly dissatisfied with the maternal care she received during her pregnancies and after birth. She said that her two very difficult pregnancies and some health challenges her children faced left her utterly disgusted with maternal and pediatric health care in Ethiopia. Nafkote recounted many heartbreaking encounters with medical professionals that left her in tears. She stated:

> Doctors are treated like gods in Ethiopia! They always painted me as the troublemaker when I asked questions or dared challenge their opinions. They regarded me with so much disdain, *niket*. More than once I have been asked, "Where is my medical degree?" Is that warranted? When I am worried about my health or the well-being of my child, do they need to treat me with such contempt?

Nafkote resented the mostly male medical professionals who portrayed her as a hysterical diaspora woman "who did not know her place." She was yet another respondent who experienced gendered frustrations, in this case during encounters with mostly male medical professionals. Nafkote mentioned that she would not have survived motherhood without the help of her husband and her extended family. After more than a decade in Ethiopia waiting for her husband's U.S. immigration paperwork to be regularized, Nafkote relocated back to Atlanta with her two children. The health needs of one of her daughters and the high cost of living in Addis Ababa motivated her move. Her husband's paperwork was still pending, but Nafkote felt she had no choice but to move without her husband. She felt compelled to engage in repeat migration despite her refusal to live away from her husband for the first ten years of their marriage.

Birtukan (F, 44) shared her experiences with return and repeat migration over coffee, seated in her kitchen while her four children watched TV in the living room. She explained the circumstances that led her family first to return and later to engage in subsequent migration back to the United States: her husband's desire to migrate coupled with the health of an elderly parent prompted both threads of migration. While Birtukan's husband is African American, he had long harbored a desire to live and work in Ethiopia. With his educational background, he was able to secure an upper administrative position in one of the educational institutions in Addis Ababa, which facilitated their relocation. At the same time, Birtukan wanted to be close to an ailing parent, for whom she became the primary caregiver. The couple moreover considered the importance of their children's upbringing in an African society, where their skin color would not mark them as outsiders. While they were in Ethiopia, Birtukan alternated between being a full-time homemaker and caretaker of her ailing father and working in the same school as her husband. "We stayed in Ethiopia for a total of seven years, and it was great for the kids. I was also able to be there for my father, whose health was deteriorating," she explained. Like Nafkote, Birtukan mentioned a number of problems she encountered with the medical system in Ethiopia, particularly in regard to maternal care (her youngest child was born in Addis) and geriatric care.

After several years, however, her father passed away, and she felt she "no longer had a reason to stay." This grief and her husband's increasing dissatisfaction with his work environment in Addis led to them exploring a remigration back to the United States. Birtukan's family lived in Ethiopia between 2007 and 2014 and eventually relocated back to the United States. At the time of the interview, Birtukan was back to being a full-time homemaker while her husband worked as a school principal. When I asked about her family's adjustment to life back in the United States, Birtukan expressed some misgivings about her older children in particular. As teenagers, they were used to their multicultural lives in Addis, and they experienced a sort of reverse culture shock upon relocating back to the United States, where they were the only Black kids at an almost all white school. Birtukan explained, "It was shocking to me at first when we returned to Ethiopia, so many things I could not get used to . . . it was a similar shock to the older ones when we came back here [to the United States]." Birtukan therefore fits within the inadvertents category as her motivations for both her initial return migration and her subsequent repeat migration were dominated by family concerns: her husband's career and desire to resettle first in Ethiopia and then in the United States, coupled with the ailing health and subsequent death of her father.

In addition to the cases I have already discussed, the following story illustrates how family dynamics can lead to unplanned repeat migration. When I first met Adil (M, 39) in 2015, he was living as a returnee in Ethiopia and arranging his family's migration back to the United States. Even though he was in the process of liquidating his assets in Addis, we spent a couple of hours talking about all the challenges his wife had encountered as a returnee. At the time, they had been married for seven years, although they had been together for much longer. They had two children together, a four-year-old and a five-year-old. When they first moved to Addis, they were both very excited. Adil saw a lot of business opportunities, and they both wanted to raise their kids in Ethiopia among their extended families. The first two years or so were good, but as time went on, it became increasingly difficult for his wife to accept some of the gender norms in Ethiopia. Adil described her as "a white girl in a *Habesha* body." When I asked him to explain, he stated, "My Ethiopian wife is too American to remain here [in Ethiopia]."

She did not understand Ethiopian culture and could not stand the constant family interference in their daily lives. She thus packed her bags and left for the United States, leaving him behind with the children. Although they were temporarily separated, with him staying behind in Addis until the children finished their school year, he was reluctantly heading back to the United States to keep the family unit together. As his wife refused to live any longer in Ethiopia, he did not see much of a choice except to relocate as well. From a gendered lens, while older migration literature is replete with the trope of the trailing wife,[13] there is less research on male spouses who follow their female partners on their migration journey. This particular family dynamic is even more interesting as the different members would fall under different repeat migrant classifications. The wife would be classified as part of the disillusioned category, while the husband and children would fit under the inadvertent category.

These stories show that repeat migration may not be a rationally considered choice made after taking a calculated stock of all possible pros and cons, pushes and pulls. Rather, repeat migration can be the result of circumstance, most times beyond migrants' control and an emotional response to those circumstances. These stories include a child who was sent back home for disciplinary reasons, an individual who returned to get married and wait for the immigration paperwork to be sorted out, a caretaker who did not stay after the death of an elderly parent as "it became unbearable" to do so, and a husband who reluctantly followed his wife in repeat migration. While emotions played a role in how these migrants understood their journeys, the migrants didn't consider their family dynamics a matter of choice.

These individuals would not have voluntarily chosen to engage in either the initial return migration or the subsequent repeat migration if they were not compelled by a close family member, such as a parent or a spouse. Although there are some similarities between the inadvertents and the disillusioned (in the sense that some type of disappointment motivated their migrations), I find it important to separate out the similarities in these respondents. The inadvertents exhibit some ambivalence in their descriptions of return and repeat migration (similar to the discussion of ambivalence in the first chapter), whereas the disillusioned present their return experience as utterly negative. The inadvertent category therefore captures the complexity of lived experience, which is not always clear cut, black and white. Moreover, the disambiguation between inadvertents and the disillusioned also highlights the effects of structural factors and family circumstances in compelled migration. The inclusion of both trends in my analysis serves to illustrate the variable role that emotion and indeed agency itself can play in motivating a variety of individuals to repeat their migration.

Migrate, Return, Repeat: The Impermanence of Return

This study diverges from the predominant model focusing solely on the economic or policy aspects of repeat migration and considering repeat migrants only as part of an available (perhaps expendable) labor force. It expands our understanding by taking into account migra-emotions within interpersonal, sociocultural, and infrastructural circumstances that motivate repeat migrants. The decisions that migrants make within a circular system of social and economic relationships should be understood through the lens of migra-emotions. For instance, emotions such as shame and disappointment drive the disillusioned to engage in repeat migration. Similarly, retirees are driven by pragmatism and acquiescence.

The four trends discussed in this chapter—young professionals, retirees, the disillusioned, and inadvertent migrants—provide a good overview of the migra-emotions and life circumstances that lead to repeat migration. While the value and hope an individual might place on work and career considerations are important motivating factors for some, family circumstances, health concerns, and a myriad of disappointments, internal and external, in return can vastly influence repeat migration. Table 5.1 outlines the primary factors motivating return and repeat migration and the prevalent migra-emotions among my sixteen repeat migrant respondents. This analysis foregrounds the life circumstances of the repeat migrants and highlights their decisions as social beings making choices within interconnected geographies.

In regard to the socio-ecology of migration, repeat migrants take advantage of opportunities in both the home and host nations, their mobility enabled for the most part by their legal documentation status. All of the

TABLE 5.1. REPEAT MIGRANTS' MOTIVATIONS FOR RETURN AND REPEAT MIGRATIONS

Characteristic	Motivation for return	Motivation for repeat migration	Prevalent migra-emotions
Young professionals	Work / career and reconnecting with the homeland / extended family	Work / career	Desire, optimism
Retirees	Life stage, retirement, and reconnecting with the homeland / extended family	Health and family (progeny)	Concession, pragmatism, community, responsibility
Disillusioned	Business opportunity and family	Failure	Anger, disappointment, shame
Inadvertents	Forced by circumstances	Compelled by circumstances	Ambivalence, acceptance

repeat migrants in this study have maintained their legal residency permits or their citizenship in the host country. As nations tighten their immigration regulations, the ease of entry and exit is a crucial factor that facilitates (or hinders) the movements of migration. Some of the returnee participants in this study have used repeat migration as a possible ready escape valve in situations of social, political, or economic duress. Therefore, the legal requirements for travel and residence in different locations are an important consideration. Along with legal privileges, we also have to consider the privileges afforded by repeat migrants' financial (economic) status. Overall, financial considerations affect the available choices for repeat migrants. The young professionals' search for better career opportunities is coupled with a search for high income levels that will enable their choice of lifestyle. The financial means to resettle in different places has given retirees flexibility and choice. For other repeat migrants, a lack of funds posed a significant problem they needed to overcome and partially led them to engage in repeat migration. For the most part, relative wealth and privilege enable these repeated migrations.

While the legal and economic conditions privilege repeat migrants, these migrants nonetheless also encounter practical disadvantages, particularly the lack of integration in either place. Some repeat migrants have a mentality of transit and lack a sense of rootedness in a singular geography as they are constantly on the move and do not put down roots in one place. Repeat migrants are sometimes therefore portrayed by non-migrants as dysfunctional, neither here nor there. Paradoxically, searching for a sense of belonging leads many migrants to return in the first place. Questions of belonging plague the repeat migrants just as they do the return migrants. While repeat migration may appear indecisive, the reality reveals that migrants develop a location-specific capital and accumulated knowledge that they can deploy selectively. Repeat migration can also indicate new dynamic arrangements of family and community.

Finally, we have to consider infrastructural differences between home and destination geographies to contextualize the experiences of repeat migrants. For instance, the availability of cheap means of transportation and communication enables migrants to remain connected to both the home and host nations regardless of their current residence. On the other hand, the medical infrastructure in the home country of Ethiopia has affected a number of migrants, in some cases prompting their repeat migration. While retirees stated that the inadequate long-term care facilities compelled them to engage in repeat migration, parents also expressed their dissatisfaction with the level of available pediatric care (in addition to the bedside manner of some of the medical professionals they encountered), which influenced their decision-making process. Therefore, the level and quality of health care, coupled with interpersonal miscommunication, have led some returnees to become repeat migrants.

Overall, repeat migrants exercise their agency in an unpredictable world with changing circumstances and evolving emotional landscapes as they move between home and host countries. They take into account their legal status, different infrastructures, their family structure, and a myriad of other issues when deciding on their subsequent migration. Noneconomic factors such as attachment to places, family circumstances, and choice of lifestyles all influence migration decisions. Moreover, just like return migration, repeat migration carries associated socioeconomic costs and advantages. Finally, repeat migrants highlight the impermanence of return migration.

Conclusion

In migration studies, there is an enduring debate about whether mobility or immobility is the norm, about which one is the pervasive aspect of human nature. Perhaps the fact that 97 percent of the world population is immobile indicates the norm. The limited magnitude of migrants globally, stable at the 3 percent mark, signals that this is an exception to the rule that warrants explanation. At the same time, human history is marked by various waves of migration, starting with the migration initiated in eastern Africa that went on to populate the rest of the world over millennia. Regardless of whether migration or immobility is the norm, migration is a phenomenon that affects not just the migrants themselves but also non-migrants in the home, host, and transit societies. Migration is therefore a permeating force that has the power to alter sociocultural dynamics, political structures, and countries' economic outlooks.

In this work, I make a number of interrelated arguments about the nature of migration and the use of the lens of migra-emotions to understand (non)migrants' decision-making. The findings from this research will better inform (1) a 360-degree view of migration, starting with non-migrants and encompassing both returnees and repeat migrants; (2) the emotional dimensions of migration experiences and decision-making; (3) the importance of positioning migra-emotions in the socio-ecology of migration; (4) *counterstreams* in migration, beyond the regional specificity and with global applicability; and (5) our understandings of transnational interconnections and modes of incorporation of (Black African) migrants in home and host societies.

In this Conclusion, I start by summarizing the main points of the 360-degree perspective on migration. I then recap the importance of migra-emotions in the decision-making processes and experiences of non-migrants, returnees, and repeat migrants. Furthermore, I locate this work within the larger socio-ecology of migration. I then discuss the benefits of studying migrant movements from the perspective of the source country, specifically centering Ethiopia. Finally, I review the importance of place and space in Ethiopian migration.

360-Degree View of Migration

The intent of this book is to provide a partial look at a complicated issue, weaving together stories of non-migrants, returnees, and repeat migrants. This research brings to light the fact that migration affects the home and host nations in different ways. The 360-degree view of migration, by shedding light on the interconnections between different locations and categories of migrants, "offers a nuanced perspective for exploring how migration changes not only people and countries, but also the social relations and processes that occur in and between societies."[1] While this book offers a groundbreaking 360-degree view of migration, it does not claim to cover all types of migration. I set out to do a number of things in this work. I start off by rejecting the misleading dichotomy between sedentary and mobile and proving that even people who have never moved from their home nation are transformed by migration and maintain a set of associations, considerations, and meanings regarding migration. The concept of "social remittances" coined by Peggy Levitt aptly captures the cultural elements (norms and behaviors) transmitted through migration.[2] Sometimes, it is practically impossible to untangle media-based and migration-driven cultural diffusion. Most scholars have been predominantly concerned with monetary remittances, and few have studied the social or lifestyle changes of non-migrants caused by their interactions with migrant kin. Yet migrants export ideas, behaviors, and other social capital back to their communities of origin, and these have a transformative effect on non-migrants' social values and lifestyles. Social remittances—a migration-driven form of cultural diffusion that alters local customs and at times reproduces social norms or expectations from the migrant's host nation—travel through identifiable pathways as migrants export their new ideas and lifestyles through communication exchanges (such as social media) while still in their host countries and as they return to visit or live in their communities of origin. While social remittance flows are one aspect of an ongoing process of cultural diffusion, the personalized and gradual character of the communication stands in contrast to the larger-scale nature of global cultural diffusion through different forms of media. Migration and social remittances are therefore inextricable symbiotic processes.

It is easy to see how non-migrants are affected by migration. Non-migrant respondents display intimate knowledge of the cultural and social life of their migrant kin's host nation. The ever-growing Ethiopian diaspora is changing the expectations, life opportunities, and outcomes of those who have not migrated. Migration is altering the social fabric of a large, cosmopolitan city such as Addis Ababa as even non-migrants increasingly adopt Western lifestyles. Migration therefore does not only pertain to those who have left the country. In fact, as non-migrants often told me, "you do not need to cross the borders of the country to be affected by migration." I encountered a competing set of values and emotions that shape the consideration of non-migrants: indignant patriotism, hopefulness, and ambivalence. Adopting a more deterministic nomenclature, one might observe that the non-migrant whose reaction is dominated by indignant patriotism and pride is a voluntary non-migrant, the non-migrant who views migration predominantly with hope and eagerness is an involuntary non-migrant, and the non-migrant whose emotional ambivalence gives way to pragmatic inaction is an incidental non-migrant. Although these three types of migra-emotions do not represent the totality of perspectives, they each echoed prominently among the subjects in this study and serve to highlight the nuances that exist in perceptions of migration.

I aim to disrupt the idea that migration can be understood as a single linear movement from origin to destination. Migration is not a one-way journey. I provide a multifaceted understanding of migration as an ongoing, contingent process that emphasizes fluidity, continuums, and nonlinearity. In this book, I do not present a linear narrative with a straightforward storyline. Reality is often fluid, dynamic, and even elusive, and there is an argument to be made about the multiplicity of stories in lived experiences. The attractions of the initial migration have been widely written about and include a better economic outlook, more stable political regimes, and more educational opportunities. The attractions of return include sociocultural belonging, better and quicker returns on investments, the proximity of family, and lifestyle. These benefits are coupled with significant drawbacks, including life in a developing country and the lack of resources (water, electricity, internet connection) that comes along with it, political instability, and the high expectations of family members and the home society more generally. To encapsulate these various dynamics, I provide a push-pull analysis of return migrations, examining conditions in both the home and host nations. Moving beyond motivations, I examine the experiences of returnees, including how they negotiate their privilege and exhibit a form of saviorism, warranted or not, once in the home nation.

Upon return, returnees justify and reify their class position and create their own separate category premised on their migration experience. Returnees thus engage in a strategic manipulation of class. Returnees have access to certain luxuries unavailable to them in host nations (such as household servants) but deal with the everyday challenges of living in a developing nation (such as unreliable electric power and internet access). Returnees enact an upper-class identity through the use of a slew of domestic servants, ostentatious displays of wealth, and other practices. Therefore, as returnees reify their class position, their habits are ingrained and taken for granted. The consumption patterns of returnees tend to reproduce and exacerbate existing inequalities. These types of behaviors can have a negative impact on countries of origin.

In general, returnees and repeat migrants, by virtue of their migration, are reckoned as a separate class or category of people. They share common characteristics of migration and, upon return, similar socioeconomic, cultural, and even political positions. Both groups see themselves (internal ascription) and are seen by non-migrants (external ascription) as different from the overall society. We should not presuppose that membership in these unique groups implies automatic similarity or internal cohesion. Rather, internal divisions and hierarchies based on place of migration, among other factors, abound. The boundaries of this community are constantly drawn and redrawn. The social status of migrants, unlike most other social statuses, opens doors within Ethiopia. Returnees in particular create and recreate their own communities based on imagined similarities premised on the migration experience. We can therefore see the centrality of im/mobility in their refashioned identity.

Finally, although returnees tend to initially engage in return in the belief that the move is permanent, conditions in the home nation, family situations, and other considerations can lead them to become repeat migrants. Return is therefore not the end of the migration cycle. The attractions of repeat migration are often the same as the attractions of initial migration: security, stability, and predictability of life, among other things. We can visualize return and repeat migration as a sort of boomerang movement where migrants leave their home country, return, and leave again. I identify four trends among the repeat migrants I studied: young professionals, retirees, the disillusioned, and inadvertents. The plurality of considerations represented among these migrants provides a nuanced understanding of the different motivations, experiences, and lifestyles of Ethiopian repeat migrants. It further enables us to interrogate belonging, privilege, and inequality in a circular system of social and economic relationships between the Global North and the Global

South. Respondents are formed and transformed through the migration process. They are both agents of change and products of migration.

The book follows a logical arc starting with non-migrants and ending with repeat migrants. We can conceptualize these three stages as a continuum (instead of mutually exclusive categories), underscoring how one potentially leads to another: non-migrants become migrants, who become returnees, who become repeat migrants. As discussed in the Introduction, the stages have a clear beginning and a cyclical nature but not necessarily a clear end point. This indicates the open-ended nature of migration. This is the inherent paradox of this work: I am constrained by the need to use discrete, somewhat limiting labels for a phenomenon that is fluid, circular, and complex and thus goes beyond existing labels.

For the sake of simplification, I have presented the three categories of non-migrants, returnees, and repeat migrants in separate chapters. However, it is important to see how each group influences the others. Most (repeat) migrants or returnees will never meet or even know their fellow comrades. Although their individual lives may never intersect, they walk the same metaphorical path as they are part of the same migrant community. Non-migrants can explain a great deal about migration, returnees can explain about both migration experiences and the home nations, and repeat migrants can explain about experiences of return. These groups are in conversation with one another, if not directly, then indirectly. None of these groups can be taken for granted as "natural," but together they can shed light on the benefits, pitfalls, and overall experiences of geographic mobility. Together, they challenge the conventional wisdom that either migration or staying put is consistently desirable, affording social mobility or ensuring belonging.

Migra-emotions

In this work, I advance a theory of migra-emotions: emotions specific to migration that are central to understanding migration decisions and experiences. I adopt a broad constructionist approach to explore how migrants feel in specific situations and how they act on those emotions within the socio-ecology of migration. Rather than seeing emotions as an unwelcome intrusion in academic analysis, I set forth emotions as a central component, recognizing their importance to human understanding. Emotions have real-life consequences, and this book has amply shown that migra-emotions affect migration decision-making and experiences. Even though individuals can only directly experience the events of their own lifetime, the amalgamation of life stories reveals a great deal about the broader sociohistorical contexts without abridging the richness of the narratives. There is a symbiotic relationship between how migra-emotions shape migration and how in turn migration experiences shape migra-emotions. Multiple cross-border movements engender different migra-emotions and vice versa. While it is impossible to draw a direct causal relationship between migra-emotions and migrant decisions, there is a clear and obvious correlation between the two. Moreover, although the relationship between migra-emotions and migration decision-making is not straightforward, significant patterns emerge. In sum, respondents' migra-emotions highly influenced their motivations for initial, return, and repeat migration.

Table C.1 summarizes the various migra-emotions of non-migrants, returnees, and repeat migrants discussed in the previous chapters. While I separated the different emotions into positive, negative, and neutral or ambivalent categories, they are not exclusive to the category of (non)migrants identified. No one group has primacy over one set of migra-emotions; the table just shows some of the emotions most commonly reported by the different groups.

In the individual chapters, I additionally highlight the importance of age and the life course to migra-emotions. The generations into which people are born and the ages they migrate heavily affect their (positive or negative) perception of migration and their ideas of home. Older Ethiopians, particularly non-migrants, tend to have more negative views of migration and therefore pity migrants and favor return. They tend to still hold on to the idea of the homeland that was established during Emperor Haile Selassie's reign. Younger Ethiopians born during the Derg regime and later hold more pragmatic and even romanticized views about migration and, by contrast, less idealized views of the homeland. Returnees are pulled to the home nation by a sense of duty and belonging and pushed from the host nation by alienation and exhaustion. Repeat migrants also experience a slew of emotions, from acquiescence to discontent, that lead them to reemigrate from the homeland.

In summary, individuals' migra-emotions influence their migration journeys in specific ways. While considering each group—non-migrants,

TABLE C.1. MIGRA-EMOTIONS SUMMARY			
	Non-migrant	Returnee	Repeat migrant
Positive	Honor, hope, optimism, pride, sense of adventure	Sense of duty, sense of belonging, excitement	Sense of accomplishment
Negative	Boredom, despair, discontent, indignation, shame	Alienation, exhaustion, fatigue	Anger, discontent, frustration, sadness
Neutral / Ambivalent	Ambivalence, pragmatism	Nostalgia	Acquiescence, resolve

returnees, and repeat migrants—within the migration continuum, we have to be cognizant of migra-emotions within the constraints of the socio-ecology of migration. The MSM (migration within the socio-ecology of migration) framework highlights the intersection and complicated relationship between micro- and macrofactors that influence migration decision-making.

Socio-ecology of Migration

It is meaningless to study migra-emotions in a vacuum; rather, it is crucial to contextualize them within the socio-ecology of migration—the ecosystem of social, political, and economic factors that alternatively enable or prohibit migration. Factors that are exogenous to the migrant have been referred to as social structures, capabilities, and assemblages. While each framework has its unique benefits and drawbacks, I find that a socio-ecological conceptualization better captures the ever-evolving local, national, regional, and international realities that migrants must navigate. For migrants, important socio-ecological factors can include national and international laws governing migration, employment opportunities, social welfare infrastructures, and immigrant integration landscapes ranging from multiculturalism to xenophobia that enable/encourage or inhibit/discourage migration.

The case studies that appear in this book invite reflection on broad demographic processes and provide insight into larger political processes. The elephant in the room thus far has been migration and citizenship laws and policies—in other words, elements within the socio-ecology of migration. The migration policy in both the home and host nation should be examined as government intervention and management have an impact in terms of the who, why, and how of migration. The state is always in the background, deciding who is formally in or out, desirable or not. Most of the participants in the study (not including non-migrants), although Ethiopian by birth, are citizens or permanent legal residents of Global North countries. This change in their legal status allows them a level of privilege compared to other Ethiopian nationals. Legal status is, however, only part of the story.[3] I do not disregard the importance of individual countries' migration policies. However, there are significant similarities in policies in Global North countries—this is known as migration policy diffusion. Consequently, I have found no significant difference in return or repeat migration regardless of where the migrants came from. This is not to imply that the migration policies of those countries have no effect or did not affect the migrants' lives while they were in the host country. However, these differences are less important by the time the migrants become returnees or repeat migrants. The returnees and repeat migrants in this study illustrate their flexibility in geographic and sociopolitical positioning. Return and repeat migrants simultaneously challenge and reify existing sociocultural and geopolitical borders through their privileged mobility, which is accessible to a select few on a global scale. It is important to question the factors that allow such seemingly unfettered mobility.

In Interlude 2, I discuss the power and various meanings of the passport as a small but mighty document that enables (and sometimes prevents) cross-border movement. It is also important to recognize how much privilege is imbued in documented migration. A passport is a unique object of migration, embedded with layers of hierarchy, cultural meaning, and sociopolitical restrictions. For most of human history, people did not need a document to migrate. The passport is a creation of our modern world and governments' impulse to control borders, ostensibly keeping "undesirable" populations out but in fact creating stratifications based on national origin and other axes of identity.

Centering Ethiopia

As I argued in the Introduction, context matters, and the primary backdrop of this study is Ethiopia. In the introduction to *The Global Ethiopian Diaspora*, a book that explores "the complicated processes involved in Ethiopian transnational migration and the making of the global Ethiopian diaspora," my colleagues Shimelis B. Gulema, Mulugetta F. Dinbabo, and I note that "migration, both internal and external, has been an essential part of the history of Ethiopia."[4] We explain that "international migration and the making of Ethiopia's international diaspora have a very old history, and contemporary cross-border movements should be seen as a continuation of a deeply entrenched tradition."[5] We identify the study of return and circular migration as a recent development in the trajectory of Ethiopian migration, one that is "disruptive of the pragmatic assumptions of migration scholarship."[6] Such studies aim "to transcend geographic, conceptual, and methodological boundaries and explore both areas [the homeland and diaspora] as two interconnected and interpenetrating spatial, conceptual, and temporal constructs in which new forms of affinities and affiliations, new imaginings and practices of belongings are made possible but also continuously recalibrated."[7] This is exactly what I set out to do in *Counterstreams*. This book tells the untold stories of Ethiopian (African) migration. My aim is to contribute in some small way to the restorying of Ethiopian (African) migration to better reflect the diversity of perspectives and experiences.

In this study, I focus on a community of migrants physically moving back and forth between the place of origin and different destinations in the Global North. Rather than focusing on destination countries or even exclusively on the home country, I highlight ongoing ties and dynamics between migrants and their places of origin. Nonetheless, the unifying factor, biggest reference point, or pole of migration circulation is the source country. I argue that it is imperative to examine return and repeat migration patterns from the perspectives of migrant-sending nations. So what do we gain from this approach? The motivations and experiences of migrants cannot be fully understood from the point of view of the destination country; we must consider the place of origin. While most works focus on the host or receiving country, this book flips the script by taking up the perspective of the source country. Doing so allows for a comparative approach that focuses on one population of (non)migrants from the same country dispersed globally. This book seeks to highlight the similarities and differences in migration experiences in different countries of the Global North. Moreover, it centers return as one of the significant counterstreams in African migration.

By squarely centering Ethiopia in the study, I contribute to various academic literatures, including (but not limited to) transnational migration and the New African Diaspora. By shedding light on privileged migration and the lifestyles of returnees in Ethiopia, I expose another side of the African migration puzzle. While Ethiopian migrants are still subject to the racialization of global migration systems, return and repeat migration subvert the prevailing system and further challenge the ghettoization of African migration.

Black African migrants are not the typical privileged migrants who move seamlessly between different territories, as they are generally marginalized. Yet the individuals in this book are generally quite well educated, skilled, and culturally familiar with their destinations. Therefore, host nations should destigmatize migration and work on the perception of migrants as drains on the resources of the nation. Rather, migrants can be seen as enterprising individuals who are beneficial to both the home and host societies. This research on immobility, return, and repeat migration expands the lens of African migration studies by breaking away from the narrow and restrictive focus of forced migration and the single-minded preoccupation with development. Sociology's focus on assimilation or integration for the majority of its history inadvertently neglected the homeland before the introduction of transnational perspectives. Global North countries, with their supposedly better economic and political development, are seen as the obvious destinations for migrants. This, however, does not hold equally true to all who reside within its borders. We should not assume that all migrants intend to settle in the host nation permanently. This research is timely and critical given current national and global events. At the international level, different migration "crises" in the Global North dominate the headlines, inciting concerns about the absorption and repatriation of new waves of migrants.

Geography Matters: Space and Place in Ethiopian Migration

It is important to recognize the multisited nature of migration; migrants live complex lives in multiple places, negotiating overlapping identities. While migration is a complex social phenomenon, the significance of space and place remains important from the perspective of (non)migrants. In this book, I make an argument about the importance of geography and territory. As migration studies is a highly interdisciplinary field, I borrow heavily from geographic perspectives on space and place. While space is a physical location, measured by latitude and longitude, it is abstract, without any substantial meaning, whereas place is a space with added value, imbued with culturally ascribed meaning. A place is the result of human entanglement derived from direct and indirect interaction through various senses (e.g., including olfactory, audiovisual, and other sensory components) and mediated through symbols. Given this understanding of space and place, there is a lot to be said about the politics of urban spaces and Ethiopian migrants' assertion of their identities and belonging in multifaceted ways.

Although there is something transgressive about return and repeat migrants crossing and crisscrossing borders, seemingly unshackled from territory, their repeated movements indicate that there is indeed a relevance tied to specific geographies. The very act of repeat migration highlights the importance of territory. Rather than being the exception that proves the rule, repeated cross-border movements raise a question: Why move unless there is a reason to move? If migrants are doing well materially and financially in either location, they must be seeking something more. Moreover, the diaspora and the returnees transform the landscape as much as it transforms them.

As discussed in the Introduction and the Appendix, this topic is close to my heart and lived experience. As an Ethiopian migrant residing in the United States, I have had plenty of interactions with other Ethiopian migrants, some considering return, some repeat migrants. I also have plenty of non-migrant friends, family members, and acquaintances who do not hesitate to tell me their opinions about migration: the good, the bad, and everything in between. I insert myself and my experiences in the analysis presented in this book, cognizant of my insider-outsider positionality, as research is embodied, lived. The geographies I describe in this book are very personal to me; they are meaningful spaces that I have inhabited at different times of my life.

In the interludes, I have provided thick descriptions of three urban spaces that are filled with significance and symbolism for Ethiopian migrants. I argue that migration is inscribed in specific geographies. In the discussion of Bolé Airport, I have highlighted how this transient space, the threshold between in and out, is imbued with its own unvoiced stratification between valuable migrants and supposedly less worthy (non)migrants. The hierarchies are present in the destinations, the Black bodies, the travelers, and the airport staff. Bolé is an equally emotive, economic, and political space where different dreams and agendas are on full display. In the comparative ethnographies of Addis Ababa and Washington, DC, I have shown how migrant dreams and realities have been inscribed on the urban landscapes of both capital cities. A multiplicity of globalization processes assumes concrete, localized forms in cities, where the mixing of the local and global is highly visible. In Addis Ababa, returnees and aspiring non-migrants have styled their businesses with a hodgepodge of names reminiscent of locations in the Global North, while names of Global South migrant destinations are conspicuously missing in the trendy parts of the city. In contrast, in one of the most populous cities of Ethiopian migrants, Washington, DC, Ethiopian ethnic businesses carry monikers from the homeland. These labels serve a double purpose: on the one hand, they are strategic names steeped in nostalgia to attract coethnic people; on the other, these exotic names captivate the imagination of a non-Ethiopian clientele seeking an "authentic" experience. Migrants simultaneously transform and are transformed by these transnational spaces. Migrants are thus creating and recreating community wherever they go. Since this is a book mostly about return, two of the interludes focus on the home country, whereas a third describes a destination hub. These places are in conversation with one another, not necessarily by design but through the individual agentic decisions of migrants, their social remittances, and the power of migration for non-migrants. In all these examples, we can clearly see the roles of aspiration, nostalgia, and memory in (return) migration as yearnings are inscribed on socio-physical spaces.

Built environments can be spaces of social struggle as they are sites for multiple negotiations, manipulations, and expressions of ownership. These are places of inclusion and exclusion, belonging and displacement. The tension between the global and the local is conspicuously visible and viscerally experienced. Not only are the three places described in the interludes—Bolé Airport and certain neighborhoods in Addis Ababa and Washington, DC—visible expressions of Ethiopian migration, they also convey the dynamism of human mobility. In these narratives, I encapsulate how these spaces enable (non)migrants to mark their place in the world. In all of these places, we can see the contradictory pull of "home" for the migrant and the "global" for both non-migrants and returnees. The meaning of place and identity in migration is an important aspect of our understanding.[8] Through these physical spaces and practices, we can demonstrate the paradox that while migration seemingly dilutes territory, it highlights the importance of geography. In other words, territory matters in contradictory ways. It enables migrants and non-migrants alike to create a "here" based on an imagined or idealized "there."

Suggestions for Future Research

The limitations of this study that I identify in the Introduction double as opportunities for future research. If governments and organizations such as the International Organization for Migration (IOM) can agree on a unified definition of return and repeat migration and start to systematically gather statistical data on these important phenomena, it would significantly advance our understanding and help us devise better policies.

I also hope that this discussion offers an important starting point for future researchers to more deeply explore migra-emotions in a variety of geographies and levels of privilege. For instance, future researchers can explore how migra-emotions affect less privileged migrants, second-generation migrants, and South–South migration. Future researchers could thus expand on potential regional differences in the patterns of return and repeat migration. Moreover, future researchers can explore a 360-degree view of migration from the perspective of less privileged, undocumented, and forced migrants (e.g., refugees). I suspect that other types of migrants will encounter different barriers and enabling factors within the socio-ecology of migration. Nonetheless, we cannot assume that migration is a one-way street even for less privileged migrants.

In this research, I highlighted the difference between Ethiopian return migrants from the Global North (the subjects of this study) and those from the Arabian Peninsula or South Africa. The latter are generally assumed to be of lower socioeconomic standing and thus are accorded less acceptance in the homeland. Moreover, as it is predominantly women who migrate to Gulf States, it would be pertinent to examine the gendered reception they experience upon return. Similarly, future research should examine the particularities of return and repeat migration among countries of similar socioeconomic standing, or South–South migration, an area of growing interest to researchers.[9] The Ethiopian case study can thus easily be compared and contrasted with other contexts (e.g., other African nations or regions). Moreover, the concept of migra-emotions is not exclusive to Ethiopian (non)migrants; it can be adapted to a number of contexts and scenarios. Finally, we have to acknowledge the contributing factors of different technologies that keep us connected in real time across borders and vast geographic spaces (time-space compression) and allow us to physically move at reasonable cost (time-cost compression). While the field research for this book ended in the prepandemic era, the COVID-19 pandemic has shown us possibilities of remote work at unprecedented levels. Does such work have the potential to engender further return? Can we potentially anticipate increasing counterstream mobilities, similar to the ones discussed in this book, as a result? In other words, how does technology influence migration movements?

All in all, this research opens up a plethora of possible inquiries for future researchers. It goes beyond geographic specificity to examine how experiences of migration are affected by migra-emotions and the socioeconomic positioning of countries of origin and destination.

Appendix

Methodological Overview

This methodological appendix provides an in-depth look at the research design and methodology of the project. I provide detailed demographic information about the non-migrants, returnees, and repeat migrants interviewed for this study. I lay out my recruitment and sampling method, as well as my interviewing technique, which emphasized gaining trust and building relationships. I then describe my ethnographic immersion in the field as a participant observant and discuss my autoethnographic approach. Last, I expand on my positionality as an insider-outsider before ending on a summary of adopting emotions as an analytical lens.

INTERVIEWS

This study draws from a total of ninety-four interviews with the following breakdown: sixty-two returnees, sixteen non-migrant kin, and sixteen repeat migrants. The largest group of respondents consisted of returnees with sixty-two individuals, twenty-seven women, and thirty-five men. Their ages ranged from twenty-two to seventy-seven years old, with the average age of forty-one years old. The majority of respondents were in their thirties (twenty-four respondents), followed by those in their twenties (twelve respondents), and forties (eleven respondents). Twenty-four were single, thirty-two were married, and five were divorced, although a number of the married folks were separated and some of the single folks were cohabitating with long-term partners. Respondents had between zero and seven children, with the average returnee having one to two children. The average year of return was 2010, ranging from 1998 as the earliest and 2018 as the latest. The average returnee spent about fifteen years abroad, with the shortest at five years and the longest at thirty-five years. The average returnee had been back in Ethiopia for an average of five years, ranging from the shortest period of one year to the longest of sixteen years. Most of the returnees (thirty-three of sixty-two) in my sample formerly lived in North America (twenty-eight in the United States and five in Canada); fewer (twenty-five) lived in different parts of Europe (seven in Britain, six in Sweden, four in Germany, three in France, three in Norway, and two in the Netherlands), and an even smaller number resided in either Australia (two) or Israel (two). For most, the country of citizenship matched the country of former residence, although some (eighteen) kept their Ethiopian citizenship and maintained a residence permit in the former host country. The average returnee was highly educated, holding at least a bachelor's degree. Seven held terminal degrees (MDs and Ph.D.s), fourteen held master's degrees, twenty-three held bachelor's degrees, nine held associate's degrees, eight had a high school degree, and one respondent only had elementary school education. Returnees exhibited a wide range of occupations and careers.

There were sixteen non-migrants, with six women and ten men, ranging in age from nineteen to sixty-eight years old, with an average age of thirty-eight years old. Average non-migrants had some level of college education and were employed in various fields, including the private sector (e.g., business owners) and nongovernmental organizations, or were outside of the labor force (e.g., students, homemakers). There were also sixteen repeat migrants, with nine women and seven men, ranging in age from twenty-three to eighty-four years old, with an average age of forty-seven. The repeat migrants had lived in their home country of Ethiopia as returnees for an average of five and a half years, ranging from two to twelve years, before emigrating once again. All returned back to their previous host country, the United States. The average repeat migrant was highly educated and had at least a bachelor's degree, with four respondents holding either a master's degree or a Ph.D. They were either outside of the labor force (e.g., student or retired) or employed in a variety of fields, including business, real estate, art, and design.

I employed different recruitment methods for the three groups of respondents and used multiple entry points. For the returnee group, respondents were recruited through a network of personal contacts and snowball sampling. As there was no central returnee organization or government database to draw from, I relied on my personal connections among returnees in Ethiopia to recruit an initial set of participants. While interviewing these respondents, I solicited further introductions and employed a nonprobability snowball sampling method to expand my sources of potential respondents. Word-of-mouth referrals are an effective means of recruitment as personal connections are an important feature of research in Ethiopian communities.

Once I started interviewing returnees, the recruitment of non-migrants was relatively simple because the non-migrants were directly related to returnees, as either family members or close friends. They were not necessarily a sample of convenience, but their direct acquaintance with migrants and returnees made them an interesting group with an informed perspective. First, although they did not have personal migration experiences, they were intimately familiar with the migration experiences of close kin, and they were better informed about the pros and cons of migration. Second, most had a more realistic chance of migrating compared to the average Ethiopian, both because of their social status (relatively wealthy) and skill or educational level and also because of their potential for sponsorship by family members under family reunification programs in the Global North. They either embraced or rejected this opportunity depending on personal preferences and circumstances. Thus, they were a select group who could offer information about non-migrants' unique views on migration.

The recruitment of repeat migrants proved to be more challenging than the other two groups. Some of the repeat migrants were initially interviewed for this project as returnees but eventually relocated back to the United States for a number of reasons and therefore were interviewed a second time and reclassified as repeat migrants. Outside of this subset, I relied on word-of-mouth advertising among my many contacts within the Ethiopian diaspora community in the United States. I also sought referrals from returnees who had spoken about family members or friends who subsequently engaged in repeat migration. Identifying, contacting, and recruiting non-migrants and returnees was relatively straightforward, but repeat migrants proved to be more elusive, harder to reach, and more difficult to convince to take part in the study. As noted in Chapter 5, even after I secured referrals and the potential respondents agreed to talk to me, they either canceled or delayed our appointments and were not very forthcoming about their experiences. Although I would have much preferred a more direct turndown, I interpreted this approach of repeated postponements, last-minute cancellations, no-shows, and ghosting as indirect refusal. Nonetheless, after a number of false starts, I was able to recruit a robust number of sixteen respondents with different experiences of repeat migration.

Although for the most part my study subjects were educated and understood the value of scientific research, there was more emphasis on the relationship with me as a researcher than on the research itself. Relationship building was a major aspect of my interaction with respondents, from the initial recruitment to the follow-up years later. I worked to build a good rapport with my respondents to gain their trust. As I discuss in more detail in the next section, my social location as an insider-outsider held significant currency in my exchanges with respondents. Incidentally, more than a handful of respondents explained that it was therapeutic to talk at length about their migration experiences. I therefore played the unintended role of confessor or psychologist for some of them.

I greatly benefited from a number of mediators who facilitated introductions, opened their social networks, lessened respondents' potential misgivings about the research, and created a conducive space for my probing questions. In an environment deemed politically charged, I had to gain the trust of the respondents and abate their suspicions to gather data. Some respondents felt they were dealing with politically sensitive subjects, which rendered them suspicious of the research projects and by extension the researcher.

As relationships were the major currency for recruitment, establishing networks became key. Potential respondents were generally willing to talk to me if a close friend or family member referred me to them. One respondent even introduced me as his niece when he referred me to one of his colleagues to be interviewed. He explained that because of their busy schedules and general misgivings about interviews, some of the high-powered businesspeople he would introduce me to would be reluctant if not outright unwilling to talk to me. As a result, he suggested a fictive kin relationship to open doors and allow me access.

To ensure that I captured a wide range of experiences, I made an effort to recruit a diverse group of non-migrants, returnees, and repeat migrants who varied along different axes of identity, such as gender, ethnicity, class, and age. Since the respondents were relatively well off, no compensation was provided to any of the participants. Offering any type of monetary compensation to this group might have been construed as offensive given their high economic resources and cultural contexts.

Addis Ababa, the capital of Ethiopia, was the return destination for most returnees.[1] Just like any other major metropolitan area, Addis Ababa does not constitute a cohesive urban space but is highly segmented by social class. Return migrants tended to socialize with others in similar socioeconomic situations. In Addis Ababa, I conducted the interviews with returnees and non-migrants in people's homes or offices (private spaces) and in cafés and restaurants (public spaces), generally letting the respondents pick a place that was convenient for them. While the returnees and their non-migrant kin were residents of Addis Ababa, Ethiopia, all of the repeat migrants were residing full-time in the

United States at the time of the interview. My interviews with repeat migrants in the United States took place mostly over the phone or in video conferences as there was a significant geographical spread. Only about one-third of the interviews with repeat migrants took place face-to-face, mostly in cafés around the Washington, DC, area, including one of the sites discussed in Chapter 5, Kaldis Social House. Almost all the face-to-face interactions took place over food or copious amounts of coffee.[2]

Interviews ranged from forty-five minutes to four hours in length, with the average interview lasting about an hour and a half. Although I had an interview protocol guideline and formatted questionnaire, the interviews were loosely structured, allowing the respondents to guide the conversation and raise topics and questions they deemed salient. Unlike rigidly structured survey questionnaires, semistructured interviews allow the flexibility to shape each interaction or subsequent question on the basis of previous answers.[3] The interviews included mostly open-ended questions, although some closed-ended questions were used to gather biographic data such as ages and dates of migration and return. When topics included in my questionnaire did not come up during the conversations organically, I asked pointed questions and probed when necessary. I also prepared follow-up and contingency questions, as well as probes to obtain an elaboration on previous answers.

The interviews covered a range of topics, from the respondents' own experiences to their general views on migration, and more specifically Ethiopian migration. All the respondents were queried on their general views on migration (and the desirability of the practice), the Ethiopian migration experience and the ensuing global diaspora, cultural understandings of migration, the comparison between documented and undocumented migration, and the cost-benefit analysis of migration, among other topics. With the exception of non-migrants, the interviews mapped out the migration life histories of the respondents, starting with their premigration lives (place of birth, upbringing, socioeconomic status), their experiences around initial migration (age of migration, reasons, contexts, reception in host country, process of integration, etc.), motivations and experiences around return, and for repeat migrants, motivations and experiences around the second or subsequent migration. I used this information to map out a life history timeline that included a record of the different migration sequences, including age of initial migration, age of return, and age of repeat migration as appropriate.

The interviews took place in Amharic and English in equal numbers.[4] My knowledge of the Amharic and English languages and ability to switch back and forth with ease became a major cornerstone of the data collection. Language is more than spoken words; it reflects a way of understanding, a way of seeing, and a way of recalling particular moments. There is a knowledge base that comes embedded in linguistic interactions. The choice of language for polyglots (multilingual individuals) reveals embedded cultural connections and subtle nuances of meaning that provide insight into the lives and meaning making of the speakers. Among my interviewees, there was a generational difference in the language of choice: while the older generation (aged forty-six and above) generally chose to speak entirely in Amharic, the younger respondents (aged forty-five and younger) either opted to be interviewed entirely in English or interjected English regularly while conversing in Amharic. The thematic coding and memos were all written in English. In the final reporting of the data, if any portion of the original interviews was conducted in Amharic, I translated it into English.

The interviews were partially audio-recorded when the respondent granted their accord. However, about half of the respondents preferred that I did not record the interviews. For the most part, older men declined the recording, while women and younger respondents (aged thirty-five or younger) agreed. As only half of the interviews were recorded, I opted not to transcribe the interviews that were, for two reasons. First, I did not want to give more weight or emphasis to the recorded interviews than to the ones for which I only had handwritten notes. Second, since the majority of the interviews switched between English and Amharic, settling on a language of transcription proved to be impractical. For consistency purposes, I therefore relied on the copious field notes I took during and after the interviews, recording the interviewees' migration patterns, motivations, and experiences, paying attention to respondents' emotional reactions. For the recorded interviews, I additionally replayed the recordings during the analysis so I could pay particular attention not just to the respondents' words but also to their intonations, pauses, laughter, and voice fluctuations.

In retrospective interviews, it is important to acknowledge that memory can be highly selective and can introduce biases or revisionist histories. There are layers of distance between the respondents and their migration experiences or memories of a place. Respondents also negotiate their past and present identities to create a meaningful narrative. As people interpret the past through the present, respondents can make certain claims, such as "I always intended to return," even though they might not have had those thoughts during the entirety of their migration journey. It is important to acknowledge that thoughts, emotions, and perceptions are not linear but rather subjective, ever evolving, shifting, constantly interpreted and reinterpreted. While I acknowledge the existence of such challenges, I took respondents at their word and recorded their thoughts, emotions, and other claims as stated to me at the time of the interview.

ETHNOGRAPHY

In addition to the interviews, I carried out a total of twenty months of ethnographic participant observation in Addis Ababa, Ethiopia, between 2011 and 2019. While the ethnography and overall data collection was spread out over the course of almost a decade, my longest continuous stay in the field was from October 2014 to July 2015, for a contiguous ten months of immersion in the field. I carried out the bulk of the first round of data collection with returnees during this period. Since 2015, I spent subsequent summers following up with respondents I had connected with during earlier trips and making new connections.

As part of the ethnography, I selected a few returnees to shadow in their everyday lives and recorded their daily interactions. Ethnographic observations allow for the study of returnees in their natural habitat and can illuminate their practices, social relationships, social groups, and overall lifestyles. Through careful ethnography, everyday personal experiences of migration can reveal a great deal about larger dynamics. I therefore spent time with these individuals in their places of work, at home with their families, and in social outings in various parts of the city. I cooked and ate with them, met their families and acquaintances, played with their children, dropped off and picked up their children from school, navigated the city with them to see Addis through their eyes, served in community service projects, participated in their events, toured their projects (whether real estate, industry, or nonprofit), frequented their businesses, and attended church with them. In other words, I was immersed in every aspect of their worlds. These types of ethnographic activities enabled me to experience firsthand the lives of Ethiopian returnees. These ethnographic observations elucidate interpersonal interactions with family members, coworkers, and non-migrants in general. Therefore, the participant observation or ethnography provided me with an accurate and detailed picture of the everyday lives of returnees. Some of my observations from the ethnography are rendered in the interludes. Drawing from the rich ethnographic data I have compiled over the years and using thick descriptions, I aim to tell a vibrant story of the migration as inscribed in space and place. In other words, the interludes help me showcase in a unique way my own emotional reading of different spaces within the socio-ecology of migration. I therefore emphasize how I experienced the different transient migrant spaces while incorporating the book's overall conceptual framework throughout.

RESEARCHER POSITIONALITY

As knowledge is socially constructed, it is important that I explicate my social position and identity vis-à-vis the research. The recognition of the embodied self and positionality with reference to the study subject helps to elucidate representation and point out potential bias. Thus, reflexivity, a common approach in qualitative research, serves to position the researcher within her own set of lived experiences.[5] In fact, "[as] reflexivity is a researcher's conscious and deliberate effort to be attuned to one's own reactions to respondents and to the way in which the research account is constructed, it helps identify and explicate potential or actual effect of personal, contextual, and circumstantial aspects on the process and findings of the study and maintain their awareness of themselves as part of the world they study."[6] Reflexivity is therefore more than "navel gazing"; it is "self-critical sympathetic introspection and the self-conscious analytical scrutiny of the self as researcher. Indeed, reflexivity is critical to the conduct of fieldwork; it induces self-discovery and can lead to insights and new hypotheses about the research questions."[7]

I was born and spent the first fifteen years of my life in the Ethiopian capital city, Addis Ababa. My family of four was uprooted to the United States in the fall of 1997 because my father was relocated for work.[8] This was a big move for our family as we had never before lived away from our home in Addis Ababa. On a dewy October morning, our closest friends and family gathered at Bolé International Airport to see us off, with the genuine apprehension that we might never see one another again.[9] We transformed the parking lot of the airport into a *lekso bet*, or a house of mourning. My aunts openly wailed "May God protect you" as they ushered us into the unknown, while my uncles stoically wiped away their silent tears. When my family left Ethiopia for the United States, it was rare for people to return for a visit, let alone to resettle. My extended family's fear that they would never see us again was therefore not unfounded.[10]

Fast-forward eleven years later to 2008; upon my father's retirement, my parents packed their belongings once more and trekked across the Atlantic back to the African continent.[11] My parents' relocation was once again prompted by my father's work; this time, he was retiring after a total of twenty-seven years of service to the United Nations. My parents returned to Ethiopia with the objective of my mother opening up a small business, a dream she had been harboring for years, while my father enjoyed his retirement. When I visited my parents in Addis Ababa after their return, they would introduce me to scores of other return migrants of different age groups and backgrounds. Between 1997, when my family left, and 2008, when my parents returned to Ethiopia (while my brother and I settled in the United States), it had increasingly become more common for Ethiopians to permanently resettle in Ethiopia.[12] The changing Ethiopian migration landscape of not only exit but also return migration inspired this research. Ethiopia was no longer just a migrant-sending nation; it was ushering in a new historical period where members of its diaspora were returning to resettle in noteworthy ways.

My own biography highlights my and my family's entanglement with migration. The above synopsis sketches the genesis of my interest in African migration and more specifically return and repeat migration. This research was not impersonal for me, nor did I approach it with clinical detachment. Instead, my family's experience with (return) migration highly influenced my perspective. My proximity to the topic was an asset rather than a disadvantage as it opened numerous doors for me. Respondents were much more responsive when they found out that members of my own family have engaged in (return) migration. For the most part, my respondents considered me an insider since I was a first-generation Ethiopian immigrant currently residing in the United States. At the same time, I was an outsider as a nonreturnee carrying out academic research on this important topic. Therefore, my insider-outsider status helped me gain important insight into the lives and motivations of Ethiopian returnees. I was keenly aware of the situational nature and malleability of identity. My identity opened some doors but also closed others. I therefore had to pay close attention to the ways my identity mattered to the work while not letting it distract me from my research questions.

It is widely understood that social hierarchies are omnipresent and deeply rooted in culture. My research subjects made certain assumptions about my (upper-middle) class background based on my educational level, my area of residence, and the social groups I frequented while in Addis Ababa. Being in a similar class position to my study subjects facilitated some of our interactions. My (perceived) class background allowed me access to certain spaces (such as expensive resorts) that most of my respondents frequented. I was also able to talk to my respondents intelligibly about places, activities, and social groups specific to the upper classes. There was also a gendered aspect to the class trappings as the women in my sample generally assumed that I would be interested in different types of spa treatments. I received numerous recommendations for different spas to visit and the types of treatments I should receive. They assumed first that I would be interested in this specific type of gendered pampering and second that I could afford the prices at the high-end resorts and spas. Their assumption was not necessarily erroneous, and it allowed me to identify the types of places they frequented and the lifestyles they led upon return. Gendered activities came into conversation most often when I was interviewing or shadowing women respondents. The most common reference was household work. The majority of the women in my sample compared the amount of time they spent doing the cooking and cleaning in the host country (North America or Europe) with the benefits of having affordable household help in Ethiopia after their return. They would draw me into solidarity with them by pointing out that they had to shoulder most of the household work in the host nation, while it could be easily outsourced in Ethiopia. They identified household help as a necessary time saver in Ethiopia, while (for most) it would have been an unheard-of luxury while in the host nation. They also tried to entice me to return by teasing about the potential of never again having to do household chores. My status as an Ethiopian migrant woman enabled me to be viewed as similar to my study respondents and facilitated my access to them.

While being an insider researcher carries such significant advantages, such as cultural familiarity, linguistic competency, in-depth understanding, ease of access, and sensitivity about representation, the drawbacks, such as community assumptions and expectations in regard to the researcher, are not negligible.[13] As insiders, some scholars refer to their research as *homework* rather than *fieldwork* as they are studying their home societies or cultures.[14] This interesting word play highlights an important binary divide between insider and outsider perspectives in research. In my case, although I am originally from Ethiopia and identify strongly with my country of origin, I have lived most of my life in the United States rather than in my home country. I maintain my connection to my homeland through regular visits, family, research, and different virtual engagements, but a certain level of disconnect and alienation comes with living as a migrant in a different country. I therefore identify as what Erin Roberts calls a "transient insider," using a more fluid and malleable conception of insider positionality.[15] Rather than positing insider and outsider positionality as discrete and binary categories, it is more useful to conceptualize them on a continuum. It was not always easy for me to identify when I was benefiting from my insider status or when my outsider positionality was affecting my perspective.

Some of my respondents assumed that I was using my research to map out the field, prepping the ground for my own eventual return migration. They wondered whether I would be joining their ranks soon enough. Some offered their assistance, while others warned me about the dangers of return. All assumed that I had a personal stake in the research. My respondents often asked me, "Are you planning on returning back too?" This repeated question resonated with me for the duration of my fieldwork and beyond. When I first started this research project, although I was curious, I had not seriously considered relocation. However, as I stayed longer in the field, I was extremely tempted by the lure of the life of a returnee. During the longest contiguous fieldwork period of ten months, I lived the life of a returnee, doing something akin to living like an expat in my own country of birth. It was a life of food, family, and luxury. I was honestly tempted to resettle. Perhaps this is an example of overidentification with research subjects, what used to be termed, rather pejoratively, "going native."[16] This occurs when the researcher identifies very highly with research subjects, their interests, and their viewpoints and loses scientific detachment. "Going native" has often been seen in a negative light where the white civilized researcher abandons all logic and joins those of the researched "other." While I call out the racist undertones of the concept of "going native," I am hyperaware of my strong identification with my respondents.[17]

While obstacles in research are always context dependent, they can also offer insight into the research topic and opportunities to expand the research focus. My awareness of my strong identification with research subjects forced me to take deliberate steps to minimize the pitfalls of researcher bias. I strongly adhered to established practices for data collection and analysis. I included people with different points of view from one another rather than relying on similar voices. I spent time away from the research site and returned periodically to reassess respondents' changes in views or perspectives. In the same vein, I received feedback from participants in subsequent visits. As an additional measure, I debated my findings with individuals who were critical of the project of return migration. Although I realize that researcher bias might not be fully overcome, I have taken the necessary steps to minimize its effects.

AUTOETHNOGRAPHY: TURNING THE LENS INWARD

Social science research has historically been presented from a seemingly objective, detached, white male perspective. With the inclusion of diverse perspectives from women and people of color in academia, there has been a significant and justified pushback against this practice since at least the 1990s. We now recognize that research is an embodied practice, and our individual lived experiences and intersectional identities influence our research questions, data collection, analysis, and interpretation of the data.

I recognize the importance of my own lived experience in elucidating larger narratives. I have accordingly discussed how personal this research has been to me since its inception. However, without including the autoethnography, I would only be telling half the story. As a migrant myself moving back and forth between the different spaces I describe in the book, I forefront my personal reflections and what these places evoke in me while demonstrating the liminality of the migration experience as an ongoing fluid continuum rather than a single point in time. In my autoethnographic writing, I reflexively explore my personal experiences around migration as a way of gaining wider sociopolitical and cultural understanding. Self-observation allows me to connect the personal to the sociocultural. My experiential point of view is an opportunity to uniquely render the social world under investigation and my own emotional state.[18] I interrogate my own experiences as a way of understanding the social world of migrants who crisscross multiple borders, both literal and figurative, and analyze what my experiences reveal about larger social structures and processes.

Autoethnography is an approach to present and systematically analyze unique cultural experiences, including that of migration.[19] As a method, autoethnography pushes back against traditional academic and epistemological boundaries and the way knowledge production has been undertaken, as a level of reflexivity and self-reflection are core components of the methodology. Located within the interpretive tradition, autoethnography is not detached; it is a critical interrogation of social life through one's personal experiences. Autoethnography is about critical reflection on personal experiences within the research topic being investigated. Autoethnography is a "genre of writing and research that displays multiple layers of consciousness," going beyond a personal report to provide an important sociocultural analysis.[20]

Adopting an autoethnographic approach in research carries a number of advantages, such as creating empathy with the research participants and providing unparalleled insight into sociocultural contexts through personal experiences. Introspection on our personal lives and experiences provides rich and personal insight into the phenomenon under study. Laurel Richardson suggests that autoethnography should be considered both a science and an art and proposes five criteria for evaluation: substantive contribution, aesthetic merit, reflexivity, the impact the narrative has on the reader, and the extent to which the narrative expresses a reality.[21] From the autoethnography, I can address a number of theoretical areas of interest, such as migration policy regimes, the social worlds of airports (border control), and the (re-)creation of community across geographies.

No method is without its limitations, however, and autoethnography is no exception.[22] The most common criticism leveled against this method is that it is introspective and self-involved and therefore is not a scientific or valuable research method. Accordingly, autoethnographers have often been accused of being too close to the phenomenon under investigation, with insufficient distance to present a detached objective reality. At the extreme, autoethnographers are sometimes seen as narcissistic navel gazers who do not make any real contribution to scientific knowledge. However, as discussed earlier, researchers have debunked the idea of any detached objective truth in research.

For me, the most challenging aspect of autoethnography is that it is deeply personal, requiring honesty and, at times, uncomfortable self-disclosure. It is not only veracity around facts but also radical sincerity, genuine forthrightness, and self-reflection. The practice of autoethnography is an exercise in vulnerability, particularly when it concerns the researcher's innermost feelings and personal thoughts. As a very private person with virtually no social media presence, I do not find it easy to disclose private details of my life in such a public format. However, in this book I provide descriptions of periods of my life that are sensitive, emotional, and sometimes still raw despite the passing of time. While the blurring of the lines between an academic project and my life can result in some justifiable anxiety, understanding the importance of telling a story larger than myself using my experiences as a starting point has helped me overcome this fear.

EMOTIONS AS A LENS

We live emotionally yet surgically excise emotion from academic spheres. Although there is still a long way to go, the works of feminist, gender, and more broadly humanities scholars are helping emotions take up their rightful place in academic research. We often contrast emotion and intellect as if they are on the opposite sides of a spectrum. However, in this work, I argue that emotion is one lens through which we experience and understand our world. Emotions and intellect work in tandem, complementing rather than opposing each other. I chose to focus on emotions as a visceral, intuitive aspect of human consciousness and cognition. When I started the research for this book, I began by looking at how individuals' intersectional identities affected their migration decisions and experiences. I theorized diverging experiences based on the migrant's gender, class, and ethno-racial identification. Although it was an interesting angle, as my research unfolded, the reality I uncovered was far more complex and was mitigated through the migrants' emotional lives. I became intrigued by the complex role feelings and emotions played in how migrants made decisions and experienced their lives. I did not initially ask specific questions about emotions, but respondents nonetheless described them in depth. My respondents also used a lot of emotional language to explain their decision-making processes.[23]

When I was in the field, I systematically recorded my respondents' emotions and emotional responses, but this did not fully register until years down the line. I did not deem emotions important enough to be a (central) focus, considering them too fluffy, not academic enough. When I coded the data, I noticed that the phrase "I feel" or some variation of it occurred more than any other explanatory variable. I initially experienced a significant amount of internal resistance to telling an emotional story of Ethiopian migrants. However, the longer I stayed with these stories—the more I presented this material, the more I discussed it with colleagues, the more I wrote and rewrote these narratives using different framing—the more the emotional lens emerged as the most appropriate. The emotional lives of respondents ended up being the focus of this book.[24]

There is no emotion metric that can accurately measure and assess people's emotions. Therefore, as a researcher, I have to rely on my respondents' self-perceived and reported emotions. In addition, I describe my own internal emotional cognizance as it relates to migration and this research in particular. Emotions therefore become a lens through which we can craft a better understanding of the process of doing research. It is also important to acknowledge the emotional resources required of ethnographers, particularly autoethnographers. As mentioned earlier, I offered an attentive listener to my respondents, who did not often have extended periods to discuss and reflect on their own migration experiences. My respondents jokingly said that I alternatively playing the role of psychologist or confessor. I was not fully aware of the emotional labor I was engaging in while in the field.[25]

DATA ANALYSIS

For my analysis, I allowed the data to guide me to generate theory. In practicality, I did not enter my field of research with preconceived notions about the outcomes. I therefore employed grounded theory, an inductive research methodology that allows the generation of theory rooted in observation and systematic research.[26] Grounded theory is particularly suited to situations where the analysis starts with the lived realities of the respondents. Grounded theory "tradition starts with and develops analyses from the point of view of the experiencing person.... Such studies aim to capture the worlds of people by describing their situations, thoughts, feelings, and actions and by relying on portraying the research participants' lives and voices. Their concerns shape the direction and form of the research. The researcher seeks to learn how they construct their experience through their actions, intentions, beliefs, and feelings."[27] Therefore, grounded theory goes beyond the accurate description of the phenomenon at hand and enables the researcher to generate concepts to capture the concerns and lived realities of the respondents.

Systematic coding is the key to achieving validity and reliability. Therefore, as part of my data analysis, I carried out different levels of coding, starting with open coding (the initial classification of concepts). On the basis of a close reading of the interview and ethnographic data, I generated a list of broad themes, which I grouped in relation to migra-emotions and the socio-ecology of migration. I systematically searched for (and color-coded) words and phrases that touched on the three main stages of migration—immobility, return and repeat migration. I then broke the broad themes down into smaller categories and used a detailed coding schema. I continued to systematically write field notes and memos during the coding process, recording both my empirical observations and my interpretations of events so I could more effectively understand and interpret migra-emotions in the socio-ecology of migration.

TIMELINE

I did not intentionally set out to do a longitudinal study; however, my research questions and the many changes in the field compelled me to return to the field multiple times over the span of almost a decade. This project started with a singular focus on returnees, with some informal conversations and interest in non-migrants and repeat migrants. However, I quickly realized that to fully understand the experiences of returnees, I would have to provide a more encompassing, 360-degree view of migration, starting with non-migrants and ending with repeat migrants. I interviewed some respondents two or three times over the course of my study, a period of years, but most were interviewed only once. Between an interview carried out in 2011 (when the political situation was relatively calm) and 2016 (when the ethnic upheavals were heightened), respondents' perspectives may have undoubtedly shifted. Although this variability can be interpreted as a drawback, the data gathered over a longer period of time (and over the course of fluctuating political and economic times) can have more validity.[28] My own perspective, emotional state, and family circumstances have also greatly evolved during this longitudinal study.

Unsurprisingly, the situation in Ethiopia has not remained constant since the beginning of my first venture into the field in 2011. In the last decade, Ethiopia has experienced significant ebbs and flows in its economy and sociopolitical landscape.[29] For instance, in 2015, Ethiopia experienced a devastating famine in parts of the country. In the summer of 2016, the underlying political tension erupted in both violent and nonviolent mass demonstrations across the country, which the government effectively suppressed. Several states of emergency were declared in 2016, 2017, and 2018, which saw the rise of a new head of state. After the 2012 unexpected death of Prime Minister Meles Zenawi, a figure who loomed large over post–Cold War Ethiopian politics and ruled the country in different capacities since 1991, he was replaced by Prime Minister Hailemariam Desalegn. Hailemariam, who was seen as a puppet ruler by many, unexpectedly quit on February 15, 2018, and was replaced by Dr. Abiy Ahmed on April 2, 2018. Oromo by birth, and widely popular at least at the beginning of his rule, the new prime minister was expected to unify the country like no other statesperson before him. As part of the peaceful transition of power, in his acceptance speech, Abiy Ahmed called on his fellow

Ethiopians in the diaspora to return to Ethiopia and contribute to its sociopolitical and economic development.

Since the palpable euphoria around his inauguration, Prime Minister Abiy Ahmed has become a divisive political character. On the one hand, he won the Nobel Peace Prize in 2019 for ending Ethiopia's long-standing war with Eritrea within weeks of taking office. His administration has worked diligently on the Green Legacy Initiative, making major infrastructural changes across the country, including the rapid changes in Addis discussed in Interlude 3. On the other hand, he continues to encounter significant opposition, and many hold him responsible for the civil conflict in Tigray that raged between 2020 and 2022, resulting in a significant loss of lives on all sides. Therefore, the economic and sociopolitical situation in Ethiopia is ever changing and marked with uncertainty. This background of constant economic, social, and political change in the homeland undoubtedly shaped my respondents' experiences, perceptions, and analysis of immobility, return, and repeat migration. The migration life histories of the respondents cannot be extracted from the public context that led to their initial migration, return, and eventual repeat migration. The home context of Ethiopia and the context of the host country therefore provide the necessary background information to these various migration experiences. At the time of publication, the political situation is still fluid. Regardless, even if the present-day situation in Ethiopia is not exactly the same as what initially motivated returnees in this study to embark on their return journey, the lessons we can draw from their experiences transcend the particularities of the case study.

I concluded all the data collection in 2019, a notable date because some major shifts happened globally and specifically in Ethiopia that significantly altered the fabric of society—namely, the COVID-19 pandemic and conflict in the northern region of Ethiopia. While I have not officially collected data in the last couple of years, I have gone back periodically (after some of the COVID-19 pandemic travel restrictions were lifted and as safety and security have permitted) for a couple of months to help me assess the changes within society, reconnect with some of my previous respondents, and immerse myself once again in the community. I remain connected to the respondents whose stories are recounted in this book, and I owe them a profound debt of gratitude.

TABLE A.1. NON-MIGRANT DEMOGRAPHIC DATA

	Pseudonym	Gender	Age	Group	Education	Occupation
1	Negussu	M	64	Indignant patriot	MA, engineering	Engineer, business owner
2	Etey Etagu	F	68	Indignant patriot	Some high school	Widowed homemaker
3	Zemenaye	F	38	Indignant patriot	MA, social science	NGO worker
4	Yosef	M	55	Indignant patriot	Some college, law	Business owner
5	Nega	M	26	Hopeful	Some college	Family business
6	Henock	M	31	Hopeful	BA, history	NGO worker
7	Micky	M	19	Hopeful	Some college	Student
8	Simon	M	28	Hopeful	Some college	Family business
9	Adonias	M	22	Hopeful	Some college	Student
10	Lilly	F	23	Hopeful	AA, teaching	Teacher
11	Aida	F	26	Hopeful	BA, nursing	Nurse
12	Teferi	M	43	Ambivalent	BA, political science	Government employee
13	Dereje	M	53	Ambivalent	BA, languages	School director
14	Haile	M	37	Ambivalent	High school	Business owner
15	Marda	F	29	Ambivalent	BA, art	Artist
16	Tsehai	F	41	Ambivalent	MA, management	Private sector

TABLE A.2. RETURNEE DEMOGRAPHIC DATA

	Pseudonym	Gender	Age	Status (marital)	No. of children	Former country of residence in the Global North	Year of return	Years abroad	Years since return at the time of interview	Highest level of education
1	Elizabeth	F	38	Single	0	Australia	2016	10	3	BA
2	Ewenet	F	33	Married	2	Australia	2018	7	1	BA
3	Konjit	F	42	Single	0	Britain	2008	6.5	7	BA
4	Desta	M	41	Married	3	Britain	2002	13	13	BA
5	Lenssa	F	22	Single	0	Britain	2013	18	2	BA
6	Dawit	M	27	Single	0	Britain	2013	6	3	BA
7	Fatima	F	32	Married	1	Britain	2013	13	2	MBA
8	Mohammed	M	36	Married	1	Britain	2013	9	2	MBA
9	Idris	M	56	Married	5	Britain	2016	22	2	MD
10	Demekech	F	61	Married	3	Canada	2007	30	7	BA
11	Ezana	M	35	Single	1	Canada	1998	11	5	BA
12	Netsanet	F	27	Single	0	Canada	2013	26	2	BA
13	Daniel	M	26	Single	1	Canada	2012	9	4	BA
14	Tekle	M	42	Married	2	Canada	2015	13	6	Ph.D.
15	Abigail	F	32	Married	1	France	2011	11	4	MA
16	Noah	M	33	Single	0	France	2013	14	2	MA
17	Musse	M	28	Single	0	France	2013	7	2	MA
18	Gebre Kristos	M	68	Married	3	Germany	2009	32	7	MA
19	Lydia	F	30	Married	0	Germany	2010	21	5	BA
20	Yonas	M	31	Single	0	Germany	2014	11	1	AA
21	Sisay	M	52	Married	3	Germany	2000	14	15	Ph.D.
22	Wubit	F	27	Single	0	Israel	2014	18	1	BA
23	Lemlem	F	29	Single	0	Israel	2013	5	2	BA
24	Biruk	M	47	Divorced	3	Netherlands	2002	18	2	AA

(*continued*)

TABLE A.2. RETURNEE DEMOGRAPHIC DATA (continued)

	Pseudonym	Gender	Age	Status (marital)	No. of children	Former country of residence in the Global North	Year of return	Years abroad	Years since return at the time of interview	Highest level of education
25	Aster	F	29	Married	0	Netherlands	2013	22	2	MA
26	Tamerat	M	45	Divorced	2	Norway	2009	7	6	MA
27	Aklilu	M	34	Married	0	Norway	2008	5	7	High school
28	Misir	F	55	Married	4	Norway	2010	15	5	High school
29	Hagos	M	34	Single	1	Sweden	2014	14	1	AA
30	Fikre	M	45	Single	0	Sweden	2009	15	7	AA
31	Almaz	F	33	Married	2	Sweden	2014	6	3	MBA
32	Makeda	F	41	Married	2	Sweden	2004	17	10	High school
33	Zelalem	M	38	Single	0	Sweden	2006	12	9	High school
34	Hiwot	F	27	Single	0	Sweden	2013	22	2	MA
35	Bogale	M	62	Married	2	United States	1998	15	16	High school
36	Mesfin	M	64	Married	3	United States	2007	30	7	MD
37	Gizaw	M	66	Married	2	United States	2008	11	6	BA
38	Nigist	F	62	Married	2	United States	2008	11	6	AA
39	Abebech	F	74	Married	7	United States	2011	7	3	Elementary
40	Kebede	M	77	Married	7	United States	2011	9	3	High school
41	Mebratu	M	71	Married	2	United States	2009	35	5	BA
42	Birhan	F	65	Divorced	3	United States	2010	24	4	AA
43	Adamu	M	43	Divorced	2	United States	2004	18	11	AA
44	Hiyawit	F	38	Single	0	United States	2010	8	4	BA
45	Alemneh	M	47	Married	3	United States	2008	21	8	MD
46	Ahadu	M	42	Single	0	United States	2003	11	11	High school
47	Samrawit	F	37	Single	0	United States	2004	11	8	MA

TABLE A.2. RETURNEE DEMOGRAPHIC DATA (continued)

	Pseudonym	Gender	Age	Status (marital)	No. of children	Former country of residence in the Global North	Year of return	Years abroad	Years since return at the time of interview	Highest level of education
48	Melkamu	M	31	Single	0	United States	2013	10	3	BA
49	Minilik	M	35	Married	2	United States	2013	14	2	BA
50	Caleb	M	46	Single	0	United States	2011	12	4	MD
51	Mahlet	F	37	Married	2	United States	2011	10	4	BA
52	Sammy	M	29	Married	0	United States	2010	19	5	MA
53	Tiruneh	M	29	Single	0	United States	2012	26	3	BA
54	Zechariah	M	32	Married	0	United States	2009	26	6	High school
55	Abtew	M	37	Married	3	United States	2005	27	10	AA
56	Beza	F	32	Married	3	United States	2005	18	10	BA
57	Ashenafi	M	34	Single	0	United States	2013	16	2	MBA
58	Robel	M	33	Married	2	United States	2009	15	6	BA
59	Meskerem	F	39	Married	0	United States	2010	12	5	MA
60	Redeit	F	28	Married	1	United States	2007	7	8	BA
61	Maaza	F	66	Single	0	United States	2007	31	12	Ph.D.
62	Zinash	F	50	Divorced	3	United States	2018	23	1	AA

TABLE A.3. REPEAT MIGRANT DEMOGRAPHIC DATA

	Pseudonym	Gender	Age	No. of years as returnee	Group	Education	Occupation
1	Rihan	F	42	5	Young professionals	MA	Economic development officer
2	Saron	F	29	2.5	Young professionals	BA, some graduate credits	Sales and marketing
3	Zema	F	39	4	Young professionals	MA	Communication PR specialist
4	Hiyaw	M	33	2	Young professionals	Ph.D.	Political scientist
5	Elelta	F	72	4	Retirees	AA	Homemaker
6	Mengesha	M	68	6	Retirees	BA	Retired from private sector
7	Agonafer	M	84	9	Retirees	MA	Retired postal worker
8	Meselu	F	65	6	Retirees	Some high school	Retired retail worker
9	Salem	F	45	5	Disillusioned	BA	Real estate / interior design
10	Nahom	M	42	10	Disillusioned	AA	Art and graphic design
11	Hunde	M	43	2	Disillusioned	BA	Finance specialist
12	Ayana	F	45	8	Disillusioned	BA	Business administration
13	Nafkote	F	37	12	Inadvertents	Some college	Small business owner
14	Birtukan	F	44	7	Inadvertents	BA	Homemaker
15	Nardos	F	23	3	Inadvertents	Some college	Student / retail worker
16	Adil	M	39	4	Inadvertents	BA	Entrepreneur

Notes

INTRODUCTION

1. Throughout this book, I include key phrases uttered by my respondents in the Amharic (Ethiopian) language transliterated in the Roman alphabet. When doing so, I note these phrases in italics, not to exoticize my native language but for ease of understanding. I also immediately provide an English-language translation.

2. All the names have been changed to pseudonyms to protect the identity of the respondents.

3. International Organization for Migration (IOM), *World Migration Report 2020* (IOM, 2020), available at https://publications.iom.int/books/world-migration-report-2020.

4. The IOM broadly defines return as "the act of going back from a country (either transit or destination) to the country of previous transit or origin." IOM, *Glossary on Migration* (IOM, 2019). This definition is too broad and lacks specificity. Various governments, nongovernmental organizations, and researchers define the category of the return migrant differently. Moreover, most nations do not distinguish between a pure, single return and circular migration.

5. Return migration can be undertaken either voluntarily or under compulsion. Forced return can include individuals who have been deported, denied asylum seekers, and so forth, while voluntary return comprises individuals who return to their home country without coercion. In addition, returnees can be (first-generation) individuals who have left the home country and returned to resettle in their own lifetime. Return migration can further include ancestral, diasporic, ethnic, or second- or later-generation return, involving children or descendants of migrants. This study focuses on voluntary, first-generation lifetime returnees only. For a discussion of forced return, see Laura Hammond, *This Place Will Become Home: Refugee Repatriation to Ethiopia* (Cornell University Press, 2004). For a discussion of ancestral return, see Takeyuki Tsuda, ed., *Diasporic Homecomings: Ethnic Return Migration in Comparative Perspective* (Stanford University Press, 2009).

6. I sought out only returnees who relocated back to Ethiopia for a minimum period of one year because they would have had sufficient time to reflect on their experiences and minimize the rosy haze of nostalgia or wishful thinking. Moreover, individuals who returned for less than one year did not qualify for this project as they might have been returning for family visits, short-term stays, or extended vacations.

7. The extended length of stay abroad (five years or more) excludes shorter stays where migrants might not have settled in the host society.

8. I chose to focus on returnees exclusively from the Global North because experiences vary greatly depending on the country or region of settlement.

9. *Gash* is an honorific title for older men.

10. See Stephen Castles and Derya Ozkul, "Circular Migration: Triple Win, or a New Label for Temporary Migration?" in *Global and Asian Perspectives on International Migration*, ed. Graziano Battistella (Springer, 2014), 27–49; Amelie F. Constant, Olga Nottmeyer, and Klaus F. Zimmermann, "The Economics of Circular Migration," in *International Handbook on the Economics of Migration*, ed. Amelie F. Constant and Klaus F. Zimmermann (Edward Elgar, 2013); Kathleen Newland, "Can Migrants, Countries of Origin and Countries of Destination All Win from Circular Migration?" (Global Forum on Migration and Development, Civil Society Day, Belgium, 2007).

11. In some Global North nations, political motivation may drive academic research with a heavy emphasis on processes of integration and perhaps even on ways to stem the flow of migrant populations.

12. Peggy Levitt and B. Nadya Jaworsky, "Transnational Migration Studies: Past Developments and Future Trends ," *Annual Review of Sociology* 33, no. 1 (2007): 129–156.

13. Amanda Wise and Selvaraj Velayutham, "Transnational Affect and Emotion in Migration Research ," *International Journal of Sociology* 47, no. 2 (2017): 116–130.

14. It is beyond the scope of this work to untangle the different components of emotions (bio-neurological versus sociocultural).

15. Sara Ahmed, *The Cultural Politics of Emotion* (Edinburgh University Press, 2004).

16. Ahmed, 119.

17. The field of social psychology as it concerns migration has for the most part been concerned with processes of assimilation, adaptation, or acculturation. This is a limited intervention despite the fact that the field of migration studies can benefit from social psychological insights.

18. Erving Goffman, *The Presentation of Self in Everyday Life* (Doubleday/Anchor Books, 1959).

19. Arlie Hochschild, *The Managed Heart: Commercialization of Human Feeling*, 3rd ed. (University of California Press, 2012).

20. See Paolo Boccagni and Loretta Baldassar, "Emotions on the Move: Mapping the Emergent Field of Emotion and Migration," *Emotion, Space and Society* 16 (2015): 73–80; Anastasia Christou, "Narrating Lives in (E)Motion: Embodiment, Belongingness and Displacement in Diasporic Spaces of Home and Return," *Emotion, Space and Society* 4, no. 4 (2011): 249–257; Maruška Svašek, "On the Move: Emotions and Human Mobility," *Journal of Ethnic and Migration Studies* 36, no. 6 (2010): 865–880.

21. Nira Yuval-Davis, Kalpana Kannabiran, and Ulrike Vieten, eds., *The Situated Politics of Belonging* (Sage, 2006): 1.

22. Aida Ibričević, "Facing Fear and Responding with Courage: Understanding How Fear Constitutes the 'Emotional Citizenship' of Voluntary Returnees to Bosnia and Herzegovina," *Migracijske i etničke teme* 2 (2019): 171–194.

23. Elizabeth M. Aranda, *Emotional Bridges to Puerto Rico: Migration, Return Migration, and the Struggles of Incorporation* (Rowman and Littlefield, 2007).

24. Ala Sirriyeh, *The Politics of Compassion: Immigration and Asylum Policy*, Global Migration and Social Change (Bristol University Press, 2018).

25. Leah Williams Veazey, *Migrant Mothers in the Digital Age: Emotion and Belonging in Migrant Maternal Online Communities*, Studies in Migration and Diaspora (Routledge, 2021).

26. Juliet Stumpf, "The Crimmigration Crisis: Immigrants, Crime, and Sovereign Power," *American University Law Review* 56 (2006): 367; Charis Thompson, "Reprotech in France and the United States: Comparisons, Reproductive Technology and Migrapolitics," *Reproductive Biomedicine and Society Online* 11 (2020): 104.

27. See Jørgen Carling, "Migration in the Age of Involuntary Immobility: Theoretical Reflections and Cape Verdean Experiences," *Journal of Ethnic and Migration Studies* 28, no. 1 (2002): 5–42; Hein De Haas, "A Theory of Migration: The Aspirations-Capabilities Framework," *Comparative Migration Studies* 9, no. 1 (2021): 1–35.

28. Asnake Kefale and Fana Gebresenbet, "Introduction: Multiple Transitions and Irregular Migration in Ethiopia; Agency and Assemblage from Below," in *Youth on the Move: Views from Below on Ethiopian International Migration*, ed. Asnake Kefale and Fana Gebresenbet (Oxford University Press, 2022), 1–20, 12.

29. Sarah F. Derbew, *Untangling Blackness in Greek Antiquity* (Cambridge University Press, 2022).

30. Shihan de S. Jayasuriya and Richard Pankhurst, eds. *The African Diaspora in the Indian Ocean* (Africa World Press, 2003).

31. David Eltis, "The Volume and Structure of the Transatlantic Slave Trade: A Reassessment," *William and Mary Quarterly* 58, no. 1 (2001): 17–46.

32. Oliver Bakewell and Hein De Haas, "African Migrations: Continuities, Discontinuities and Recent Transformations," in *African Alternatives*, ed. Leo de Haan, Ulf Engel, and Patrick Chabal (Brill, 2007), 95–117.

33. Kwesi Kwaa Prah, *Back to Africa: Afro-Brazilian Returnees and Their Communities* (Center for Advanced Studies of African Society, 2009).

34. Colin Grant, "Marcus Garvey: 'Africa for the Africans,'" in *The Pan-African Pantheon: Prophets, Poets, and Philosophers*, ed. Adekeye Adebajo (Manchester University Press, 2021), 104–117.

35. Dominik Frühwirth, "'Repatriation: Yes! Migration: No!': Back-to-Africa in Rastafarian Thought and Practice," in *Cultural Mobilities between Africa and the Caribbean*, ed. B. Englert, B. Gföllner, and S. Thomsen (Routledge, 2021).

36. Sedi Soga, "'Homegoing': Mobility, Diaspora, and Ghana's Year of Return" (MA Thesis., Université d'Ottawa / University of Ottawa, 2003).

37. Colin Clarke, Ceri Peach, and Steven Vertovec, eds., *South Asians Overseas: Migration and Ethnicity* (Cambridge University Press, 1990); Andrew Arsan, *Interlopers of Empire: The Lebanese Diaspora in Colonial French West Africa* (Oxford University Press, 2018).

38. A. Adepoju, "Issues and Recent Trends in International Migration in Sub-Saharan Africa," *International Social Science Journal* 52 (2000): 383–394.

39. Marie-Laurence Flahaux and Hein De Haas, "African Migration: Trends, Patterns, Drivers," *Comparative Migration Studies* 4 (2016): 1–25, 1.

40. Flahaux and De Haas, 2.

41. Kwadwo Konadu-Agyemang, Baffour K. Takyi, and John A. Arthur, eds., *The New African Diaspora in North America: Trends, Community Building, and Adaptation*

(Lexington Books, 2006); I. Okpewho and N. Nzegwu, *The New African Diaspora* (Indiana University Press, 2009).

42. *Voluntary* African migration needs to be qualified. While contemporary African migration is not a direct result of enslavement as it was in the past, it has to be understood within the context of political instability, failed states, underdeveloped economies, and other issues, most of which are legacies of hundreds of years of enslavement and European colonization.

43. Kassahun H. Kebede, ed., *Identity and Transnationalism: The New African Diaspora Second Generation in the United States* (Routledge, 2020).

44. Toyin Falola and Adebayo Oyebade, eds., *The New African Diaspora in the United States* (Routledge, 2017).

45. See Laura Nader, "Up the Anthropologist: Perspectives Gained from Studying Up," in *Reinventing Anthropology*, ed. Dell Hymes (Pantheon Books, 1972), 284–311.

46. See Gayatri Chakravorty Spivak, "Imperialism and Sexual Difference," *Oxford Literary Review* 8, no. 1 (1986): 225–244.

47. Julian Go, "For a Postcolonial Sociology," *Theory and Society* 42, no. 1 (2013): 25–55.

48. Gayatri Chakravorty Spivak and Sarah Harasym, *The Post-colonial Critic: Interviews, Strategies, Dialogues* (Routledge, 1990), 166.

49. C. Wright Mills, *The Sociological Imagination* (1959; repr., Oxford University Press, 2000).

50. While the modernizing preoccupation persisted, there was also an understanding of migration as exile during the time of Emperor Haile Selassie. Stories abound of individuals who lamented their fate and sent emissaries to the emperor, pleading to be allowed to stay within Ethiopia and not be forced out of the country, even for short periods of time.

51. Bahru Zewde, *Pioneers of Change in Ethiopia: The Reformist Intellectuals of the Early Twentieth Century* (Ohio University Press, 2022).

52. Solomon Addis Getahun, *The History of Ethiopian Immigrants and Refugees in America, 1900–2000: Patterns of Migration, Survival, and Adjustment* (LFB Scholarly, 2007).

53. Tassé Abye, "Ethiopian Elites Trained in the USSR and Socialist Countries: Fading from View?" *Cahiers d'etudes Africaines* 226, no. 2 (2017): 289–312.

54. See Richard Danzinger, "Voting with Their Feet? Why Young Africans Are Choosing Migration over the Ballot Box," IOM, July 11, 2017, available at https://www.weforum.org/agenda/2017/07/the-biggest-cause-of-african-migration-might-not-be-what-you-think/.

55. See Hassen Hussein, "If Ethiopia Is So Vibrant, Why Are Young People Leaving?" Al Jazeera, April 28, 2015, available at http://america.aljazeera.com/opinions/2015/4/if-ethiopia-is-so-vibrant-why-are-young-people-leaving.html.

56. The TPLF supposedly represents the Tigray people, who are a minority group in terms of numbers, making up only about 6 percent of the total Ethiopian population.

57. Shimelis Bonsa Gulema, Hewan Girma, and Mulugeta F. Dinbabo, eds., *The Global Ethiopian Diaspora: Migrations, Connections, and Belongings* (University of Rochester Press, 2024).

58. Getahun, *History of Ethiopian Immigrants*. Ethiopians are the second-largest African immigrant group in the United States, after Nigerians. The Ethiopian government, together with the IOM, preliminarily mapped out the size and spread of the Ethiopian diaspora in the United States. See IOM, *Mapping of Ethiopian Diasporas Residing in the United States of America* (IOM, 2018).

59. Bina Fernandez, "Cheap and Disposable? The Impact of the Global Economic Crisis on the Migration of Ethiopian Women Domestic Workers to the Gulf," *Gender and Development* 18, no. 2 (2010): 249–262.

60. For instance, in December 2013, the Saudi government expelled over 150,000 Ethiopians after a crackdown on foreign workers. See "Saudis Expel 100,000 Ethiopians," *Al Jazeera*, December 6, 2013, available at http://www.aljazeera.com/news/africa/2013/12/saudis-expel-100000-illegal-ethiopians-201312591727221329.html. The mass expulsion of Ethiopians from Saudi Arabia was repeated again in the summer of 2017, when around thirty thousand migrants were repatriated to Ethiopia. See "Saudi Arabia To Release 1,000 Ethiopian Prisoners," *Al Jazeera*, May 20, 2018, available at https://www.aljazeera.com/news/2018/5/20/saudi-arabia-to-release-1000-ethiopian-prisoners. Again in 2020 and 2021, this time because of the COVID-19 pandemic, Ethiopian migrants from different Gulf States were deported unceremoniously back to their home country. See, for example, Samuel Getachew, "Ethiopian Workers Are Being Expelled from Saudi Arabia and UAE on Coronavirus Suspicions," *Quartz Africa*, April 14, 2020, available at https://qz.com/africa/1837457/ethiopians-expelled-from-saudi-arabia-uae-for-covid-19. Researchers have estimated that at least half-a-million Ethiopians have been deported from Saudi Arabia between 2017 and 2022. See Girmachew Adugna, "Half a Million Ethiopian Migrants Have Been Deported from Saudi Arabia in 5 Years—What They Go Through," *The Conversation*, December 4, 2022, available at https://theconversation.com/half-a-million-ethiopian-migrants-have-been-deported-from-saudi-arabia-in-5-years-what-they-go-through-195378. In general, those who return from Saudi Arabia or other Gulf States do not experience the same privileges and luxuries as those described in this study. For an academic analysis of the experiences of returnees from Saudi Arabia, see Marina De Regt and Medareshaw Tafesse, "Deported before Experiencing the Good Sides of Migration: Ethiopians Returning from Saudi Arabia," *African and Black Diaspora: An International Journal* 9, no. 2 (2016): 228–242. For a journalistic rendering of the situation, see Benno Muchler, "Ethiopian Migrants Expelled by Saudis Remain in Limbo Back Home," *New York Times*, January 7, 2014, available at https://www.nytimes.com/2014/01/08/world/africa/ethiopian-migrants-expelled-by-saudis-remain-in-limbo-back-home.html.

61. IOM, *Mapping of Ethiopian Diasporas Residing in the United States*.

62. Sonja Fransen and Katie Kuschminder, "Migration in Ethiopia: History, Current Trends and Future Prospects" (Migration and Development Country Profiles, Maastricht Graduate School of Governance, 2009).

63. Patrick McSharry et al., "Setting the Stage: Growth and Convergence in Ethiopia," in *Ethiopia's Great Transition: The Next Mile-Country Economic Memorandum*, ed. World Bank (World Bank, 2022), 10–25. Ethiopia is part of what is known as the new PINE emerging economies, which include the Philippines, Indonesia, Nigeria, and Ethiopia. The acronym is modeled after the BRICS nations (Brazil, Russia, India, China, and South Africa). Ethiopia (along with Egypt, Indonesia, Iran, and the United Arab Emirates) eventually joined the BRICS as a member state in its expansion in 2024.

64. Ethiopia's average annual income or gross domestic product per capita is about $1,000 World Development Report 2019. Washington, D.C.: World Bank Publications.

65. For instance, in April 2015, Ethiopians across the globe were shocked by the release of an internet video showing thirty Ethiopian migrants beheaded as part of a death campaign by ISIS in the deserts of Libya. The event highlighted the vulnerability of the Ethiopian migrants who take dangerous routes to reach the coveted shores of Europe. The deaths of these thirty Ethiopian migrants have sent ripple waves through the

Ethiopian community at home and abroad. The brutal loss of lives in extraordinary circumstances provoked discussion about identity (both religious and national) and civic and political responsibility. It put those in power on the defensive as accusations of political negligence (or impotence) ran rampant.

66. *Hakim* is an Amharic title, derived from Arabic, meaning "physician" or "doctor." *Hakim* Workeneh left Ethiopia at a very young age, taken by British soldiers who assumed he was an orphan. After spending about thirty years of his life in different parts of the British Empire, including present-day Pakistan and Scotland, *Hakim* Workeneh returned to Ethiopia to pioneer reforms in the political and education sphere. For more detail, see Bahru Zewde, *Pioneers of Change in Ethiopia: The Reformist Intellectuals of the Early Twentieth Century* (James Currey, 2002).

67. Tekle returned to Ethiopia after spending close to twenty years in Russia, partly in a military academy. Upon return, Tekle held various political positions, including the roles of governor and minister, and he even drafted the first Constitution of Ethiopia under Emperor Haile Selassie.

68. The ancient Roman god Janus is a god of duality usually depicted as having two faces.

69. United Nations High Commissioner for Refugees, *Global Trends: Forced Displacement in 2019* (Geneva: UNHCR, 2019), available at https://www.unhcr.org/media/unhcr-global-trends-2019.

70. Gulema, Girma, and Dinbabo, *Global Ethiopian Diaspora*.

71. I offer a more detailed explanation of my methodology in the Appendix.

72. The specific nature of and changes in economic, social, and political situations and their effects on the respondents are discussed in subsequent chapters.

73. The lack of statistical data is not unique to Ethiopia or characteristic of African nations in general. Rather, statistical data on return and repeat migration is hard to come by in most regions of the world since sufficient attention has not been accorded to these phenomena.

74. B. G. Glaser and A. L. Strauss, *The Discovery of Grounded Theory: Strategies for Qualitative Research* (1967; repr., Aldine Transaction, 1999).

75. Grounded theory is particularly suited to situations where the terms and concepts are highly contested, as is the case here. The grounded theory "tradition starts with and develops analyses from the point of view of the experiencing person.... Such studies aim to capture the worlds of people by describing their situations, thoughts, feelings, and actions and by relying on portraying the research participants' lives and voices. Their concerns shape the direction and form of the research. The researcher seeks to learn how they construct their experience through their actions, intentions, beliefs, and feelings." Kathleen Marian Charmaz, "The Search for Meanings: Grounded Theory," in *Rethinking Methods in Psychology*, ed. J. A. Smith, R. Harre, and L. V. Langenhove (Sage, 2007), 27–49, 30.

76. I position myself, and by extension this work, within larger social and historical processes. This is not about self-involved navel gazing, but it needs to be clear that I am implicated in the story. I am not presenting a cold and detached report to which I bear no emotional connection. Abstraction can be disengaging, which would be a disservice to the stories countless individuals have shared with me.

77. My family first migrated to the United States in the late 1990s, when I was a teenager. When I was in my midtwenties, my parents relocated back to Ethiopia upon my father's retirement while I settled in the United States. Within the span of a decade, it had increasingly become more common for Ethiopians to engage in return migration

and semipermanently resettle in Ethiopia. Another decade later, at the writing of this book, my parents split their time equally between Ethiopia and the United States, spending about six months of the year in each location, following seasonal patterns and generally seeking out warmer weather in both locations.

78. See Abdi M. Kusow, "Beyond Indigenous Authenticity: Reflections on the Insider/Outsider Debate in Immigration Research," *Symbolic Interaction* 26, no. 4 (2003): 591–599.

79. Chinua Achebe as quoted in Bacon, 2000.

80. Adichie, Chimamanda, "The Danger of a Single Story," TED Talk, July 2009, available at https://www.ted.com/talks/chimamanda_ngozi_adichie_the_danger_of_a_single_story.

CHAPTER 1

1. Kerilyn Schewel, "Understanding Immobility: Moving beyond the Mobility Bias in Migration Studies," *International Migration Review* 54, no. 2 (2020): 328–355, 330n.

2. Schewel, 328–355.

3. See Jørgen Carling, "Migration in the Age of Involuntary Immobility: Theoretical Reflections and Cape Verdean Experiences," *Journal of Ethnic and Migration Studies* 28, no. 1 (2002): 5–42.

4. Reza Azarian, "Potentials and Limitations of Comparative Method in Social Science," *International Journal of Humanities and Social Science* 1, no. 4 (2011): 113–125; Irene Bloemraad, "The Promise and Pitfalls of Comparative Research Design in the Study of Migration," *Migration Studies* 1, no. 1 (2013): 27–46, available at https://doi.org/10.1093/migration/mns035.

5. In terms of numbers, of the sixteen non-migrants interviewed for this project, four are indignant patriots, seven are hopefuls, and five are ambivalents. While the hopeful category contains the largest number, the indignant patriot and the ambivalent categories put together outnumber it.

6. *Gashe* is an endearing term of respect for older men.

7. Although a contested designation, *Habesha* is a general term that Ethiopians and Eritreans use to refer to themselves.

8. Bahru Zewde, *Pioneers of Change in Ethiopia: The Reformist Intellectuals of the Early Twentieth Century* (Ohio University Press, 2002).

9. Hewan Girma, "Songs of Sidet: An Insight into Ethiopia's Culture of Migration through Song Lyrics Analysis," in *The Global Ethiopian Diaspora: Migrations, Connections, and Belongings*, ed. Shimelis Bonsa Gulema, Hewan Girma, and Mulugeta F. Dinbabo (University of Rochester Press, 2024).

10. *Eteye* is an Amharic honorific title for older women.

11. Girma, "Songs of Sidet," 303–329.

12. See "Full English Transcript of Ethiopian Prime Minister Abiy Ahmed's Inaugural Address," OPride, April 3, 2018, available at https://www.opride.com/2018/04/03/english-partial-transcript-of-ethiopian-prime-minister-abiy-ahmeds-inaugural-address/.

13. For a more detailed analysis, see Girma, "Songs of Sidet."

14. Although in the Ethiopian context older generations exhibit a stronger preference for staying rather than migrating, in a different context, other researchers have shown that younger populations sometimes aspire to stay. For instance, Sara Wyngaarden and colleagues discuss Honduran youths' immobility aspirations and practices, which

they keep despite some of the challenges that persist in their home country. See Sara Wyngaarden, Sally Humphries, Kelly Skinner, Esmeralda Lobo Tosta, Veronica Zelaya Portillo, Paola Orellana, and Warren Dodd, "'You Can Settle Here': Immobility Aspirations and Capabilities among Youth from Rural Honduras," *Journal of Ethnic and Migration Studies* 49, no. 1 (2022): 212–231, available at https://doi.org/10.1080/1369183X.2022.2031922.

15. Daniel Mains, *Hope Is Cut: Youth, Unemployment, and the Future in Urban Ethiopia* (Temple University Press, 2012).

16. See Cecilia Macaulay, "African Brain Drain: '90% of My Friends Want to Leave,'" BBC News, June 2, 2022, available at https://www.bbc.co.uk/news/world-africa-61795026.

17. Ray, Julie and Anita Pugliese, "Desire to Migrate Remains at Record High," Gallup News, October 31, 2024, available at https://news.gallup.com/poll/652748/desire-migrate-remains-record-high.aspx.

18. Carling and Schewel, 945–963.

19. Charles Piot, *Nostalgia for the Future: West Africa after the Cold War* (University of Chicago Press, 2019).

20. See Onoso Imoagene, *Structured Luck: Downstream Effects of the US Diversity Visa Program* (Russell Sage Foundation, 2023).

21. Peggy Levitt, "Social Remittances: Migration Driven Local-Level Forms of Cultural Diffusion," *International Migration Review* 32, no. 4 (1998): 926–948.

22. Mains, *Hope Is Cut*.

23. Asnake Kefale and Fana Gebresenbet, eds., *Youth on the Move: Views from Below on Ethiopian International Migration* (Oxford University Press, 2021).

24. See David H. Shinn, "Ethiopia: The 'Exit Generation' and Future Leaders," *International Journal of Ethiopian Studies* 1, no. 1 (2003): 21–32.

25. The hopefuls were the largest group of non-migrants interviewed for this project.

26. Roberto Patricio Korzeniewicz and Timothy Patrick Moran, *Unveiling Inequality: A World-Historical Perspective* (Russell Sage Foundation, 2009).

27. Milena Belloni, "Cosmologies of Destinations: Roots and Routes of Eritrean Forced Migration towards Europe" (Ph.D. diss., University of Trento, 2015).

28. For a more detailed analysis, see Paul A. Silverstein, "Immigrant Racialization and the New Savage Slot: Race, Migration, and Immigration in the New Europe," *Annual Review of Anthropology* 34 (2005): 363–384.

29. Migrants can be separated into two major categories: internal migrants stay within the borders of the same country, while international migrants cross an international border. Migrants can also be subdivided between voluntary and forced migrants, where the latter are generally compelled by war, conflict, natural disaster, or another type of instability in their homeland.

30. Catrin Lundström, *White Migrations: Gender, Whiteness, and Privilege in Transnational Migration* (Springer, 2014); C. Lundström, "The White Side of Migration," *Nordic Journal of Migration Research* 7, no. 2 (2017): 79–87.

31. Peter Redfield, "The Unbearable Lightness of Ex-pats: Double Binds of Humanitarian Mobility," *Cultural Anthropology* 27, no. 2 (2012): 358–382.

32. Kimberlé Crenshaw, *#SayHerName: Black Women's Stories of Police Violence and Public Silence* (Haymarket Books, 2024).

33. Zygmunt Bauman, *Modernity and Ambivalence* (Cornell University Press, 1991); Neil J. Smelser, "The Rational and the Ambivalent in the Social Sciences: 1997 Presidential Address," *American Sociological Review* 63, no. 1 (1998): 1–16; Katarina Wegar, "The

Sociological Significance of Ambivalence: An Example from Adoption Research," *Qualitative Sociology* 15, no. 1 (1992): 87–103.

34. Hewan Girma, "Language, Culture and Hierarchies of Migration," *International Journal of Ethiopian Studies* 12, no. 2 (2018): 79–96.

35. The Agazi are federal special police generally deployed to different parts of Ethiopia in situations of unrest.

INTERLUDE 1

1. James Clifford, "Traveling Cultures," in *Cultural Studies*, ed. Lawrence Grossberg et al. (Routledge, 1992), 96–116.

2. For comparison, New York's JFK Airport serves sixty million annual passengers, and London Heathrow serves eighty million.

3. The previous airport located around Lideta was replaced because of a need for longer runways. After the relocation of the airport, the plush neighborhood of the previous airport was unimaginatively renamed Old Airport.

4. The phrase "where my umbilical cord is buried" (*etebete yetekeberebet*) implies a strong and continued attachment to the home country or region regardless of present residence.

5. Brenda Chalfin, "Sovereigns and Citizens in Close Encounter: Airport Anthropology and Customs Regimes in Neoliberal Ghana," *American Ethnologist* 35, no. 4 (2008): 519–538.

CHAPTER 2

1. Olivia Guntarik, "Homecoming: The Enigma of Returning," *Asian Ethnicity* 14, no. 1 (2013): 99–105, available at https://doi.org/10.1080/14631369.2012.726140.

2. Jørgen Carling, "Myth of Return," in *The Wiley Blackwell Encyclopedia of Race, Ethnicity, and Nationalism*, ed. John Stone et. al. (John Wiley and Sons, 2015), 1507–1508.

3. William Safran, "Diasporas in Modern Societies: Myths of Homeland and Return," *Diaspora: A Journal of Transnational Studies* 1, no. 1 (1991): 83–99.

4. Giulia Sinatti, "'Mobile Transmigrants' or 'Unsettled Returnees'? Myth of Return and Permanent Resettlement among Senegalese Migrants," *Population, Space and Place* 17 (2011): 153–166.

5. Mary Goitom, "The Epistemological Significance of Tizita and Sam-ennä warq in Understanding the Return-Thinking Processes and Psychosocial Wellbeing among Ethiopian Migrants in Toronto, Canada," *International Journal of Ethiopian Studies* 12, no. 2 (2018): 143–169.

6. Luis Eduardo Guarnizo, "The Emergence of a Transnational Social Formation and the Mirage of Return Migration among Dominican Trans-migrants, Identities," *Global Studies in Culture and Power* 4, no. 2 (1997): 281–322.

7. Francesco P. Cerase, "Expectations and Reality: A Case Study of Return Migration from the United States to Southern Italy," in "Policy and Research on Migration," special issue, eds. Daniel Kubat, Anthony H. Richmond and Jerzy Zubrzycki, *International Migration Review* 8, no. 2 (1974): 245–262.

8. Russell King, "Return Migration: A Neglected Aspect of Population Geography." *Area* 10, no. 3 (1978): 175–182.

9. Dino Cinel, *The National Integration of Italian Return Migration, 1890–1929* (Cambridge University Press, 1991).

10. Osman Balkan, "Burial and Belonging," *Studies in Ethnicity and Nationalism* 15, no. 1 (2015): 120–134.

11. Ernest George Ravenstein, "The Laws of Migration," *Journal of the Royal Statistical Society* 52, no. 2 (1889): 241–305; Everett S. Lee, "A Theory of Migration," *Demography* 3, no. 1 (1966): 47–57, available at https://doi.org/10.2307/2060063.

12. The attraction of a growing economy to returnees is not unique to Ethiopia. Takeyuki Tsuda (2003) details how ethnic Japanese relocated en masse from Brazil to Japan at the height of Japan's manufacturing boom in the late 1980s and 1990s. The government of Japan took an active role in recruiting ethnic Japanese to work in low-skill and low-wage manufacturing jobs. See Takeyuki Tsuda, *Strangers in the Ethnic Homeland: Japanese Brazilian Return Migration in Transnational Perspective* (Columbia University Press, 2003).

13. Lillian Trager, ed., *Migration and Economy: Global and Local Dynamics* (AltaMira, 2005).

14. See Maryamawit Engdawork, "Ethiopia: Double-Digit Economic Growth," *Reporter* (Addis Ababa), March 14, 2015, available at http://allafrica.com/stories/201503161818.html.

15. The narratives of "Africa Rising" have been tainted between 2011, when the *Economist* ran a hopeful cover story by the same title, and 2016, when the *New York Times* pointed to the inconsistencies of development and the coexistence of economic growth with widespread political repression, particularly in Ethiopia. See "Africa Rising: After Decades of Slow Growth, Africa Has a Real Chance to Follow in the Footsteps of Asia," *Economist*, December 3, 2011, available at http://www.economist.com/node/21541015; Jeffrey Gettleman, "'Africa Rising'? 'Africa Reeling' May Be More Fitting Now," *New York Times*, October 17, 2016, available at http://www.nytimes.com/2016/10/18/world/africa/africa-rising-africa-reeling-may-be-more-fitting-now.html?_r=0.

16. See Amen Teferi, "Ethiopia Is Burning the Midnight Oil," *Ethiopian Herald*, January 3, 2017, available at http://allafrica.com/stories/201701040542.html.

17. See "Ethiopia-Djibouti Electric Railway Line Opens," BBC, October 5, 2016, available at http://www.bbc.com/news/world-africa-37562177.

18. The East Asian Tigers are the four nations of Hong Kong, Singapore, South Korea, and Taiwan, which transformed their economies between the 1960s and 1990s to become developed or highly industrialized.

19. The PINE (Philippines, Indonesia, Nigeria and Ethiopia) acronym was devised by Michael Schuman, who argues that the BRICS nations (Brazil, Russia, India, China, and South Africa) are experiencing a slowdown in their development and emerging economies such as the PINEs are the countries to watch in the coming years. While the BRICS nations are globally recognized for their significant economic growth, the acronym PINE has not gained similar ground. Michael Schuman, "Forget the BRICS, Meet the PINES," *Time*, March 13, 2014, available at http://time.com/22779/forget-the-brics-meet-the-pines.

20. Elizabth Chacko and Peter H. Gebre, "Engaging the Ethiopian Diaspora: Policies, Practices and Performance," in *Africa and Its Global Diaspora: The Policy and Politics of Emigration*, ed. J. Mangala (Springer, Palgrave Macmillan, 2017), 219–250.

21. See http://www.bamboostar.net.

22. The information in this paragraph is gleaned from an interview with an individual working in the Diaspora office in the Ethiopian Ministry of Foreign Affairs,

Addis Ababa, Ethiopia, August 2016. Moreover, see Dawit Endeshaw, "Ethiopia Passes Law to Open Banking to Foreign Competition," Reuters, December 17, 2024, available at https://www.reuters.com/business/finance/ethiopia-passes-law-open-banking-for eign-competition-2024-12-17.

23. See Sherri Sharma, "Beyond Driving while Black and Flying while Brown: Using Intersectionality to Uncover the Gendered Aspects of Racial Profiling," *Columbia Journal of Gender and Law* 12, no. 2 (2003): 275–309; Angela Anita Allen-Bell, "The Birth of the Crime: Driving while Black (DWB)," *Southern University Law Review* 25, no. 1 (1997): 195–226.

24. *Habesha* is a general term that Ethiopians and Eritreans use to refer to themselves. The term is contested by some ethnic minorities for its lack of overall representation. For a more detailed discussion, see Mohammed Hamid Mohammed, "Imagining and Performing Habasha Identity: The Ethiopian Diaspora in the Area of Washington, DC" (Ph.D. diss., Northwestern University, 2006).

25. Peter Hansen, "Circumcising Migration: Gendering Return Migration among Somalilanders," *Journal of Ethnic and Migration Studies* 34, no. 7 (2008): 1109–1125.

26. Steve Garner, "The European Union and the Racialization of Immigration, 1985–2006," *Race/Ethnicity: Multidisciplinary Global Contexts* 1, no. 1 (2007): 61–87.

27. Sarah Jaffe, "The Collective Power of #MeToo," *Dissent* 65, no. 2 (2018): 80–87.

28. Loretta Baldassar, Cora Vellekoop Baldock, and Raelene Wilding, *Families Caring across Borders: Migration, Ageing and Transnational Caregiving* (Springer, 2006).

29. Man Guo, Iris Chi, and Merril Silverstein, "Intergenerational Support of Chinese Rural Elders with Migrant Children: Do Sons' or Daughters' Migrations Make a Difference?" *Journal of Gerontological Social Work* 52, no. 5 (2009): 534–554.

30. Katharine M. Donato and Donna Gabaccia, *Gender and International Migration: From the Slavery Era to the Global Age* (Russell Sage Foundation, 2015).

31. Anastasia Christou, "Migrating Gender: Feminist Geographies in Women's Biographies of Return Migration," *Gender and Globalism* 17 (2003): 1–22.

32. See Nicole Maurantonio, "Remembering Rodney King: Myth, Racial Reconciliation, and Civil Rights History," *Journalism and Mass Communication Quarterly* 91, no. 4 (2014): 740–755.

33. Christian Dustmann, "Children and Return Migration," *Journal of Population Economics* 16, no. 4 (2003): 815–830.

34. Slobodan Djajić, "Immigrant Parents and Children: An Analysis of Decisions Related to Return Migration," *Review of Development Economics* 12, no. 3 (2008): 469–485.

35. Push-pull models of migration identify a list of reasons migrants are repelled or pushed out of their home nation (e.g., conflict, persecution, and unemployment) and reasons migrants are attracted or pulled into host nations (e.g., work, educational opportunities, and democracy).

36. Guido Dorigo and Waldo Tobler, "Push-Pull Migration Laws," *Annals of the Association of American Geographers* 73, no. 1 (1983): 1–17.

37. Mohamed-Abdullahi Mohamed and Asmat-Nizam Abdul-Talib, "Push–Pull Factors Influencing International Return Migration Intentions: A Systematic Literature Review," *Journal of Enterprising Communities: People and Places in the Global Economy* 14, no. 2 (2020): 231–246.

38. Translated in David G. Stern, "Heraclitus' and Wittgenstein's River Images: Stepping Twice into the Same River," *Monist* 74, no. 4 (1991): 579–604, 580.

39. Thomas Wolfe, *You Can't Go Home Again* (Simon and Schuster, 1940 / 2011).

INTERLUDE 2

1. See U.S. Department of State, Reports and Statistics, Valid Passport in Circulation by Fiscal Year (1989–2024), available at https://travel.state.gov/content/travel/en/about-us/reports-and-statistics.html.
2. Nelson Mandela, *Long Walk to Freedom: The Autobiography of Nelson Mandela* (Back Bay Books, 1995).
3. Mandela, 1995.
4. Nicole Constable, *Passport Entanglements: Protection, Care, and Precarious Migrations* (University of California Press, 2022).
5. Laila Lalami, *Conditional Citizens: On Belonging in America* (Pantheon, 2020).
6. For a detailed analysis of the Ethiopian Origin Identity Card, see Metka Hercog and Katie Kuschminder, "The Power of the Strong State: A Comparative Analysis of the Diaspora Engagement Strategies of India and Ethiopia" (UNU-MERIT Working Paper, 2011).

CHAPTER 3

1. Kate Torkington, *Defining Lifestyle Migration* (Dos Algarves, 2010), 19, 99–111.
2. Jean-Pierre Cassarino, "Theorising Return Migration: The Conceptual Approach to Return Migrants Revisited," *International Journal on Multicultural Societies* 6, no. 2 (2004): 253–279; Christian Dustmann, "Return Migration, Uncertainty, and Precautionary Savings," *Journal of Development Economics* 52, no. 2 (1997): 295–316.
3. Peggy Levitt, *The Transnational Villagers* (University of California Press, 2001).
4. Michaela Benson and Nick Osbaldiston, eds., *Understanding Lifestyle Migration: Theoretical Approaches to Migration and the Quest for a Better Way of Life* (Palgrave Macmillan U.K., 2014).
5. Michaela Benson, "Negotiating Privilege in and through Lifestyle Migration," in Benson and Osbaldiston, *Understanding Lifestyle Migration*, 47–68.
6. Benson.
7. Michaela Benson and Karen O'Reilly, "Migration and the Search for a Better Way of Life: A Critical Exploration of Lifestyle Migration," *Sociological Review* 57, no. 4 (2009): 608–625.
8. See Laura Nader, "Up the Anthropologist: Perspectives Gained from Studying Up," in *Reinventing Anthropology*, ed. Hymes Dell (Pantheon Books, 1972), 284–311.
9. The birr is the Ethiopian currency.
10. Madeleine Wong, "Navigating Return: The Gendered Geographies of Skilled Return Migration to Ghana," *Global Networks* 14, no. 4 (2014): 438–457.
11. In terms of terminology, studies of economic distribution have placed emphasis on "class" and then "stratification" before reaching the current preoccupation with "inequalities." The change in terminology is a response to criticism from previous eras. However, even if the terminology has evolved, researchers are still trying to analyze and understand the same phenomenon of privilege and economic hierarchies within and between societies.
12. Iain Walker and Thomas F. Pettigrew, "Relative Deprivation Theory: An Overview and Conceptual Critique," *British Journal of Social Psychology* 23, no. 4 (1984): 301–310.
13. Hewan Girma, "The Salience of Gender in Return Migration," *Sociology Compass* 11, no. 5 (2017), available at https://doi.org/10.1111/soc4.12481.

14. Oyeronke Oyěwùmí, *The Invention of Women: Making an African Sense of Western Gender Discourses* (University of Minnesota Press, 1997).

15. M. Cristina Alcalde, "Gender, Autonomy and Return Migration: Negotiating Street Harassment in Lima, Peru," *Global Networks* 20, no. 1 (2020): 25–41.

16. Oyeronke Oyewumi, "Conceptualizing Gender: The Eurocentric Foundations of Feminist Concepts and the Challenge of African Epistemologies," *Jenda: A Journal of Culture and African Women Studies* 2, no. 1 (2002): 1–9, 2.

17. The overlap between gender and age as social categories can be exemplified through the Amharic language, which has no gendered pronouns for the formal form, for older or respected people. To illustrate, there are equivalents for the terms "she/her" and "he/him," but the equivalent for the "vous" in French or "usted" in Spanish is not gendered.

18. Helene K. Lee, "'I'm My Mother's Daughter, I'm My Husband's Wife, I'm My Child's Mother, I'm Nothing Else': Resisting Traditional Korean Roles as Korean American Working Women in Seoul, South Korea," *Women's Studies International Forum* 36 (2013): 37–43.

INTERLUDE 3

1. The phrase "where my umbilical cord is buried" (*etebete yetekeberebet*) implies a strong and continued attachment to the home country or region regardless of present residence.

2. Peggy Levitt, "Roots and Routes: Understanding the Lives of the Second Generation Transnationally," *Journal of Ethnic and Migration Studies* 35, no. 7 (2009): 1225–1242.

3. See Anooradha Iyer Siddiqi, *Architecture of Migration: The Dadaab Refugee Camps and Humanitarian Settlement*, Theory in Forms (Duke University Press, 2023).

4. Shimelis Bonsa Gulema, "City as Nation: Imagining and Practicing Addis Ababa as a Modern and National Space," *Northeast African Studies* 13, no. 1 (2013): 167–214.

5. Gulema, 188.

CHAPTER 4

1. Presca Wanki, Ilse Derluyn, and Ine Lietaert, "'Let Them Make It Rain and Bling': Unveiling Community Expectations towards Returned Migrants in Cameroon," *Societies* 12, no. 1 (2022): 8, available at https://doi.org/10.3390/soc12010008.

2. Milena Belloni, *The Big Gamble: The Migration of Eritreans to Europe* (University of California Press, 2019).

3. Adele Galipo, *Return Migration and Nation Building in Africa: Reframing the Somali Diaspora* (Routledge, 2018).

4. Katarzyna Grabska, "Threatening Miniskirts: Returnee South Sudanese Adolescent Girls and Social Change," in *Africa's Return Migrants: The New Developers?* ed. Lisa Åkesson and Maria Eriksson Baaz (Zed Books, 2015).

5. Pierre Bourdieu, "Distinction: A Social Critique of the Judgement of Taste," in *Inequality: Classic Readings in Race, Class, and Gender*, ed. D. Grusky (Routledge, 2006), 287–318.

6. Hewan Girma, "Language, Culture and Hierarchies of Migration," *International Journal of Ethiopian Studies* 12, no. 2 (2018): 79–96.

7. Nicole Constable, *Passport Entanglements: Protection, Care, and Precarious Migrations* (University of California Press, 2022).

8. The Ethiopia Origin Identity Card, colloquially referred to as the "Yellow Card" came into effect in 2005. It is modeled after the "Overseas Citizenship of India" (OCI) card, where the holder can expect certain privileges such as owning property, entry without visa requirements. One of the limitations on the card holder is that it prohibits involvement in the political sphere, where a yellow card holder cannot vote or hold public office. For a more detailed analysis of the Ethiopian Origin Identity Card, see Hercog & Kuschminder, 2011.

9. Milena Belloni, "Cosmologies and Migration: On Worldviews and Their Influence on Mobility and Immobility," *Identities* 29, no. 5 (2022): 557–575.

10. Belloni, Milena, *The Big Gamble: The Migration of Eritreans to Europe* (University of California Press, 2019), 47.

11. The GERD, previously known as the Millennium Dam, is a hydroelectric dam on the Blue Nile River. The Ethiopian government used mostly crowdfunding and internal fundraising to cover the estimated cost of upward of US$5 billion. Despite resistance from Egypt and Sudan and after over ten years of construction (2011–2023), the gradual filling of the reservoir began in July 2020. The symbolic and geopolitical importance of the GERD cannot be overstated.

12. Ethiopia fought against European colonization twice in the span of less than fifty years, first winning a decisive victory against the Italian colonial invasion at the Battle of Adwa during the First Italo-Ethiopian War (1895–1896) and again in 1936 during the Second Italo-Ethiopian War (1935–1936).

13. Known as the father of Ethio-jazz, Mulatu Astatke (born 1943) is a prolific musician with a career spanning decades.

14. Mekdes Haddis, *A Just Mission: Laying Down Power and Embracing Mutuality* (InterVarsity, 2022).

15. Frantz Fanon, *Black Skin, White Masks*, trans. Richard Philcox (1952; repr., Grove, 2008).

16. Kipling's poem was a praise to colonialism portraying colonized peoples as "half devil and half child." It has been widely criticized for its endorsement of colonialism and white supremacy. Kipling, Rudyard, "The White Man's Burden," *McClure's Magazine*, February 1899.

17. Michele Mitchell, "'The Black Man's Burden': African Americans, Imperialism, and Notions of Racial Manhood, 1890–1910," *International Review of Social History* 44, no. S7 (1999): 77–99.

18. Teju Cole, "The White-Savior Industrial Complex," *Atlantic*, March 21, 2012.

19. M. B. Akpan, "Black Imperialism: Americo-Liberian Rule over the African Peoples of Liberia, 1841–1964," *Canadian Journal of African Studies / La Revue Canadienne des études Africaines* 7, no. 2 (1973): 217–236.

20. Akpan, 217–236.

21. Akpan, 217–236.

22. Joseph Nye coined the term and concept of "soft power," which is defined as the ability to obtain your own goals because others admire your ideas and want to emulate your example. Soft power is not relegated solely to the context of political entities and international relations. It has been studied in relation to international students and study abroad programs. Joseph S. Nye, "Soft Power," *Foreign Policy* 80 (1990): 153–171; Joseph S. Nye Jr., *Soft Power: The Means to Success in World Politics* (Public Affairs, 2004).

23. Osman Antwi-Boateng, "The Transformation of the US-Based Liberian Diaspora from Hard Power to Soft Power Agents," *African Studies Quarterly* 13, no. 1/2 (2012): 55.

24. Åkesson and Baaz, *Africa's Return Migrants*, 15.

25. Robert B. Potter and Joan Phillips, "Both Black and Symbolically White: The 'Bajan-Brit' Return Migrant as Post-colonial Hybrid," *Ethnic and Racial Studies* 29, no. 5 (2006): 901–927, available at https://doi.org/10.1080/01419870600813942.

26. Joan Phillips and Robert B. Potter, "'Black Skins—White Masks': Postcolonial Reflections on 'Race,' Gender and Second Generation Return Migration to the Caribbean," *Singapore Journal of Tropical Geography* 27, no. 3 (2006): 309–325.

INTERLUDE 4

1. Mohammed Hamid Mohammed, "Imagining and Performing Habasha Identity: The Ethiopian Diaspora in the Area of Washington, DC" (Ph.D. diss., Department of Performance Studies, Northwestern University Evanston, 2005); Samantha Friedman et al., "Race, Immigrants, and Residence: A New Racial Geography of Washington, DC," *Geographical Review* 95, no. 2 (2005): 210–230; Elizabeth Chacko, "Identity and Assimilation among Young Ethiopian Immigrants in Metropolitan Washington," *Geographical Review* 93, no. 4 (2003): 491–506.

2. Elizabeth Chacko, "Ethiopian Ethos and the Making of Ethnic Places in the Washington Metropolitan Area," *Journal of Cultural Geography* 20, no. 2 (2003): 21–42; Mussa S. Idris, "The Multidimensional Roles of Food and Culture-Centered Entrepreneurship among Ethiopian and Eritrean Migrants: Ethnographic Case Studies in Washington, D.C.," *African and Black Diaspora: An International Journal* 8, no. 1 (2015): 55–70.

3. Shelly Habecker, "Not Black, but Habasha: Ethiopian and Eritrean Immigrants in American Society," *Ethnic and Racial Studies* 35, no. 7 (2012): 1200–1219.

4. Nebiy Mekonnen, የእኛ ሰው በአሜሪካ *(Yegna Sew Be America)* [An Ethiopian in the United States], 1995.

5. Dinaw Mengistu, *Children of the Revolution* (Vintage Books, 2009).

6. To learn more about other efforts to create Little Ethiopias in North America, see Alpha Abebe, "Politicking about Ethiopian Cuisine with *The Simpsons*," *Focus on the Horn* (blog), January 12, 2013, available at https://focusonthehorn.wordpress.com/2013/01/12/politicking-about-ethiopian-cuisine-with-the-simpsons.

7. Paul Schwartzman, "Shaw Shuns 'Little Ethiopia,'" *Washington Post*, July 25, 2005, available at https://www.washingtonpost.com/archive/local/2005/07/25/shaw-shuns-little-ethiopia.

8. Elizabeth Chacko, "Translocality in Washington, DC and Addis Ababa: Spaces and Linkages of the Ethiopian Diaspora in Two Capital Cities," in *Translocal Geographies: Space, Places, Connections*, ed. Katherine Brickell and Ayona Datta (Routledge, 2011), 163–178.

9. "Spotlight: D.C. Honors Ethiopian Community with 'Little Ethiopia' Resolution," *Tadias Magazine*, December 24, 2020, available at http://www.tadias.com/12/24/2020/spotlight-d-c-honors-ethiopian-community-with-little-ethiopia-resolution.

CHAPTER 5

1. According to the legend, when Kaldi noticed that his goats were excited after nibbling on the bright red coffee berries, he started investigating. Kaldi shared the berries with either a Christian or an Islamic monk from a nearby monastery, who initially disapproved of their use but later enjoyed their ability to increase alertness. The beans were

later roasted, brewed, and shared widely from their African birthplace in Ethiopia to Asia, Europe, and the Americas.

2. Amelie F. Constant, Olga Nottmeyer, and Klaus F. Zimmermann, "The Economics of Circular Migration," in *International Handbook on the Economics of Migration*, ed. Amelie F. Constant and Klaus F. Zimmermann (Edward Elgar, 2013); Graeme Hugo, "What We Know about Circular Migration and Enhanced Mobility," *Migration Policy Institute* 7 (2013): 55–74.

3. Stephen Castles and Derya Ozkul, "Circular Migration: Triple Win, or a New Label for Temporary Migration?" in *Global and Asian perspectives on international migration*, ed. Graziano Battistella (Springer, 2014), 27–49; Constant, Nottmeyer, and Zimmermann, "Economics of Circular Migration"; Kathleen Newland, "Can Migrants, Countries of Origin and Countries of Destination All Win from Circular Migration?" (Global Forum on Migration and Development, Civil Society Day, Belgium, 2007).

4. Castles and Ozkul, "Circular Migration," 27–49; Piyasiri Wickramasekara, "Circular Migration: A Triple Win or a Dead End" (Global Union Research Network Discussion Paper 15, 2011).

5. Florin Vadean and Matloob Piracha, "Circular Migration or Permanent Return: What Determines Different Forms of Migration?" in *Migration and Culture 8*, ed. Gil S. Epstein and Ira N. Gang (Emerald Group, 2010), 467–495.

6. A total of nine women and seven men repeat migrants were included in this study. The average age was forty-eight, with a range of twenty-three to eighty-four years old. On average, repeat migrants stayed as returnees for a period a little over five years. The average repeat migrant was educated with at least a bachelor's degree, working in various fields from sales and marketing to homemaking.

7. AnnaLee Saxenian, "Brain Circulation. How High-Skill Immigration Makes Everyone Better Off," *Brookings Review* 20, no. 1 (2002): 28–31; Ugo Fratesi, "Editorial: The Mobility of High-Skilled Workers—Causes and Consequences," *Regional Studies* 48, no. 10 (2014): 1587–1591.

8. Amelie F. Constant and Klaus F. Zimmermann, "Circular Migration: Counts of Exits and Years away from the Host Country" (SOEP Papers on Multidisciplinary Panel Data Research 40, Deutsches Institut für Wirtschaftsforschung, Berlin, 2007).

9. The parable of the prodigal son is a biblical story (Luke 15:11–32) of a young man who leaves his home and family in search of a better life. After facing numerous trials, he returns to his father's house, repentant. While his father welcomes him with open arms, the prodigal son is resented by his non-migrant, older brother, who feels left out. The prodigal son is a story of homecoming (i.e., return migration) and redemption.

10. Mohammed Girma, "Whose Meaning? The Wax and Gold Tradition as a Philosophical Foundation for an Ethiopian Hermeneutic," *Sophia* 50, no. 1 (2011): 175–187.

11. Hein De Haas, Tineke Fokkema, and Mohamed Fassi Fihri, "Return Migration as Failure or Success?" *Journal of International Migration and Integration* 16, no. 2 (2015): 415–429.

12. Sending children back home is a situation widely written about in different African contexts. For instance, in Somalia, children sent back for a period of cultural reorientation are known as *dhaqan celis*, which translates to "return to culture." See Farah Bakaari and Xavier Escandell, "Ambivalent Returns: Dhaqan Celis and Counter-diasporic Migration among Second-Generation Somalis," *Global Networks* 22, no. 1 (2021): 51–64. See also Pamela Kea and Katrin Maier, "Challenging Global Geographies of Power: Sending Children Back to Nigeria from the United Kingdom for Education," *Comparative Studies in Society and History* 59, no. 4 (2017): 818–845.

13. Aileen Stockdale, "From 'Trailing Wives' to the Emergence of a 'Trailing Husbands' Phenomenon: Retirement Migration to Rural Areas," *Population, Space and Place* 23, no. 3 (2017): e2022.

CONCLUSION

1. Tiffany D. Joseph, *Race on the Move: Brazilian Migrants and the Global Reconstruction of Race* (Stanford University Press, 2015), 155.

2. See Peggy Levitt, "Social Remittances: Migration Driven Local-Level Forms of Cultural Diffusion," *International Migration Review* 32, no. 4 (1998): 926–948; Peggy Levitt and Deepak Lamba-Nieves, "Social Remittances Revisited," *Journal of Ethnic and Migration Studies* 37, no. 1 (2011): 1–22. While Levitt hypothesizes that cultural and geographic proximity partly explains the strength of social remittances, the Ethiopian case study aptly demonstrates that social transmissions are not limited or inhibited by such things. Ethiopia is thousands of miles away from the United States, both geographically and culturally, but this African country still endures the sociocultural tug of U.S. global dominance.

3. For instance, legal status is only an enabling factor, not a determinant of belonging. Borders are a geopolitical reality to be navigated, but citizenship and other forms of political membership do not automatically translate into belonging. While other analyses of belonging have favored the nation-state and migrants cannot escape the reality of territorial boundaries or the state's ability to police its geopolitical border, a passport is less and less an attestation of belonging, as belonging is more complex than a legal document.

4. Shimelis Bonsa Gulema, Hewan Girma, and Mulugeta F. Dinbabo, *The Global Ethiopian Diaspora: Migrations, Connections, and Belongings* (University of Rochester Press, 2024), 13, 1.

5. Gulema, Girma, and Dinbabo, 5.

6. Gulema, Girma, and Dinbabo, 13.

7. Gulema, Girma, and Dinbabo, 13.

8. Victoria A. Lawson, "Arguments within Geographies of Movement: The Theoretical Potential of Migrants' Stories," *Progress in Human Geography* 24, no. 2 (2000): 173–189.

9. Oliver Bakewell, Hein de Haas, Stephen Castles, Simona Vezzoli, and Gunvor Jónsson, "South-South Migration and Human Development: Reflections on African Experiences" (Human Development Research Paper Series: United Nations Development Programme, 2009); Katja Hujo and Nicola Piper, "South–South Migration: Challenges for Development and Social Policy," *Development* 50, no. 4 (2007): 19–25.

APPENDIX

1. Adamnesh Atnafu, "Aspects of Ethiopian Return Migration" (MA thesis, Addis Ababa University, 2006).

2. I often offered to buy coffee or treat my respondents to a meal during or after the interview; however, with the exception of only a handful of participants, most refused and, almost without fail, ended up treating me instead. This is typical of Ethiopian welcoming culture and reinforces the social relationship building aspect.

3. M. Crouch and H. McKenzie, "The Logic of Small Samples in Interview-Based Qualitative Research," *Social Science Information* 45, no. 4 (2006): 483–499.

4. Amharic is one of the most widely spoken local languages in Ethiopia. I am equally fluent in Amharic and English.

5. B. Bourke, "Positionality: Reflecting on the Research Process," *Qualitative Report* 19, no. 33 (2014): 1–9; W. Pillow, "Confession, Catharsis, or Cure? Rethinking the Uses of Reflexivity as Methodological Power in Qualitative Research," *International Journal of Qualitative Studies in Education* 16, no. 2 (2003): 175–196; G. Rose, "Situating Knowledges: Positionality, Reflexivities and Other Tactics," *Progress in Human Geography* 21, no. 3 (1997): 305–320.

6. R. Berger, "Now I See It, Now I Don't: Researcher's Position and Reflexivity in Qualitative Research," *Qualitative Research* 15, no. 2 (2015): 219–234, 221.

7. K. V. L. England, "Getting Personal: Reflexivity, Positionality, and Feminist Research," *Professional Geographer* 46, no. 1 (1994): 241–256, 244.

8. My father, who worked for the United Nations (UN) for close to thirty years, moved from the African regional headquarters (Economic Commission of Africa) in Addis Ababa to the global headquarters of the UN in New York City, transitioning to a different role within the same organization.

9. Bolé Airport was the only international airport serving the entire country of Ethiopia at the time.

10. Thanks to family visits funded by the UN for its international staff, we were fortunate enough to return every two years like clockwork to see our extended families in Ethiopia.

11. The Atlantic crossing had acquired a new (racialized) meaning to me during my decade-long stay in the United States.

12. Between 2008, when my parents returned to Ethiopia, and the early 2020s, at the writing of this research, my parents split their time between the United States and Ethiopia, spending about six months of the year in each location.

13. Abdi M. Kusow, "Beyond Indigenous Authenticity: Reflections on the Insider/Outsider Debate in Immigration Research," *Symbolic Interaction* 26, no. 4 (2003): 591–599.

14. Esther R. Anderson, "Positionality, Privilege, and Possibility: The Ethnographer 'at Home' as an Uncomfortable Insider," *Anthropology and Humanism* 46, no. 2 (2021): 212–225; Ayça Ergun and Aykan Erdemir, "Negotiating Insider and Outsider Identities in the Field: 'Insider' in a Foreign Land; 'Outsider' in One's Own Land," *Field Methods* 22, no. 1 (2010): 16–38; Iskender Gelir, "Can Insider Be Outsider? Doing an Ethnographic Research in a Familiar Setting," *Ethnography and Education* 16, no. 2 (2021): 226–242; Debarati Sen, "Locations: Homework and Fieldwork," in *Everyday Sustainability: Gender Justice and Fair Trade Tea in Darjeeling* (State University of New York Press, 2017), 29–42.

15. Erin Roberts, "The 'Transient Insider': Identity and Intimacy in Home Community Research," in *Emotion and the Researcher: Sites, Subjectivities, and Relationships*, ed. T. Loughran and D. Mannay, Studies in Qualitative Methodology 16 (Emerald, 2018), 113–125.

16. Valli Kalei Kanuha, "'Being' Native versus 'Going Native': Conducting Social Work Research as an Insider," *Social Work* 45, no. 5 (2000): 439–447; M. S. Lewis-Beck, A. Bryman, and T. Futing Liao, eds., *The SAGE Encyclopedia of Social Science Research Methods* (SAGE, 2004), s.v. "going native."

17. Kanuha, "'Being' Native versus 'Going Native,'" 439–447.

18. Carolyn Ellis, "Evocative Autoethnography: Writing Emotionally about Our Lives," in *Representation and the Text: Re-framing the Narrative Voice*, ed. William G. Tierney and Yvonna S. Lincoln, (State University of New York Press, 1997), 115–139.

19. Anderson, "Positionality, Privilege, and Possibility," 212–225.

20. Arthur Bochner and Carolyn Ellis, *Evocative Autoethnography: Writing Lives and Telling Stories* (Routledge, 2016), 65.

21. Laurel Richardson, "Evaluating Ethnography," *Qualitative Inquiry* 6 (2000): 253–255.

22. Mariza Méndez, "Autoethnography as a Research Method: Advantages, Limitations and Criticisms," *Colombian Applied Linguistics Journal* 15, no. 2 (2013): 279–287; Richardson, "Evaluating Ethnography," 253–255; S. Wall, "Easier Said than Done: Writing an Autoethnography," *International Journal of Qualitative Methods* 7 (2008): 38–53.

23. Yvonne Jewkes, "Autoethnography and Emotion as Intellectual Resources: Doing Prison Research Differently," *Qualitative Inquiry* 18, no. 1 (2012): 63–75.

24. Jewkes, 63–75.

25. Arlie Russell Hochschild, *The Managed Heart: Commercialization of Human Feeling* (University of California Press, 2019).

26. B. G. Glaser and A. L. Strauss, *The Discovery of Grounded Theory: Strategies for Qualitative Research* (1967; repr., Aldine Transaction, 1999).

27. K. Charmaz, "The Search for Meanings: Grounded Theory," in *Rethinking Methods in Psychology*, ed. J. A. Smith, R. Harre, and L. V. Langenhove (Sage, 2007), 27–49, 30.

28. J. C. Hermanowicz, "The Longitudinal Qualitative Interview," *Qualitative Sociology* 36, no. 2 (2013): 189–208.

29. A detailed timeline of Ethiopia's history, including the political upheavals of recent years, is available at http://www.bbc.com/news/world-africa-13351397.

Index

Abiy Ahmed, Prime Minister of Ethiopia, 40, 195–196
Achebe, Chinua, 27
Addis Ababa, 30–31, 115–119, 142–143, 146, 187
Adichie, Chimamanda, 27, 46
Affective, 2, 6, 61
Africa, 17–21, 28, 83, 103, 121, 129–136
African, 17–21, 28, 46, 71–72, 104, 112, 116, 179
African American, 129–130, 145–146
African Union, 116, 131
Africa Rising, 67
Afro-pessimism, 19
Ageism, 77, 112, 114
Ahmed, Sara, 9
Airport, 30, 55–59, 181. *See also* Bolé International Airport
Ambivalent, 48–54, 140
Ambivalence, 11–13, 38, 48–54, 167, 176
Arabian Peninsula, 24–25, 128, 182
Aspirations, 12–14, 36, 44, 47, 54, 129
Assemblage, 14
Axum/Axumite, 56–58, 131, 146

Belonging, 10–12, 39–40, 46, 69, 72, 77, 87, 114, 137–141, 163, 169, 176, 180

Black, 3–4, 18–19, 22, 56, 70–72, 83–84, 130–132, 135–137, 143–146, 179
Black Lives Matter, 52, 146
Bolé International Airport, 30, 41, 55–59, 180–181
Bourdieu, Pierre, 123, 125
BRICS (Brazil, Russia, India, China, South Africa), 68
Burnout, 31, 69, 73, 87. *See also* dissatisfaction

Capability/capabilities, 13–14, 177
Care (caregiving/caretaking), 75–76, 85, 87, 98, 155, 165, 169
Career, 74, 81, 125, 151–154, 168
Carling, Jørgen, 13, 43
Child/children, 21, 40, 75, 79, 81–85, 87, 98, 103–104, 156, 164–167
Chores, 97–100
Circular, 5, 7, 28, 32, 149–150
Citizen, 39, 164
Citizenship, 55, 57, 91–92, 127, 177
Class, 16, 46, 98–100, 113–114, 123–126, 174
Compression, time-space and time-cost compression, 57, 182
Cosmologies of destinations, 47, 129

COVID-19, 182
Culture of migration, 2

De Haas, Hein, 13, 19
Deportation, 24, 63, 87
Deprivation, 102
Development, 23, 32, 65–67, 127, 135, 153, 179
Disappointment, 159-160, 162–163, 168
Discontent, 24, 46, 176
Discrimination, 112
Disillusioned, 150–151, 156–163, 167–168
Dissatisfaction, 12, 73–74, 87, 158. *See also* burnout
Diversity Visa, 20, 23, 43–44

Elder respect, 77, 112
Embodied, embodiment, 62–63, 113, 180
Emerging economy, 24, 65–66, 68
Emotion, 2, 9–13, 14–16, 26, 30, 38, 48–50, 53–54, 86–87, 151, 168, 171, 173–176
Emotional labor, 10, 194
Ethiopian Airlines, 56
Ethiopian Origin Identity Card, 92, 127. *See also* Yellow Card
Ethnicity, 103–104
Ethnography, 27, 189

Frustration, 101, 104

Garvey, Marcus, 17–18
Gender, 70, 76, 80, 98, 104–112
Gender policing, 104, 107–108, 110–112, 114
Ghana, 18, 121
Goffman, Erving, 9–10
Global North, 4, 16, 21, 24, 28, 32, 72, 94, 114, 121–122, 127–129, 151, 177, 179
Global South, 16, 21, 32, 102, 117–118, 127, 129, 151, 181
Good life, the, 95–96
Grand Ethiopian Renaissance Dam, 67, 131
Greenfield, 66
Grounded theory, 27, 194
Gulf States, 24–25, 47, 129, 182

Habitus, 123
Hailemariam, Mengistu, 22
Haile Selassie, emperor, 2, 21–22, 39, 90, 176
Hierarchy, 54, 122–123, 178
History, 21–22, 39, 90–91, 145–146, 178
Hochschild, Arlie, 10

Homesickness, 78, 87, 143
Hopeful, 43–47, 54, 139–140
Hopefulness, 43–47, 54

Identity, 16, 27, 45, 70–71, 100, 114, 131, 181
Immobility, 2–3, 7–8, 35–36, 43, 171
Impermanence, 6, 148, 150, 168–170
Inadvertents, 150–151, 163–167
Incidental, 54
Indian Ocean world, 17
Indignant Patriot, 38–43, 54, 139, 173
Inequality, 32, 91–92, 101–102, 119, 123–125, 138, 151
Insider, 27, 180, 187, 191–192. *See also* positionality
In/voluntary, 35–36, 43, 53–54, 62

Labor, 10, 17, 25, 77, 97–100, 168
Levitt, Peggy, 115, 172
Liberia, 17–18, 121, 136–137
Life stage, 64, 75–77, 85, 87, 168
Lifestyle migration, 94
Linear, 7, 173
Little Ethiopia, 142–146
Luxury, 96, 99–101, 103

Mandela, Nelson, 90
Marriage, 80–81, 85, 87
Mental health, 72, 78
Migra-emotions, 9–13, 14–15, 53–54, 168, 171–172, 175–177, 182
Mobility, 3, 7–8, 21, 35–36, 57, 91, 127, 171, 175. *See also* immobility
Myth of return, 61–62

Nader, Laura, 20, 95
New African Diaspora, 19, 179
Non-migrant, 2–3, 8, 35–38, 53–54, 121, 128, 137–140, 172–173

Othering, 72, 87
Outsider, 27, 132, 144, 165, 180, 187, 191–192. *See also* positionality

Pan-African, 18, 56, 146
Passport, 55, 89–92, 94–95, 127–128, 178
PINE (Philippines, Indonesia, Nigeria, Ethiopia), 68
Police, 51–52, 54, 70
Positionality, 50, 180, 190–192. *See also* insider; outsider

Postcolonial sociology, 21
Poverty, 19, 55, 101–102, 144
Privilege, 28, 94–95, 97, 100, 102, 110, 113, 123, 127–128, 169, 178–179, 182
Push-pull, 85–87

Qualitative methods, 26

Race, 52, 70–71, 136, 145
Racism, 69–72, 84, 103
Rastafari, 18, 130
Rat race, 4, 16, 73, 96
Repeat Migrant, 4–6, 24, 149–151, 168–170, 174–176
Retirees, 77, 151, 154–156, 168
Retirement, 5, 62, 76–77, 87
Return Migration, 4, 62–64, 85–87

Saviorism, 133–137, 140–141
Sexism, 106, 109–110, 114
Sierra Leone, 17–18
Single story, 27
Social capital, 32, 123, 140, 150, 172

Social construction, 72
Social remittances, 7, 45, 172–173, 181
Socio-ecology of migration, 13–14, 14–16, 88, 177
Sociology, 21, 179
South Africa, 24, 68, 90, 182
South-South migration, 182
Spivak, Gayatri Chakravorty, 21
Stayee, 3, 35
Storying, restorying, 27–28, 178

Teddy Afro, 41
Transatlantic slave trade, 17, 19

U.S. race relations, 52, 130

Xenophobia, 13, 69–72, 84, 87

Year of the Return, 18
Yellow Card, 92, 127–128.
    See also Ethiopian Origin Identity Card
Young Professionals, 150–154, 168

Hewan Girma is Associate Professor of African American and African Diaspora Studies at the University of North Carolina Greensboro. She cofounded and codirects the Ethiopian, East African, and Indian Ocean Research Network. She is coeditor of *The Global Ethiopian Diaspora: Migrations, Connections, and Belongings* and *Naming Africans: On the Epistemic Value of Names.*

www.ingramcontent.com/pod-product-compliance
Lightning Source LLC
Chambersburg PA
CBHW022011300426
44117CB00005B/135